The History and Tradition of Accounting in Italy

T0298942

Italian accounting has a long and honourable tradition of theoretical and applied analysis of the accounting and reporting function, perceived and defined much more broadly than in the Anglo-Saxon tradition. The high point of this perhaps, is the creation of what is known as Economia Aziendale (EA). The antecedents, genesis and later developments are presented here in detail by highly knowledgeable specialists in the field.

EA takes as a prerequisite the necessity of the business (entity/azienda) to ensure its own long-run survival. This requires that the necessary resources are retained and preserved, so operating capital maintenance, by definition future-oriented, is essential. It requires a focus on the particular business organization, entity-specific and consistent with today's notion of the business model. Entity-specific information relevant to current and future cash flows is a necessary pre-requisite for ensuring long-run survival, which historical cost accounting, or fair value (being market-specific not entity-specific) satisfactorily achieve.

Flexibility of valuation and of reporting, always relevant to the specific asset at the specific time in the specific place, is a necessary condition for effective management. This is exactly the focus of EA and its analysis and tradition. Scholars and advanced students of international regulation and accounting, as well as accounting history, will find this an invaluable guide to a vibrant, scholarly tradition of great practical relevance today.

David Alexander is Emeritus Professor of Accounting, Department of Accounting, Business School, University of Birmingham, England, and author of many articles, and several textbooks, in the field of international accounting and its theories and regulation.

Stefano Adamo is Full Professor of Accounting, Business Administration and Business Management, Department of Economics, Management, Mathematics and Statistics, University of Salento, Italy, and author of many articles and textbooks in the field of financial accounting and regulation.

Roberto Di Pietra is Full Professor of Accounting, Business Administration and Business Management, Department of Business and Law, University of Siena, Italy, pro tempore President of the Italian Society of Accounting History (Società Italiana di Storia della Ragioneria, SISR) and author of many articles and textbooks in the fields of financial accounting and accounting history.

Roberta Fasiello is Associate Professor of Accounting, Business Administration and Business Management, Department of Economics, Management, Mathematics and Statistics, University of Salento, Italy, and an emerging expert in theoretical and international aspects of financial accounting and reporting.

Routledge Studies in Accounting

The History and Tradition of Accounting in Italy

Edited by David Alexander,
Stefano Adamo, Roberto Di Pietra and
Roberta Fasiello

Routledge
Taylor & Francis Group

LONDON AND NEW YORK

First published 2017 by Routledge

2 Park Square, Milton Park, Abingdon, Oxfordshire OX14 4RN

52 Vanderbilt Avenue, New York, NY 10017

Routledge is an imprint of the Taylor & Francis Group, an informa business

First issued in paperback 2019

British Library Cataloguing in Publication Data
A catalogue record for this book is available from the British Library

Library of Congress Cataloging in Publication Data
Names: Adamo, Stefano, editor. | Alexander, David, 1947 June 16– editor. | Di Pietra, Roberto, editor.
Title: The history and tradition of accounting in Italy / [edited by] Stefano Adamo, David Alexander and Roberto Di Pietra.
Description: Abingdon, Oxon ; New York, NY : Routledge, 2017. | Includes bibliographical references and index.
Identifiers: LCCN 2017002732 (print) | LCCN 2017018811 (ebook) | ISBN 9781315616971 (eBook) | ISBN 9781138671508 (hardback : alk. paper)
Subjects: LCSH: Accounting–Italy–History.
Classification: LCC HF5616.I8 (ebook) | LCC HF5616.I8 H57 2017 (print) | DDC 657.0945–dc23
LC record available at https://lccn.loc.gov/2017002732

ISBN: 978-1-138-67150-8 (hbk)
ISBN: 978-0-367-87767-5 (pbk)

Typeset in Times New Roman
by Wearset Ltd, Boldon, Tyne and Wear

Contents

Illustrations

Figures

Tables

Contributors

Stefano Adamo, University of Salento, Italy.

David Alexander, University of Birmingham, UK.

Paolo Andrei, University of Parma, Italy.

Stefano Azzali, University of Parma, Italy.

Adele Caldarelli, University of Napoli "Federico II", Italy.

Silvano Corbella, University of Verona, Italy.

Stefano Coronella, Parthenope University, Naples, Italy.

Antonio Costa, University of Salento, Italy.

Luciano D'Amico, University of Teramo, Italy.

Pierluca Di Cagno, University of Salento, Italy.

Roberto Di Pietra, University of Siena, Italy.

Roberta Fasiello, University of Salento, Italy.

Luca Fornaciari, University of Parma, Italy.

Francesco Giaccari, University of Salento, Italy.

Enrico Gonnella, University of Pisa, Italy.

Francesca Imperiale, University of Salento, Italy.

Alessandro Lai, University of Verona, Italy.

Riccardo Palumbo, University of Chieti-Pescara, Italy.

Antonella Paolini, University of Macerata, Italy.

Sara Saggese, University of Naples "Federico II", Italy.

Michela Soverchia, University of Macerata, Italy.

Alessandra Tafuro, University of Salento, Italy.

Riccardo Viganò, University of Napoli "Federico II", Italy.

Introduction

Stefano Adamo, David Alexander, Roberto Di Pietra and Roberta Fasiello

This chapter has several objectives. In no particular order of priority, these are as follows:

1   Give an outline and overview.
2   Explain the need for this book, and in particular

    a   the importance to the Italian tradition of increasing awareness of its intellectual and educational achievements, and;
    b   the importance to the wider community of the thinking.

3   Argue for the very significant relevance of the tradition, and of the contribution to understanding which it can and should make towards solving the manifest problems of accounting and reporting regulation and practice, in multinational, international and global contexts of today and tomorrow.

The tradition is known under the title of Economia Aziendale (EA). There is an immediate, and difficult, issue: what does this mean? Many Italian academics distribute two-sided business cards, claiming membership of a Dipartimento di EA on one side, and a Department of Business Administration on the other. An official translation exists, made by the Italian National University Committee (CUN): "SECS-P/07 EA is translated as Business Administration and Management". The Italian publisher RIREA describes its *Rivista* journal, in English, as the "Italian journal of Accounting and Economia Aziendale", which seems to try to avoid the problem.

Azienda (plural aziende) can be reasonably well understood as "entity". So, perhaps, "the economia of the business entity". But equating economia with administration seems to us highly misleading. Business economics is closer than business administration. In the EA tradition, the entity is perceived as a unitary and dynamic system aimed at economic production. The three elements (disciplines) necessarily involved in making operational an effective "system aimed at economic production", that is operations (gestione), organization (organizzazione) and accounting (rilevazione), can only be studied, and can only be applied, as a coherent indivisible whole (Zappa 1927: p. 31, see Chapter 4). It is in this sense that the English word "economic" must be understood.

Note that accounting is explicitly a part of EA, so the *Rivista* self-description is perhaps partly internally repetitive. In EA, accounting is regarded as an entirely economics-related discipline and it is to be applied with its focus very much on the azienda, or business entity. In fact there are two major elements to EA, first the various but always coordinated aspects of managing the azienda (the three disciplines of the previous paragraph), and second the question of valuation bases and performance measurement and reporting. The entity/institution is represented by a set of elements that make up the structure, coordinated in order to achieve the conditions for a balanced preservation and performance of the production activity in the long run. Having done our best to translate the untranslatable, we generally use the original Italian term to represent this uniquely Italian concept.

The chapters in this book are all written by experts with a particular interest in the scholar concerned. There is a long theoretical tradition in Italian accounting, going back several hundred years, out of which the EA tradition can be said to have grown. This is in contrast to the Anglo-Saxon world, where accounting, both narrowly and broadly defined, can be seen largely as a pragmatic development. To provide a proper context, we outline the development of this early thinking.

Indeed, overstepping the phase (fifteenth to eighteenth centuries) when the studies connected with the development of the accounting method and of accounting in general took place, the nineteenth century represents a period in which fruitful theoretical developments occurred. In particular, starting from the first half of the century there are some forward-looking studies, even if coming before the rising of the "Ragioneria scientifica italiana" (Italian scientific Ragioneria), in which signals of the future theories that will be elaborated by Fabio Besta and Gino Zappa, and which form the major focus of this book, can be traced. Among these studies the ones made by Lodovico G. Grippa, Francesco Villa, Francesco Marchi, Giuseppe Cerboni and Giovanni Rossi are of particular importance. Indeed, in their studies, beyond the sometimes major differences in the approaches and in the methods, some apparent attempts to combine the merely bookkeeping studies with the "business administration" ones can be identified.

Moreover, the study of the Italian accounting theoretical tradition cannot disregard (in a civil law country) the legal regulation on financial accounting. Indeed, just during the twentieth century it is possible to identify deep interventions of the legislator regulating the drawing up of the financial statements. More precisely, the economic–accounting theories didn't find obstacles until the national legislation started to regulate, first in general and later in greater detail, the rules concerning the financial statements.

With reference to the regulatory framework of the Civil Code, the first comprehensive organization was made in 1942. In this period the relevance of the financial statements as an information tool for external parties had a more significant importance and this led to case-law decisions (at the end of the sixties) and to consequent regulatory interventions (1974–1975). These interventions were characterized by a legal–formal nature, aimed at protecting third parties and limiting management discretion, with the affirmation of reporting and evaluation processes not always consistent with the EA interpretation, and the latter was only in part recovered by the rising national accounting standards issued by the standard setters of that time, that is the National Committee of Accountants (Consiglio Nazionale dei Dottori Commercialisti and Consiglio Nazionale dei Ragionieri – CNDC–CNR).

Moreover, this phase introduced two successive changes in the law:

* Initially, the accounting European Directives (No. 78/660 and No. 83/349 as subsequently amended) implemented in Italy only in 1991, preserved the interpretative and integrative function of national accounting standards issued by CNDC-CNR (starting from 2001 the Italian standard setter was the Organismo Italiano di Contabilità – OIC).
* After 2002–2003 the implementation of the International Accounting Standards (IAS)/International Financial Reporting Standards (IFRS), that were targeted for annual and consolidated financial statements drawn up by listed companies, banks. These were introduced by the EU regulations No. 1606/2002 and No. 1725/2003, and substantially led to a dual model of financial statements (the Italian/European model and the IAS/IFRS one).

Having said that, the chapters in this book concern the period starting with the beginning of 1900 until 1975 and they highlight to what extent the Italian accounting doctrine was able to elaborate theoretical approaches that definitely anticipate some models and technical solutions subsequently introduced in the current international evaluation systems.

The chapters are arranged in broadly chronological sequence. The universally accepted founder of EA (even by his opponents) is Gino Zappa, the subject of Chapter 4. He developed his thinking, over a gradual 20-year process, as growing out of the work of his own professor and "Maestro", Fabio Besta. Besta was a great exponent of what is known as the patrimonialist school – the emphasis was on capital and asset valuation. Chapters 2 and 3 address this school in general, and Besta in particular. Chapter 1 explores the important and at the time highly visionary thinking of a "pure" economist, Maffeo Pantaleoni. His economics-based logic was far ahead of the contemporary work by the more "accounting-based" thinkers of this period (late nineteenth century). As you will see on reading through the book, it took several chapters for the accounting function (broadly defined in the Italian sense) to catch up. Zappa, eventually, rejected the patrimonialist philosophy fundamentally, arguing for an income-based (reddito) analysis designed essentially to ensure the long-run survival of the entity (azienda). This obviously, to him, was not a purely accounting issue, involving also the essential contributions of the other two disciplines, organization and management. But the accounting was central, and valuation was required to be focused on providing information to ensure the long-run capacity of the azienda to maintain and reproduce its necessary operating resources.

The appropriate valuation basis in any particular situation was to be a flexible and pragmatic choice (in today's parlance an entity-specific "business model" type choice). In the general case this would be unlikely to be the historical cost, though Zappa was very careful to avoid any semblance of suggesting any one particular "usually suitable" valuation basis as necessary in order to achieve this entity-focused operational–maintenance objective.

Following the general, but not universal, acceptance of the basic ideas developed by Zappa, a large number of followers, often seen as first and then second generation "disciples" rose to prominence. The remaining chapters, 5 to 12, present a variety of their developments, applications and extensions of the essential EA theorization. These are not always fully consistent with each other, but all accept, develop and extend the broad basis of the EA tradition.

Information about national traditions, often powerful and deep-seated in themselves, is not well disseminated across nations. This volume takes one of the most fascinating examples, that of Italy. The discipline and the tradition of EA, despite major changes in environment and context, is still very much alive. At one level, it is reasonable to suggest that the advent of International Accounting Standards, and European Union Directives, has rendered such a national theory less important. At another level, however, this proposition is not generally valid, for two reasons. The first is that the Italian accounting world, both theoretical and professional, is very much having to deal with the stresses, tensions and differences between the various strong traditions. The second is that there are extremely important and interesting inter-relationships between the Italian tradition and its rigorous and high-quality thinking and analysis, on the one hand, and the mass (or morass?) of documents, proposals and required standards emerging at the international level, on the other. This book will emphasize the very real relevance of the EA tradition to the understanding, and hopefully the improvement, of current and upcoming theoretical development and practical regulation in the Anglo-Saxon and international contexts.

In the existing literature the lack in the Anglo-American accounting of a space and time coordination (primary elements of the pure theory of entity/azienda and of the EA) is highlighted and an accounting relativism, consisting in a conceptual variety of approaches to the concept of the firm and the income calculation, emerges comparing the Italian tradition of EA with the US accounting tradition (Zambon and Zan 2000), even if the existence of a complementarity with some postulates of EA was revealed (Capalbo and Clarke 2006; Leoni and Florio 2015). A comparative analysis referring to the relationships existing between theory and practice in the USA and in Italy in the period 1930–1990 is presented in Zambon and Girella, 2016.

The discipline and the tradition of EA is much studied in Italy, even if at international level some books (Galassi in Hopwood and Schreuder 1984; Galassi in Chatfield and Vangermeersch 1996; Mattessich 2003; Mattessich 2008; Biondi and Zambon 2013) show very clearly that the broad philosophy behind EA is very relevant to a number of other country scenarios, and mainly to European ones (see in particular the chapters written by E. Viganò and

A. Canziani in Biondi and Zambon 2013 and Chapters 5 and 6 in Mattessich 2008). The EA discipline, even if with different labels, is established in some continental European countries and these theoretical traditions relating to the *azienda* are missing in the academic Anglo-Saxon accounting (Zambon 1996; Canziani 2009).

In particular in these international publications, some contributions by the major Italian accountants are discussed (see also Zan 1994; Viganò 1998; Galassi and Mattessich 2004; Cinquini and Marelli 2007; Viganò and Mattessich 2007; Alexander and Servalli 2011; Gonnella 2012), even if these are often limited by selecting the most prominent and relevant Italian contributions or are focused only on a single scholar, even if less known at international level. Examples include Fabio Besta in Paglietti 2009, Sargiacomo *et al.* 2012 and Alexander and Fasiello 2014; Alberto Ceccherelli in Antonelli and Sargiacomo 2015; Lorenzo De Minico in Cinquini and Marelli 2002 and in Fiume 2007; Gino Zappa in Galassi 1980, Bianchi 1984, Canziani 1994 and Guarini *et al.* 2013; Aldo Amaduzzi in Melis 2007 and Angeloni 2013).

This book contributes to the existing literature providing an in-depth and chronological analysis of the evolution of the business accounting traditions through a presentation and discussion of the different schools of thought and the scholars' theories developed in Italy in the twentieth century. In the existing literature some scholars whose theories are presented in this book were only mentioned and most of the above mentioned literature at the international level is examined in the chapters, together, importantly, with the larger literature at national level that remains virtually unknown outside Italy. Thanks to the latter issue this book can be considered a valuable addition to the accounting literature because it expresses the views contained in Italian sources not available at an international level (in a book review written by Chatfield in 1982 the articles written by some Italian masters were criticized because they summarized American developments in accounting already well-known by an informed American reader; here in contrast this book presents theory and models developed in Italy with detailed and documented sources in the main part unknown by international readers and relevant to today's discussion). This book represents a specific attempt to break out of this restrictive situation, mainly but not totally due to language reasons (see Lai *et al.* 2015).

In summary, this volume presents a historical outline of the coherent Italian accounting tradition which is largely unknown by international readers, showing how its knowledge and understanding are relevant in theory and in practice in the current accounting debate at international level.

The concepts of *azienda* and EA are mainly explored in this book for the contributions in the field of financial accounting starting from 1900 until 1975. Other publications explore the accounting history developments in Italy mainly after this period (Zambon and Saccon 1993; Vagnoni 2002; Zambon 2002; Cinquini *et al.* 2008). Some Italian academics already presented in English publications the relevance of the Italian studies on EA comparing institutionalisms (Dagnino and Quattrone 2006) or in other fields such as:

- Stakeholder Management Theory and Corporate Social Responsibility (Contrafatto and Rusconi 2005; Signori and Rusconi 2009) or Catholic Social Teaching (Costa and Ramus 2012), exploring the application of the thinking of some of the historical scholars of the Italian EA in the ethical debate providing an appreciable framework for Corporate Social Responsibility and ethics studies (Caldarelli *et al.* 2014).
- Strategy and strategic management, exploring the contribution of Italian studies and of EA founded by Gino Zappa (see in particular the journal special issue edited by Di Pietra and Faraci in 2010 – including the contributions of some Italian academics such as Cafferata, Lorenzoni and Caselli – and also Colombo 2000).
- Management accounting, cost accounting and performance management, transfer pricing (Bergamin Barbato *et al.* 1996; Antonelli *et al.* 2009; Mura and Clive 2010; Cinquini and Nørreklit 2015): showing how Italian accountants were familiar with different methods of transfer pricing and how they contributed to the field, elaborating original solutions almost until the diffusion of Zappa's theories, when the debate stopped.
- Public management (Meneguzzo 2007).

As a "map" to guide the reader through the detailed contents of this volume, we now present summaries of each of the 12 chapters, showing their interrelationships, and generally how the EA model arose and became widely accepted, but also was continually developed, and in a sense continually renewed, over the following decades. In this volume we aim to collect the most relevant theoretical contributions of the Italian doctrine on the problem of financial valuation. In this respect, the different contributing authors have approached this topic referring to the most prominent Italian scholars and their theoretical proposals developed during the twentieth century. Along these chapters we will mainly follow a time sequence starting from the contribution of precursors and founders of the Italian EA.

The contribution of the eclectic economist, Maffeo Pantaleoni, is the subject proposed by D'Amico and Palumbo in Chapter 1. In particular, they have examined the essay published by Pantaleoni in 1904 and entitled "Some observations on the value assignments in the absence of market prices". This chapter has had a large influence in the Italian accounting scholarly environment.

The "value-based accounting theory" developed by Fabio Besta was the topic chosen by Paolini and Soverchia in Chapter 2. According to this theory, Besta developed a precise and detailed set of financial valuations rules on the basis of which it is possible to understand the meaning and the role that Besta gave to the accrual and the prudence principles. Moving from the theoretical contribution of Besta, Coronella has centered Chapter 3 on the advances proposed by Vittorio Alfieri, Gino Zappa and Francesco De Gobbis. These scholars have developed a general theory on valuations, justified the utilization of a plurality of evaluative criteria within one financial statement, set up guide-lines of a "precautionary" nature to guarantee the integrity of the capital, explained the role of goodwill, and displayed the goodwill valuation according to logics and contemporary rules.

Following this line, Alexander, Fasiello and Giaccari have explored the pivotal contribution of Gino Zappa to the development of EA. In Chapter 4 the main focus is on the distinction between Zappa's versus Besta's thoughts, following the development of Zappa's gradual move away from a balance sheet (patrimonialist) emphasis, and towards an income statement (reddito) emphasis.

As a consequence of the theoretical approaches developed by Besta and Zappa the following chapters have examined the proposals and contributions of other Italian scholars directly or indirectly related to them. In Chapter 5 Gonnella has referred to the theoretical contribution of Alberto Ceccherelli and his "theory of functional valuation" and the subsequent refinements of Egidio Giannessi. In this approach it was stated that the value of assets depends on the economic function they perform within the specific enterprise. The "functional value" does not refer directly to a real economic transaction, but is rather a value in use deriving from an entity-specific valuation based on the examination, for each category of asset, of ad-hoc quali-quantitative information.

Costa and Tafuro have focused their attention on the original contribution proposed by Aldo Amaduzzi and his theoretical model of financial statements. This scholar deeply investigated aspects of financial and economic nature related to management, compared to which capital and income are merely derived aspects. Amaduzzi also devoted his researches to the interests that gravitate inside and outside of the company affecting the conditions of the *general equilibrium* and the preparation and interpretation of financial statements. Lino Azzini was a scholar who has greatly contributed to the development of Zappa's theory. In Chapter 7 Azzali and Fornaciari have examined the Azzini studies with a particular focus on Income Determination, Capital Maintenance Methodologies and Group Accounting, based on Entity Theory, as widely recognized in the literature.

In Chapter 8 Andrei and Corbella have described the theoretical contribution of Carlo Masini, whose thinking is characterized by his wide-eyed attention to the systemic vision, which leads him – albeit in the footsteps of Zappa's paradigm – to make significant progress, spurred by his constant need to interpret the "part" as a component of the "whole", where only the "whole" can help us understand the part. The chapter places particular emphasis on the non-recurring revaluations, the accounting models based on historical costs and/or current values, goodwill and the so-called business unit. The contribution of Domenico Amodeo is the focus of Saggese, Caldarelli and Viganò in Chapter 9. In particular, these authors have discussed Amodeo's theorization on financial valuation issues and the relationship between income and capital by emphasizing the pivotal role played by the author in the development of the modern Italian accounting theory.

Chapter 10 is devoted to the contribution of Paolo Emilio Cassandro. This scholar had a personal and independent position in the national scientific context. This position is the result of the combination of different influences (F. Besta,

E. Schmalenbach, G. Zappa and A. Amaduzzi). In this case, Adamo, Di Cagno and Imperiale have oriented their discussion on the financial valuation system identified in the estimated direct and indirect future realizable values as rational valuation bases and, at the same time, the impairment reference for the rational assessment of the fundamental economic quantities (income and capital). Di Pietra has approached the studies of Guido Ponzanelli and his contribution referring to the definition and determination of goodwill, which constitutes an aspect of great interest. On this subject Guido Ponzanelli's contribution provides an original and innovative viewpoint, which seems to limit the role of development through paradigms cited in the case of business-related disciplines.

Finally, in Chapter 12 Lai has investigated the contribution of Edoardo Ardemani referring to the main principles to determine this kind of income, legitimizing earnings management (as the greater part of his colleagues did around Italy), as a direct consequence of the idea of unity "in the space" and "across the time" that management should have. The concept of "consumable income" was particularly widespread in Italy, until the new standards deriving from the new European Accounting Directives overcame it definitively.

Some more detailed comments are necessary in this introduction in relation to the thinking and contribution of Pietro Onida (1902–1982). Within the Italian accounting and EA tradition Pietro Onida is unanimously considered the most orthodox of Gino Zappa's disciples. The merit of having improved the EA framework elaborated by Gino Zappa must be given to Onida. His approach is particularly effective in defining the economic conditions and the theory of accounting and reporting methods.

Having regard to the latter issue, Pietro Onida takes into account with particular emphasis the theory of different financial statements, discussed below in Chapter 1, elaborated by Maffeo Pantaleoni (however already recognized by Besta and Zappa). In his studies (which, starting from the thirties, were considered a common reference point by Italian scholars) Onida develops and analyses, in a critical and comparative perspective, the different possible frameworks of financial statements (in terms of the relationship existing between purpose and evaluation logics), giving rise, at the beginning of the seventies, to a very interesting scientific discussion with R.J. Chambers on the concept of measurement and of evaluation in accounting (Onida 1973a, 1973b; Chambers 1973; Gonnella and Talarico 2014).

Lastly in this introduction we develop the proposition, which we very strongly believe, that EA has much to offer theorists, but especially national and international regulators, in the twenty-first century. We suggested above, quoting Lai in Chapter 12, that "the new standards deriving from the new European Accounting Directives overcame (the concept of consumable income) definitively". But of course in the context of history, "definitive" is a relative term. More importantly, there are certainly a number of significant problems, uncertainties, debates and disagreements arising from "the new standards deriving from the new European Accounting Directives", especially when considered in the appropriate international context. We suggest that there are helpful overlaps, links, and positive lessons to be derived from the EA tradition that would significantly strengthen both the theoretical analysis and the practical operation of financial reporting, and the concomitant management of businesses, over the coming decades. We aim at helpful hints and suggestions, not anything remotely claimed as a "blueprint".

First of all, we summarize some major facets and issues relating to current regulatory thinking and practice. The question of asset valuation and income measurement is certainly crucial. Both IFRS, and the 2013 European Directive (Number 34), with a mixture of options and requirements, contain a variety of bases, giving a wide spectrum of possibility as between historical cost and current valuations of various kinds. There are debates about who the users, the "customers" of financial reporting, are, and what their differing needs are. The notion of the business model has jumped into prominence. The role, and indeed the meaning, of "prudence" produce disagreements. The dangers of "short-termism" are much warned against. All of these considerations introduce uncertainty, and potential flexibility, into the standards and practices of financial reporting.

The reader is likely to be reading this introduction before reading the detailed chapters. But even our cursory summary given above surely allows us to underline a strong general relevance of the EA tradition and its detailed variations to the current issues of the twenty-first century. Financial reporting requires a true and fair view, fair presentation, or to use the Italian terms, quadro fedele, in modo veritiero e corretto *of the entity*. Belatedly, the entity-specific implications of this seem to be recently recognized by the sudden explosion of interest in the "business model". So our first proposition is absolutely clear: relevant financial reporting requires a focus on the entity (or azienda). The entire EA tradition, not only Zappa but also his precursors and successors, provides exactly this focus. The "going concern" principle, to use post-Zapparian parlance, is truly observed in both long and short run, EA takes as a prerequisite the necessity of the business (entity/azienda) to ensure its own long-run survival. This of course requires that the necessary resources are retained and preserved, so operating capital maintenance, by definition future-oriented, is the order of the day. It is easy to show that historical cost accounting fails to achieve this.

This is not to imply that any other single valuation basis would solve the problems. EA, in different detailed ways, takes the "entity-specific" notion to its individualistic conclusions: the appropriate valuation basis may be unique to a particular asset/resource, in a particular place (entity) and at a particular time (the accounting date). At the same time, it is the relationship of the item under consideration to the entire organization, considered as a unitary operation, which is crucial. This concept of the entity as an indivisible whole may go against the needs of a number of stakeholders for individual valuations (on any of a variety of bases), of individual assets. But as an indicator of economic performance, of the contribution to increasing the stock of wealth held by a community, which for better or for worse has given its scarce resources into the control of the entity and its management, entity specificity is crucial and a report on the entity as a single, singular, indivisible and whole unity is fundamental. This is exactly the focus of EA. It is exactly what is needed to inform managers and decision-makers about the implications of ensuring the economic "health and safety" of the business in a dynamic long-run perspective. The emphasis on entity long-term survival and long-term performance, together with the clear understanding that historical cost so visibly fails to achieve this, is exactly what is needed as a standard (not necessarily perfectly achievable of course) against which second and third-rate expedients and approximations should be judged.

The final point to emphasize in this all-too-brief synopsis is that it is not only the uniqueness of time, place and business context which the analytical flexibility of EA is able to take into account, but also the variability of user needs. The point can be generalized. Context is all. The most useful financial information in any, necessarily and by definition unique, situation is a flexible factor requiring relevant realism. Subjectivity, logically and intelligently applied, is needed. A careful study of this book provides no instant solutions. But it provides exposure to a way of thinking, analysing, applying, and therefore regulating, which is far removed from the current status quo and, we suggest, of considerable analytical and logical power and rigour. Read on and see for yourself.

References

Alexander, D. and Fasiello, R. (2014) "Valore reale, fair value and the business model: was Besta best after all?", *Proceedings of the 9th International Conference Accounting and Management Information Systems*, Bucharest: Editura ASE, 703–723.

Alexander, D. and Servalli, S. (2011) "Economia Aziendale and financial valuations in Italy: some contradictions and insights", *Accounting History*, 16, 3: 291–312.

Angeloni, S. (2013) "Aldo Amaduzzi: one of the best Italian scholars in the business disciplines", *Revista de Management Comparat International*, 14, 3, July: 367–376.

Antonelli, V. and Sargiacomo, M. (2015) "Alberto Ceccherelli (1885–1958): pioneer in the history of accounting practice and leader in international dissemination", *Accounting History Review*, 25, 2: 121–144.

Antonelli, V., Boyns, T. and Cerbioni, F. (2009) "The development of cost accounting in Italy, c.1800 to c.1940", *Accounting History*, 14, 4, November: 465–507.

Bergamin Barbato, M., Collini, P. and Quagli, A. (1996) Management accounting in Italy: evolution with tradition, in Bhimani A. (ed.) *Management Accounting: European Perspectives*, Oxford: Oxford University Press: 140–163.

Bianchi, T. (1984) "The founding of Concern Economics: the thought of Gino Zappa", *Economia Aziendale*, 3, 3: 255–272.

Biondi, Y. and Zambon, S. (eds) (2013) *Accounting and Business Economy. Insights from National Traditions*, London: Routledge.

Caldarelli, A., Fiondella, C., Maffei, M., Spanò, R. and Zagaria, C. (2014) "Banking for the common good: a case study", *International Journal of Business Governance and Ethics*, 9, 4: 330.

Canziani, A. (1994) Gino Zappa (1879–1960) Accounting revolutionary, in Edwards, J.R. (ed.), *Twentieth-Century Accounting Thinkers*, London: Routledge.

Canziani, A. (2009) Economia Aziendale and Betriebswirtschaftlehre as autonomous sciences of the firm, in Biondi Y., Canziani A. and Kirat T. (eds) *The Firm as an Entity: Implications for Economics, Accounting and the Law*, London: Routledge: 107–130.

Capalbo, F. and Clarke, F. (2006) "The Italian economia aziendale and Chambers' CoCoA", *Abacus*, 42, 1: 66–86.

Chambers, R.J. (1973) "Misurazioni, stime e valutazioni nelle decisioni finanziarie" *Rivista dei dottori commercialisti*, 24, 6: 1001.

Chatfield, M. (1982) "Papers on business administration", *The Accounting Review*, 57, 1: 208–209.

Cinquini, L. and Marelli, A. (2002) "An Italian forerunner of modern cost allocation concepts: Lorenzo de Minico and the logic of the 'flows of services'", *Accounting, Business & Financial History*, 12, 1: 95–111.

Cinquini, L. and Marelli, A. (2007) "Accounting history research in Italy, 1990–2004: an introduction", *Accounting, Business & Financial History*, 17, 1: 1–9.

Cinquini, L. and Nørreklit, H. (2015) "Research perspectives in Performance Management", *Management Control*, special issue, 2.

Cinquini, L., Marelli, A. and Tenucci, A. (2008) "An analysis of publishing patterns in accounting history research in Italy, 1990–2004", *The Accounting Historians Journal*, 35, 1: 1–48.

Colombo, G. (2000) "Les études de stratégie en Italie", *Management International*, 4, 2, Spring: 47–59.

Contrafatto, M. and Rusconi, G. (2005) "Social accounting in Italy: origins and developments", *Social and Environmental Accountability Journal*, 25, 2: 3–8.

Costa, E. and Ramus, T. (2012) "The Italian Economia Aziendale and Catholic Social Teaching: how to apply the common good principle at the managerial level", *Journal of Business Ethics*, 106, 1, March: 103–116.

Dagnino, G.B. and Quattrone, P. (2006) "Comparing institutionalisms: Gino Zappa and John R. Commons' accounts of 'institution' as a groundwork for a constructivist view", *Journal of Management History*, 12, 1: 36.

Di Pietra, R. and Faraci, R. (2010) "Antecedents of entrepreneurial governance within firms: the Italian contribution to strategic management", special issue of *Journal of Management & Governance*, 14, 3: 195–197.

Fiume, R. (2007) "Lorenzo De Minico's thought in the development of accounting theory in Italy: an understated contribution", *Accounting, Business & Financial History*, 17, 1, March: 33.

Galassi, G. (1980) *Capital-Income Relations: A Critical Analysis. Gino Zappa, founder of Concern Economics*, Bologna: Accademia Italiana di Economia Aziendale: 25–49.

Galassi, G. (1984) Accounting research in Italy: past, present and future, European contributions to accounting research. The achievements of the last decade, in Hopwood A.G. and Schreuder H. (eds) *European Contributions to Accounting Research: The Achievements of the Last Decade*, Amsterdam: Free University Press: 163–187.

Galassi, G. (1996) Italy, after Pacioli, in Chatfield M. and Vangermeersch R. (eds) *The History of Accounting: An International Encyclopedia*, New York: Garland Publishing: 347–350.

Galassi, G. and Mattessich, R. (2004) "Italian accounting research in the first half of the 20th century", *Review of Accounting and Finance*, 3, 2: 62–83.

Gonnella, E. (2012) "Financial statement valuations in Italian accounting thought between the 19th and the 20th century: from exchange value to historical cost", *Journal of Modern Accounting and Auditing*, 8, 9: 1255–1271.

Gonnella, E. and Talarico, L. (2014) "Teleological and non-teleological perspectives in financial statement: the debate between P. Onida and R.J. Chambers in 1973", paper presented at JHMO Conference, 26–28 March, Paris.

Guarini, E., Magli, F. and Nobolo, A. (2013) *From Accounting to "Economia Aziendale": Innovation in the Thought of Gino Zappa (Italy, 1879–1960)*, Rirea: Roma.

Lai, A., Lionzo, A. and Stacchezzini, R. (2015) "The interplay of knowledge innovation and academic power: lessons from 'isolation' in twentieth-century Italian accounting studies", *Accounting History*, 20, 3: 266–287.

Leoni, G. and Florio, C. (2015) "A comparative history of earnings management literature from Italy and the US", *Accounting History*, 20, 4: 490–517.

Mattessich, R. (2003) "Accounting research and researchers of the nineteenth century and the beginning of the twentieth century: an international survey of authors, ideas and publications", *Accounting, Business and Financial History*, 13, 2: 125–170.

Mattessich, R. (2008) *Two Hundred Years of Accounting Research*, Routledge: London.

Melis, A. (2007) "Financial statements and positive accounting theory: the early contribution of Aldo Amaduzzi", *Accounting, Business & Financial History*, 17, 1: 53–62.

Meneguzzo, M. (2007) The study of public management in Italy, in Kickert W. (ed.) *The Study of Public Management in Europe and the US: A Competitive Analysis of National Distinctiveness*, London: Routledge.

Mura, A. and Clive, E. (2010) "Transfer pricing: early Italian contributions", *Accounting, Business and Financial History*, 20, 3: 365.

Onida, P. (1973a) "Alcuni punti di dissenso col pensiero di R.J. Chambers espressi in una mia pubblicazione del 1970: 'I moderni sviluppi della dottrina contabile nord americana e gli studi di economia aziendale'", *Rivista dei Dottori Commercialisti*, 6: 995–1000.

Onida, P. (1973b) "Replica all'articolo di RJ CHAMBERS", *Rivista dei dottori Commercialisti*, 24, 6: 1023.

Paglietti, P. (2009) "Exploring the role of accounting history following the adoption of IFRS in Europe. The case of Italy", *De Computis: Revista Española de Historia de la Contabilidad*, 11: 83–115.

Sargiacomo, M., Servalli, S. and Andrei, P. (2012), "Fabio Besta: accounting thinker and accounting history pioneer", *Accounting History Review*, 22, 3: 249–267.

Signori, S. and Rusconi, G. (2009) "Ethical thinking in traditional Italian Economia Aziendale and the Stakeholder Management Theory: the search for possible interactions", *Journal of Business Ethics*, 89, supp. 3: 303–318.

Vagnoni, E. (2002) "Critical accounting studies in Italy: some personal notes", *Critical Perspectives on Accounting*, 13, 4: 527–532.

Viganò, E. (1998) "Accounting and business economics tradition in Italy", *The European Accounting Review*, 7, 3: 381–403.

Viganò, E. and Mattessich, R. (2007) "Accounting research in Italy: second half of the 20th century", *Review of Accounting and Finance*, 6, 1: 24–41.

Zambon, S. (1996) "Accounting and business economics traditions: a missing European connection?", *European Accounting Review*, 5, 3: 401–411.

Zambon, S. (2002) *Locating Accounting in its National Context: The Case of Italy*, Milan: FrancoAngeli.

Zambon, S. and Girella, L. (2016) "Accounting theory and accounting practice as loosely coupled systems: a historical perspective on the Italian case (1930–1990)", *Financial Reporting*, special issue 1: 95–133.

Zambon, S. and Saccon, C. (1993) "Accounting change in Italy: fresh start or Gattopardo's revolution?", *European Accounting Review*, 2, 2: 245–284.

Zambon, S. and Zan, L. (2000) "Accounting relativism: the unstable relationship between income measurement and theories of the firm", *Accounting, Organizations and Society*, 25, 8: 799–822.

Zan, L. (1994) "Toward a history of accounting histories", *European Accounting Review*, 3, 2: 255–307.

Zappa, G. (1927) *Tendenze nuove negli studi di ragioneria. Discorso inaugurale dell'anno accademico 1926–27 nel R. Istituto Superiore di Scienze Economiche e Commerciali di Venezia*, Milan.

1 The contribution of Maffeo Pantaleoni in the field of financial valuation

Luciano D'Amico and Riccardo Palumbo

1 Introduction

Maffeo Pantaleoni (1857–1924) was a distinguished Italian economist and politician.

After his doctorate in law at the University of Rome (1881) he became fond of Economics and Finance. He obtained a licence for teaching Finance in 1884, then he taught in several Italian universities.

Although he had many disciples, he didn't found any "school". His aversion to the formation of "schools" is well known; he said there are only two schools "the school of those who know economics and the school of those who do not" (Pantaleoni 1897: p. 158).

The contribution of Maffeo Pantaleoni to the development of Economics has been studied by many scholars; in particular in relation to the development of the theory of value, considerably influenced by the great attention to empirical studies.

Maffeo Pantaleoni actively participated in the political life of his time. In 1901 he became part of the Chamber of Deputies. He was Minister of Finance in the government of Gabriele D'Annunzio in Fiume (1919). In 1923 he entered the Senate and was a member of the League of Nations.

Maffeo Pantaleoni's bibliography is remarkable. In 1904 Pantaleoni published in the *Giornale degli economisti* an essay entitled "Some observations on the valuations in the absence of market price formation" (*"Alcune osservazioni sulle attribuzioni di valori in assenza di formazione di prezzi di mercato"*).

This essay plays a leading role in the theory of value applied to the financial statements.[1]

Maffeo Pantaleoni is the first economist quoted by Fabio Besta in the *"Prolegomeni"* [Introduction] of his "La Ragioneria" (Besta 1922). Besta does not quote this specific essay. The work of the illustrious economist has contributed to the cultural background of Besta marginally, i.e. in relation to the general theory of value and not to financial statement valuation. Differently, Pantaleoni's "Observations" greatly influenced the work of Gino Zappa and of his disciples.

The essay consists of propositions and proofs.

Among the cases of valuations in the absence of market prices, Pantaleoni focuses on the case relating to the preparation of financial statements of a company. Pantaleoni poses a first research question: "What amount of money, having legal tender status, should be allocated to the various assets and liabilities of financial statements of a firm ['*azienda economica privata*'] where there is no formation of prices in a market?" (Pantaleoni 1904: p. 199).

To answer this question, he formulates the following five propositions:

- *first proposition*: "The end (or purpose) for which financial statements are prepared solely and entirely gives meaning to the valuations that constitute its assets and liabilities" (Pantaleoni 1904: p. 199);
- corollary to the first proposition: "The same set of rights constituting an asset, not only can, but must, receive allocations of different values, depending on the purpose of the valuation" (Pantaleoni 1904: p. 203);
- *second proposition*: "A financial statement forecast, in the absence of a specified purpose, is subject to only one absolute rule, that is, being able to approximate as much as possible what the final statement will actually be" (Pantaleoni 1904: p. 205);
- *third proposition*: "Valuations that consist of forecasted values, (i.e. are forecasted values about the price of actual future realization), have nothing to do with current market or cost prices, no matter how manipulated" (Pantaleoni 1904: p. 208);
- *fourth proposition*: "Valuations in line with forecasts of actual realization should not suffer degeneration for reconciliation with criteria other than the terms of research" (Pantaleoni 1904: p. 219);
- *fifth proposition*: "With financial statements different purposes can be achieved, but these then need to be compatible with each other; if not, different statements should be drawn up for the same company" (Pantaleoni 1904: p. 225).

2 The first proposition

First of all, Pantaleoni states that valuations depend upon the end or purpose for which financial statements are prepared. This means that, when interpreting a statement, readers ascribe an explicit or implicit purpose to their interpretation (Pantaleoni 1904: p. 201); a reader can interpret the "symbols" contained in a financial statement, only by knowing its purposes:

> A financial statement is a set of symbols: the meaning of each symbol is linked to the purpose of the statement: it is illogical to interpret those symbols with criteria that are not linked to the purpose of the statement, even though these criteria are or might be valid in other cases.
>
> (Pantaleoni 1904: p. 199)

Therefore the purposes that underlie the choice of assesment criteria for the preparation of financial statements are the same purposes that allow the interpretation of the financial statement itself:

If *one* criterion inspired the construction of the financial statement (i.e. the valuation) no *other* criteria can be used for its intepretation. If no conscious *criterion*, albeit implicitly, inspired the financial statement valuations, the statement lacks any sense and has nothing but the outward appearance of a statement.

(Pantaleoni 1904: p. 202)

When defining the purposes to be ascribed to the statement that the editor of the financial statement not only *can*, but *must* take into consideration during the valuation process, Pantaleoni clearly distinguishes between liquidation and going-concern hypotheses (i.e. "a company … [that] is fully performing its *physiological* functions").

The distinction between liquidation and going concern is linked to the formation of reserve funds.

In fact … reserve funds (*fondi*), inter alia, serve as coefficients of transformation of the value of a going concern into the value of the same concern, in case of liquidation.

The reserve fund in question is therefore necessary to preserve the capital in case of a writedown deriving from the liquidation of a company (Pantaleoni 1904: p. 224).

One of the most important purposes of a financial statement in a going-concern hypothesis is the dividend calculation. In such a hypothesis we must consider that,

the members of a company are not only the current shareholders, but also the future ones, as corporations, having a separate legal entity and thus being independent from the individuals composing them, represent also the interests of those individuals that might join the company in the future. The current dividend must be neither lower nor higher than the current income. If lower, the current shareholders would be disadvantaged compared to the future ones; the opposite occurs if the current dividend happens to be higher.

(Pantaleoni 1904: p. 201)

3 The second proposition

Going to the second proposition, Pantaleoni clarifies the concept of "forward looking operating statement". The scholar states that "a financial statement forecast, in the absence of a specified purpose, is subject to only one absolute rule, that is, being able to approximate as much as possible what the final statement will actually be"; in such a context, "financial statement forecast" stands for the statement drawn up in the case of a going concern, while "final statement" refers to the statement drawn up in the case of liquidation of the company.

In order to better define these concepts, the author describes and classifies companies according to their production process, that is the "destruction of direct goods aimed at producing capital goods that, in turn, are re-transformed into direct goods" (Pantaleoni 1904: p. 208).

So, at one end of the spectrum, he puts what he defines as "companies with an annual-oriented gestation period", i.e. those companies "whose total assets, originally liquid, will be reconverted into liquid assets within a budget period; namely, one year"; on the other end of the spectrum he defines the "companies with a strongly multi-year-oriented gestation period", i.e. "those companies whose asset transformation process requires a longer period" (Pantaleoni 1904: pp. 205–208).[2]

4 The third proposition

In his third proposition, Pantaleoni states that the valuation should be carried out in accordance with the "forecasted realization values" rather than with the "current prices" or with the "cost values"; no relationship of dependency occurs between the former and the latter. In this way he criticizes both jurists and accountants, who "usually believe they can use a couple of rules as a *passe par tout*"[3] and he stands against the so-called "legalistic-conservative model" (Perrone 1997), disregarding the rule according to which assets must be assessed at the lower of cost and current price.

The arguments provided by Pantaleoni in order to prove the ineffectiveness of the above-mentioned rule can be summarized as follows.

a   Entrepreneurs evasive behaviour:

> This old rule has always been taught but never been applied.... The rule does not hold up, because it does not pursue its own purpose.... Let us consider business owners who have, in their financial statements, some assets that costed less than their current market price; it is impossible for them to value their assets according to this criterion without disregarding the law which might require, for example, a different valuation based on costs. They can only *sell and buy again* their own asset.... In case of securities and values bound with a published price – or in case of goods that generally belong to an organized market – the inadequacy of this rule is so clear that it is usually not prescribed by law; it does only apply in the case of real assets, or movable properties treated as real assets.
>
> (Pantaleoni 1904: pp. 209–210) (here he refers to the Swiss law)

b   "Arbitrariness" when determing the production costs linked to the allocation of indirect costs:

> The rule does not hold up, because a cost is often the result of a combination of expenses that might be arbitrarily allocated to one product

rather than the other. When, for example, there is more than one product resulting from the same technical process, or when the production of a set of products is so interconnected that the expenses incurred for the first product are definitely linked also to the production of the second and the third ones, it is impossible to allocate the whole total cost to just one of these products....

Effectively, specific expenses, such as any raw material incorporated into a specific product, represent in most businesses just the lowest share of expenses and it is certainly not wrong to say that all kinds of expenses are general charges.

(Pantaleoni 1904: pp. 210–212)

c   The "retrospective" meaning of "cost":

a cost is the result of produced and marketed quantity and so it is sub-sequent to the drawing up of the financial statements, unless the statement is just a mere balance-sheet.

(Pantaleoni 1904: p. 212)

d   Complementary factors of production:

When calculating assets according to costs or to current market prices, the concept of utility of products is not taken into consideration. This happens because products are usually grouped according to their complementarity. Jurists and – mostly – accountants have always ignored the latest economic developments on this topic to their own detriment, considering that these studies reflect facts and data collected within the industrial and commercial environment.

Do the single clock gears, taken individually, have the same value as they can achieve by being complementarily assembled into a clock? Does their value equal to their cost? Can they find a selling price regardless of their nature of mutually complementary goods? Does the Retvisan, after being attacked by the Japanese torpedo, have the same value it had before? Does its value equal the sum of the costs of each single part minus those which have been destroyed or deformed by the torpedo? Or is it more likely that each single element composing the Retvisan has been reduced almost to its raw material price? Can a grain milling company, a yarn factory, or a glass manufacturer be evaluated as the sum of each cost or selling price of every single element composing them? And each of these elements, which together constitute a set, is it not in turn a set, so that no one could, in any way, split the whole in any parts and achieve an equal accounting result? Is not every single element a set of complementary goods? Has a patent, before being bought and used, the same value it will acquire after being implemented into a set of complementary goods? Could a patent related to an electric drive mechanism of a factory ... be recorded into the accounts of another factory at the same price, even though the latter does not deal with electrical systems? Or this might only occur if the same patent passes from one electric power company to another, with higher or lower potentials, i.e. if it is implemented in a different system of complementary goods? Any economic asset, either tangible or intangible, changes its value when changing possession; that is the bedrock of the exchange theory. If not, how is it possibile that every system of exchange of goods (from barter to ownership sharing or concentration) creates value as much as a technical transformation process does? Cost theorists must consider this: is the arm of a labourer or the head of a thinker worth the same if amputated from the body or not? If a single complementary element of an asset has been destroyed, compromising the functioning of the asset as a whole, are the liquidated damages commensurate only with the cost or the price of that single element damaged? Creating fruitful interaction among goods that, taken individually, would be fruitless, is the key point in the production of capital goods. And every cost-based or price-based valuation follows a real or hypothetical destruction of the interaction between the single elements of a whole economic assets, i.e. a valuation that does not tell us what the total value actually is.

(Pantaleoni 1904: pp. 212–214)

e   "In many cases, costs do not exist":

> Let us consider, for example, how many banks rediscount their whole portfolio. A bank that rediscounts its portfolio, by acting as endorsee, assumes all the risks, should the acceptor fail to pay. This risk must be covered by the reserve fund. Is there a cost?
>
> (Pantaleoni 1904: p. 214)

When disavowing the effectiveness of the "legalist-prudential" model, Pantaleoni does not want to unconditionally deny that "there might be a special purpose for which the financial statements must be drawn up on a cost basis", that is "a purpose that requires a valuation based upon the current value, at the balance-sheet date".[4] He affirms that, together with those "special purposes"[5] statements, "companies still have to keep drawing up economic-oriented financial statements".[6]

Let us consider, in conclusion, the following statements:

> There is but one fundamental thing: a purpose, an aim, a *special objective*, known and clear, to be achieved.

> But, if we have a different aim, if the purpose of a financial statement is to inform about the actual future revenues, a cost-based statement is useless. There is no link beetween costs and future revenues.

The day on which we sell the stocks ... the price will solely and fully be determined by the match between the demand and the supply curve, on that very same day. It might also vary at different times during the day.... This price, the actual realization price, is influenced by the day and the subject of the valuation!

Costs, current prices at the balance-sheet date, or a current price average, calculated on a weekly (or on a longer period) basis, are therefore useless....

Except in case of a special purpose – that should, however, be mentioned – valuations are not calculated on the basis of current market prices at the balance-sheet date, applied to some or all the different type of assets.

It is therefore clear that, for each portion of stock and for each product to be sold, we must assign a value that equals the future forecasted realization price, discounted at the balance-sheet date.

Do operators know such a price? Of course! Otherwise – unless they had a reasoned opinion on that price, i.e. they hoped to achieve a given price in a given time or in a given period – which realization price per quantity of goods, which criterion were they pursuing when producing and buying?! Which was their speculation? Why did they buy at that price and at that quantity?

By reasoning in this way, they have foreseen a reasonable likelihood over one or more prices, for a given quantity and within a given period. This estimated likelihood has constantly been adjusting, from the purchase date until the balance-sheet date, the latter being the more reliable than the former.

(Pantaleoni 1904: pp. 216–219)

5 The fourth proposition

With the fourth proposition Pantaleoni focuses on the importance of an unaltered valuation, i.e. on the importance of avoiding "degenerative criteria" that might modify values "compliant to the actual forecasts of real realization".

Hence "degenerations" might lead to the formation of hidden reserves, even though they do meet the criterion affirming "that it is prudent to create reserves" (Pantaleoni 1904: p. 219).

Pantaleoni explains that there are two ways of creating reserves, i.e. by write-downs "that alter the valuation"; or "patently" (by allocating profits deriving from a valuation in line with the "forecast of real realization"). He adds that it is undeniably true "that it is prudent to create reserves" and condemns the first way because of the potential risk associated with their "hiddenness":

in order to create reserves, or to be in line with the forecasts, it is necessary to have a benchmark below which reserves will eventually be free to float, ... when reserves affect the valuations, by making them hidden, we lose the main, maybe the only, effective guarantee i.e. the informativity for those who are interested in assessing a financial statement ... when reserves mix with other financial statement figures, we actually have two overlapped statements. These two statements are both known to the board of directors, while only the overlapping one is publicly accessible.

(Pantaleoni 1904: p. 219)

Pantaleoni openly criticizes once again the legal reserve fund required in many legislations[7] and supports the possibility to create different reserves for different purposes ("by stating that a reserve can have many functions, we imply there can be many reserves that differ in size and composition"). After stating that "a reserve represents a processing coefficient of financial statement figures into liquidation values", as already mentioned, the author focuses on another function of a reserve, that is, its role as leveller of dividends.

On this subject, the eminent economist introduces a further classification of firms based on their "generative" process. On the one hand he puts those firms "most capable of delivering more frequent or considerably longer excess earnings" that are "those same companies that deliver more frequent or considerably longer under earnings". On the other hand he puts those firms whose earnings are relatively stable over time (Pantaleoni 1904: p. 224).

On the concept of "under earnings" and, consequently, of "excess earnings", the author affirms:

In case of tangible capital goods ... the lowest earning benchmark ... is achieved whenever the capital good cannot perform its original purpose or any other purpose that might allow to reach a price even remotely close to the original one.

The reasons for such under earnings – and their amount – depend on the obstacles that stand in the way of their disposal, on the one hand, and of their re-investment on the other, i.e. the difficulties in transforming A into B.

(Pantaleoni 1904: p. 223)

Within the second type of firm, "there are no major difficulties in transforming A into B", "prices and costs are proportional", therefore reserve funds do not occur; the second type of firm, instead, "in order not to disappear completely during under-earning periods, should have collected enough reserve funds during the excess-earning periods to cover the under-earnings" (Pantaleoni 1904: p. 224). As a result, the first type of firm must "reduce current profits ... in order to create a reserve able to allow an equal re-allocation of profits in the future" to the extent determined by the "deterioration coefficients linked" (Pantaleoni 1904: p. 223).

6 The fifth proposition

In his fifth proposition Pantaleoni explains the "variety of statements" deriving from the incompatibility of the different "purposes" pursued by a statement.

> A statement can have many "purposes". The exact number of these purposes depends on the circumstances of each individual case....
>
> If the law, or any commercial interest, requires a statement to pursue a variety of purposes, these purposes might not be simultaneously displayed on a single statement.
>
> We need, therefore, to draw up various statements. Each of them will be compliant with one or more compatible purposes.
>
> ... all kind of statements might appear as "trustworthy". At first sight, a single statement might appear "trustworthy" from one point of view, and "untrustworthy" from another. If the statement has been drawn up without a review of its purposes and their compatibility or incompatibility, it will end up being an "untrustworthy" mishmash for all of the interested parties....
>
> The core point does not lie in the selection of one criterion rather than another. The core point is: the stakeholders of a statement must not be confused or misled from the statement itself into a fallacy by hasty simplistic generalization or by an informal accidental mistake.
>
> Commercial companies, in fact, do always keep a different range of statements simultaneously.
>
> (Pantaleoni 1904: p. 199)

The economist explains then who are the different stakeholders of a financial statement and he points out that "financial statements answer a wide range of questions" and "what conceals this fact is that the relevant question changes depending on the kind of firm involved". He consequently gives a classification of both the involved stakeholders and, accordingly, of the potential purposes of a statement.

Among the stakeholders of a financial statement – for whom different statements are drawn up according to their different interests – Pantaleoni includes, first of all, the "shareholders", interested in the "dividends allocation" ("That is, in fact, the main reason why they decide to be shareholders"); then, for "some companies" (e.g. insurance companies and banks) the "consumers of the actual products produced by the company" that are often in a credit position, and, finally, the "actual creditors", i.e. "creditors in the strictest sense of the term".

The purposes ascribable to a statement can be divided into three categories:

> first: the purposes imposed by law; second: the economic purposes that the owner of the company wants to achieve; third: the purposes that the third parties are entitled to expect – ascribable to the first group – or the purposes in which the third parties have an interest. In the latter case, these purposes

will be respected, as they belong to the second category, i.e. an *enlightened* owner is interested in their fullfillment; this is because a company can benefit more from the behaviour of the third parties, of the public, of the creditors, of the competitors than from its economic policy.

(Pantaleoni 1904: p. 233)

A variety of statements is, therefore, desirable because "there might be an incompatibility among the elements of these categories or even among the elements within the same category".[8]

7 Conclusion

The reading of the five propositions and "demonstrations", allows us both to summarize the economist's way of thinking and to make some assumptions.

The *first consideration* arises from the following question: if "jurists" and, with Besta, "accountants" were already dealing with financial statement valuations, why did Pantaleoni start addressing the issue? First of all, a statement, being regulated by the Commercial Code, is worth being considered as "collective" interest. It is no coincidence that Pantaleoni, on the one hand, openly criticizes both the "possibility" of intervention by the legislator during the drawing up of the valuation and the legislation resulting from the Code; on the other hand, he specifically refers to "corporations" (Pantaleoni 1904: p. 199).

The reference entity is a "firm-corporation", with a legal status separated from the one of the shareholders, i.e. with its own "financial autonomy", whose statement must be drawn up from the company itself accordingly to an "objective" interest that takes into consideration the "subjective" interest of *current* and *future* shareholders.

Pantaleoni clarifies that "The current dividend must be neither lower nor higher than the current income. If lower, the current shareholders would be disadvantaged compared to the future ones; the opposite occurs if the current dividend happens to be higher".

From a legal perspective based upon the company's "autonomy", Pantaleoni separates the interests of the company from those of the current owners: "corporations, having a separate legal entity, are independent from the natural persons composing them; they must therefore also represent the interests of those eventual natural persons that might join the company in the future". This lays the basis for an academic discussion on the different degrees of interests converging in a financial statement.[9]

Second, the financial statement is worthy of scientific interest because both "jurists" and "accountants", "have always ignored the latest economic developments on this topic to their own detriment, considering that these studies reflect facts collected within the industrial and commercial environment".

Therefore, economists study "facts" collected within the industrial and commercial environment; "facts" on which Pantaleoni's "Observations" on financial statement valuations are based.

The provided "demonstrations" suggest that, even though referring to a "production process" which is "regular in terms of destruction of direct goods aimed at producing capital goods that, in turn, are re-transformed into direct goods", Pantaleoni considers these "facts" as mostly linked to the market. This lays the foundation for an "economic-fact-driven analysis" for statement valuations.

Since he could not define valuation criteria regardless of those facts, Pantaleoni considers it appropriate to classify companies according to the characteristics of their production process.

Depending on what he defines a company's "gestation period" that can be "annual-oriented", "strongly multi-year-oriented" or classifiable on a continuum between the two, a statement can take on a different "prospective" value: "Each statement drawn up within an interim period is just a forecast; each statement is therefore an estimate and not proper financial statement"; depending on the higher or lower "predisposition" of a company to "deliver" more frequent, or "considerably longer excess-earnings and under-earnings", the formation of "adequate reserves" takes on a different meaning (if we want to avoid that "the firm, or the company with a 'higher predisposition' [will] completely disappear during under-earning periods").

A *second point* concerns the peculiar "role" of the purpose for which the financial statements are drawn up.

A statement is a "set of symbols", i.e. the "merging[10] of a signifier with a code" in order to become a "signified"; conventionally and implicitly, so that "when interpreting a statement, readers ascribe an explicit or implicit purpose to their interpretation".

The purposes on which valuations are determined can be classified into the following categories:

a   "inform" in the case of liquidation, depending on the different purposes of the liquidation itself;
b   "inform" in the case of a going concern, depending on the different "terms determining demand and supply of goods and each element constituting … the factors of production".

Among the purposes to be ascribed to a statement of a going concern, Pantaleoni distinguishes between:

• "dividends calculation";
• "preparation for a merger with another company", or the "participation in a syndicated loan" or "a credit transaction with a bank or with the general public".

It should be noted that, when comparing the value of a company with the value of others or when meeting with the expectations of third parties, "it is necessary to focus on pluriennal [statement] outcomes" and, for the analysis of the financial situation, on criteria that differ from focusing on the accrued values of a given year.

A *third consideration* deals with the "prospective" value of a statement and with the related "complementary properties" of the "factors of production". Pantaleoni clearly explains the meaning of "prospective". He claims that a statement drawn up in the case of a going concern is an "estimated financial statement"; this happens because of the time gap between the "destruction of direct goods" and their "re-tranformation into new direct goods".

This "prospective" approach to the statement leads Pantaloni to choose "a forecast of real future realization prices"; this preference is opposed with both "costs" and "current prices"; it is, therefore, in open contrast with the "legalistic-conservative model" that suggests to choose the lower between the two values (according to the well-known rule of Savary) (Savary 1676).

Pantaleoni refuses Savary's "rule" for the entrepreneurs evasive behaviour (which is, however, a highly topical issue) and for the following further reasons:

- With reference to "cost":

  - he notes the arbitrariness of the determination of production costs due to the allocation of indirect costs;
  - he looks at a "retrospective" meaning of "cost", hence cost being "in function of the produced and disposed quantity", and therefore clearly incompatible with the "prospectivity" of the financial statement.

- with reference to both "cost" and "current prices":

  - he detects their inability to express the actual "utility that goods achieve after merging together in groups with other complementary elements"; "complementarity" of economic goods is also supported, as aforementioned, by Besta. Besta, at a later stage, will "dismiss" this theory by deviating from the "decision utility" model and by approaching the "legalistic-conservative" one. Pantaleoni clearly explains the meaning of "complementary properties" and, in his view, "economic goods" are actual "factors of production".

- in relation to the principle of "complementarity" further remarks are needed:

  - the total value cannot be separated from its "allocation"; this total value changes even by "being transferred from one company ... to another, of higher or lower potential, i.e. if it becomes part of a different system of complementary goods";
  - each valuation based on "cost" or "selling price" must be rejected because "it *follows* a real or hypothetical destruction of the interaction between the single elements of a whole economic assets", i.e. it does not comply with the "total value".

This creates the basis for shifting our "point of view": from a total value given by the sum of assets and liabilities, to a total value consisting of "complementary factors".

Pantaleoni expresses a completely coherent theory, not only with the "prospective-financial model", but also with the "decision utility" one.

Companies must determine profits without opportunistic writedowns and must pay dividends "equal to profits" (in order to avoid inequalities between "current" and "future shareholders"), unless there are "obstacles" to the "transformation process". In such a case it is necessary to create reserves.

With the concepts of "under-earnings" and "excess-earning", Pantaleoni anticipates the concept of "economic life" of the factors of production and lays the foundation for a longer debate on earnings management.[11]

"Excess earnings" and "under earnings" occur in those companies operating within "unstable" enviroments; during "good" economic cycles we have "excess earnings" because of a "growing gap" between the selling price and the unit cost of production; obviously, the opposite happens in periods of "downturn".

A *final* brief *consideration* concerns once again the key role of Pantaleoni's "Observations" within the Italian academic discussion on the opposition between the necessity of a "single" balance sheet and a "variety" of documents.[12] He underlines the "incompatibily" between the different "purposes" ascribable to a balance sheet (i.e. among different assessing criteria) and states that, in order to have reliable statements, "we need to draw up various statements ... each of them will be compliant with one or more compatible purposes".

Notes

1 For a more detailed analysis see D'Amico 1999, Palumbo 2003 and Palumbo 2005.
2 "This classification of companies," states Pantaleoni,

> mainly shows us how surreal this harmonization process actually is; a process that aims at standardizing all of the valuation criteria for corporation statements, and also at classifying assets and liabilities into similar categories. Yet, this is the purpose of accountants and bookkeepers and we cannot exclude that, in the future, this nonsense will also be consecrated, i.e. made mandatory by law, as it already happened.
>
> (Pantaleoni 1904: p. 208)

3 Someone will say: "we must evaluate on a current price basis"; others will say, instead, "we must evaluate on a selling price basis", or on a production cost basis. Some will complicate this simple rule and say: "here [we consider] current prices, there [we consider] costs".

> (Pantaleoni 1904: pp. 208–209)

4 In that case

> there is no reason not to draw up a statement that way! We just need to avoid misinterpretations. We just need not to mistake a mule for a donkey or for a horse. But, if we need a mule, let's produce a mule! And we cannot a priori exclude that this might be a convenient result.
>
> (Pantaleoni 1904: p. 215)

5 These "special purposes" might eventually meet the information requirements of the international statistician or of the legislator.

6 "Purposes," adds Pantaleoni,

> that differ from a statistical purpose. Let us assume that the law preferred a single statement of a particular sort by imposing its publication, while exempting directors from the current obligation to draw up further statements (i.e. statements related to the different directors' legal liability deriving from different Codes of Commerce). This would clearly eliminate any chance of control, even if trying to create an effective one.
>
> (Pantaleoni 1904: p. 215)

7 The law imposes the collection of at least one twentieth of the net income, until reaching one fifth of the asset. But why one twentieth of the net income?... The same law does not define the net profit calculation, not even in relation to the formation of a reserve fund; therefore this reserve represents the 5% of an X value, no equation given. In such case, isn't this legislative requirement meaningless? Doesn't it compel the administration to calculate incomes with regard to the reserve, i.e. to calculate incomes in relation to the given values of that arbitrary variable represented by the statutory reserve, instead of proceeding inversely?... The law, in addition, refers to just one reserve. But, by stating that one reserve has many functions, we imply there can be many reserves that differ in size and composition.

(Pantaleoni 1904: p. 222)

8 "The most ambiguous case," adds Pantaleoni, "occurs when incompatibility arises among elements of the first category i.e. those imposed by law. And the law contradicts itself frequently, when it has many purposes" (Pantaleoni 1904: p. 233). With reference to the Italian Code of Commerce of that time, when affirming that its requirements "respond to the interests of the third parties and to those of the owner", the author says:

> Our law sets the following conditions in relation to valuations. Essential is the art. 89 of the (1882) Code of commerce, which provides that the memorandum and the articles of association must include the provisions regulating the formation of the statement and the profit valuation. They must also state the value of the receivables and of any other contributed fund ... with this provision ... in the absence of others, the owner can, in full freedom ... choose the provisions best suited to their interest..., The only safeguard for the right of third parties is the publicity of these criteria. This is, however, a sufficient guarantee.... [even though] it is claimed that, along with this provision, there are others that might restrict the owner's freedom. The main limitation is considered to be the one provided for in art. 176 that affirms that: the statement must truthfully highlight the *actual* generated profits and incurred losses. But, what are the "*actual* generated profits?"
>
> (Pantaleoni 1904: pp. 233–235)

9 On this topic, see, in particular: Amaduzzi 1949.

10 In its original meaning, with reference to its use in Ancient Greece, [the symbol] was a mean of identification and control obtained by unevenly splitting an object in two parts, so that only the owner of one of the two parts could be identified by matching them ... [From] Greek "sýmbolon", derivation of "symbállō", i.e. "combine".

11 See Canziani 1997 and Pini 1991.

12 See D'Oriano 1993.

References

Amaduzzi, A. (1949), *Conflitto ed equilibrio di interessi nel bilancio dell'impresa*, Cacucci, Bari.

Besta, F. (1920), *La Ragioneria, Parte prima, Ragioneria generale*, Vol. III, Milano: Vallardi.

Besta, F. (1922), *La ragioneria, ristampa della II ed. riveduta ed ampliata col concorso dei proff. Vittorio Alfieri, Carlo Ghidiglia, Pietro Rigobon*, Milano: Vallardi.

Canziani, A. (1997), "Per il ritorno a una concezione classica in tema di bilancio di esercizio", *Scritti di economia aziendale in memoria di Raffaele D'Oriano*, t. 1, Padova: CEDAM.

D'Amico, L. (1999), *Profili del processo evolutivo negli studi di economia aziendale. Schema di analisi per "paradigmi" e "Programmi di Ricerca Scientifici"*, Torino, Giappichelli.

D'Oriano, R. (1993), "Sulla visione 'classica' del bilancio d'esercizio", in *Scritti in Onore di Carlo Masini*, tomo terzo, Milano: EGEA.

Palumbo, R. (2003), *Profili della teoria del valore negli studi di ragioneria: dall'affermazione del paradigma bestano alla proclamazione delle tendenze nuove*, Torino: Giappichelli.

Palumbo, R. (2005), *Approcci prospettivo, retrospettivo e prudenziale nella elaborazione dei paradigmi contabili. Sviluppo scientifico e conflitti di paradigma*, Torino: Giappichelli.

Pantaleoni, M. (1897), Del carattere delle divergenze d'opinione esistenti tra economisti, Vol. 1, in Pantaleoni, M. (1925), *Erotemi di economia*, Bari: Laterza

Pantaleoni, M. (1904), "Alcune osservazioni sulle attribuzioni di valori in assenza di formazione di prezzi di mercato", Giornale degli economisti, I, 1904, reprinted in *Scritti varii di Economia, serie seconda, 1909, and in Erotemi di economia*, Bari, 1925.

Pantaleoni, M. (1925), *Erotemi di economia*, Bari: Laterza.

Perrone, E. (1997), *La ragioneria ed i paradigmi contabili*, Padova: CEDAM.

Pini, M. (1991), *Politiche di bilancio e direzione aziendale*, Milano: Etas.

Savary, J. (1676), *Le parfait négociant ou Instruction générale pour ce qui regarde le Commerce de toute sorte de Marchandises, tant de France, que des Pays Étrangers*, Geneva.

2 Fabio Besta

Financial valuations at the beginning of the twentieth century in Italy

Antonella Paolini and Michela Soverchia

1 Introduction and contextualization

Fabio Besta (Teglio di Valtellina, 1845–Tresivio di Sondrio, 1922) is today renowned as one of the greatest Italian scholars of accounting.

An accounting teacher, first at the Technical Institute of Accountants of Sondrio (1871), and then from 1872 to 1920 at Venice's Scuola Superiore di Commercio – the first post-secondary school for commerce in Italy – he combined teaching with a passion for study and research, researching a wide range of accounting issues (Antoni 1970).

Besta's period of activity and scientific production runs from the final decades of the nineteenth century to the first decades of the twentieth. It was a distinctive period, given that Italy had only recently achieved political unification, and the socio-economic environment in which Besta lived was in the midst of tremendous change. In fact, Italy was transitioning from a mainly agriculture-based economic system towards a more industrial economy, with a growing amount of technological progress in production processes; Italians were moving from being craftspeople towards capitalists, characterized by a growing dynamism in which production was separated from distribution (Catturi 1997).

Exactly between the late nineteenth century and early twentieth, and following a period of decline, the study of accounting and the debate surrounding it resumed in full force in Italy, largely due to Besta, who dealt with a broad array of themes, as evidenced by the titles of his publications (see Table 2.1). *La Ragioneria* is certainly his most important publication: it is a voluminous work, consisting of three volumes dedicated to a very broad spectrum of accounting issues, including the history of accounting (Sargiacomo *et al.*, 2012).

An analysis of Fabio Besta's works reveals the extent to which he also devoted his efforts to public accounting, specifically State accounting. This emerges both from his teaching activities – he taught State accounting for many years – as well as his participation in reform discussions that, over the years, also came to include Italian State accounts and budgets. Besta was also a member of a commission – constituted in 1904 by the then-Minister of the Treasury Luzzatti – tasked with developing a project aimed at restoring the

Table 2.1 Fabio Besta's principal publications

Year	Original title	English translation
1872	*Sulla capitalizzazione continua degli interessi*	About continuous capitalization of interests
1880	*La Ragioneria – Prolusione*	Accounting – inaugural address
1886–1887	*Computisteria mercantile*	Business arithmetic
1886–1887	*Registri e registrature*	Registers and registration
1891–1916	*La Ragioneria* (volumi I, II, III)	Accounting (Volumes I, II, III)
1897–1898	*Contabilità di Stato (dispense litografate)*	Government accounting
1908	*Sulle riforme proposte ai nostri istituti di contabilità di Stato: prolusione letta nella solenne apertura degli studi per l'anno 1908–1909 dal prof. Fabio Besta*	On the proposed reforms to our public accounting institutes: introductory essay, read on the solemn occasion of the opening of the academic year 1908–1909 by Prof. Fabio Besta
1909	*Sulle riforme proposte ai nostri istituti di Contabilità di Stato (prolusione letta nella solenne apertura degli studi per l'anno scolastico 1908–1909)*	Proposed reforms of State accounting issues
1912	*Ragioneria: le società anonime*	Accounting: limited public companies
1920	*Lezioni di Ragioneria: trattati speciali*	Accounting lessons: special treatises

double-entry bookkeeping method in Italian State accounting (Besta 1909a: p. 28 ss.; Anselmi 2006: p. 96 ss.), born of the previously non-too-successful application of logismography by Giuseppe Cerboni in the second half of the nineteenth century.

2 Fabio Besta's accounting theory

Besta is the scholar who roots accounting in its full scientific dimension. He takes a positivist approach, using historical and experimental methods, believing there is a fundamental incompatibility between science and practice. As a result, theoretical development must be based on real, observed facts.

The construction of his theoretical system also benefits from advances in knowledge, as evidenced during the nineteenth century through the works of such scholars as Francesco Villa and Giuseppe Cerboni, notwithstanding that the latter's accounting theories and applications – taking an idealistic approach – are harshly criticized by Besta in light of the positivist conception of science permeating his entire work.

For Besta, the *azienda* represents

the sum total of phenomena, or business, or relationships to manage relative to an accumulation of wealth forming a whole unto itself, or an individual, or a family, or any group, or even only a separate class of those phenomena, business, or relationships.

(*la somma di fenomeni, o negozi, o rapporti da amministrare relativi ad un cumulo di capitali che formi un tutto a sé, o a una persona singola, o a una famiglia o ad un'unione qualsivoglia, od anche soltanto una classe distinta di quei fenomeni, negozi o rapporti.*)

(Besta 1909b: p. 3)

He divides *aziende* into two main categories: on the one hand there are businesses (whether commercial, banking, agricultural, manufacturing, etc.), where the goal, means and management's purpose is to accumulate valuable material possessions, given that capital is a means to their creation. On the other hand, there are all other *aziende* in which this accumulation is merely a means for satisfying the needs of one or more people. Such wealth can be known, as in domestic companies with a fixed amount of income at their disposal, or indefinite (but not unlimited) as with State and other public entities, possessing a variable amount of wealth according to their citizens' contributions (Besta 1909b: p. 16 ss.).

The common thread running through the various classes of *aziende*, then, is the use and care of wealth: one cannot conceive of a company without the existence of a substance, or wealth "and every business has wealth, whether small or large" (Besta 1909b: p. 4).

The *azienda*, broadly understood, is therefore the goal of "economic administration" (amministrazione economica), namely "the governance of the phenomena, negotiations, and relevant relationships impacting the cycle of wealth within the *aziende*" (Besta 1909b: p. 5). It represents a vast and diverse scientific field, in which we can discern three distinct phases, namely: operations (activities relating to acquisition, use, and transmission of wealth); management (activities regulating and governing operations); and control (assessing and analysing causes and effects of operations in order to manage "economic labour") (Besta 1909b: p. 26).

In the first two phases the administrative functions are very dissimilar from the many kinds of *azienda* that Besta observed, a source of conflict with Cerboni who instead argued that one could trace everything back to the same functions. Notwithstanding, according to Besta, operations and management lack unity, and therefore scientific autonomy (Paolini 1990: p. 21; Ferraris Franceschi 1994: p. 64).

While operations and management vary significantly from one kind of *azienda* to another (think about public entities), economic control is a feature common to all economic units. Besta wants to examine every kind of *azienda*:

only economic control – a feature common to all economic units – could be the object of scientific observation and conclusion. Accounting, according to Besta, rises to the rank of science, and – compared with the unitary characteristics – it becomes the "science of economic control" for each kind of *azienda*. Thus,

> accounting's theoretical aspect identifies and sets forth the laws of economic control in every kind of *azienda*, and from there extrapolates the rules to be followed to enable truly effective, persuasive, and complete control; where – as a practical matter – such rules are applied in an orderly fashion.
>
> (Besta 1880: p. 20)

Economic control – nourished by its dual functions of understanding or registration of the various events of the *azienda*'s life, on the one hand, and labour constraints, on the other – studies a defined object: wealth. Besta's accounting theory seeks to investigate the *azienda*'s wealth, that is the complex of resources composed of positive (assets) and negative (liabilities) aspects at a given point in its life.

That complex and measurable goal through budgets, accounting bookkeeping and financial statements: the amount of the *azienda*'s wealth and its related variations generated by administrative events is subject to continuous monitoring. The economic result is a synthesis of changes in the wealth's positive and negative components, from start to close of the relevant period. Specifically, assets are goods and rights from use and possession that impact net wealth (equity); liabilities, on the other hand, are obligations from use and holding that impact equity. The difference between positive and negative elements yields the wealth (net worth), emphasizing wealth's static dimension.

Besta is known as the founder of the so-called "value-based accounts theory" (*teorica dei conti a valore*), based on the fact that wealth's elements, given their intrinsic variety and heterogeneity, can only be properly considered under the uniform aspect that makes them comparable, i.e. their value, expressed in their own currency. In this sense, Besta continues the work of Francesco Villa, the main representative of the Lombardy School of Accounting, who viewed accounting as part of a broader administrative process. For the latter, value – the monetary measurement of physical elements – is an innovative approach compared to other contemporaneous accounting theories such as those of Francesco Marchi and Giuseppe Cerboni, which were linked to the accounts personification. Both Cerboni's theoretical approach as well as Besta's highlight wealth's key role: Cerboni's personalistic approach utilizes a legal framework, while Besta's approach uses an economic or value-based one (Melis 1950: p. 773; Coronella 2007: p. 151).

According to Besta, wealth must be controlled across all of its variations.

Besta's approach (a patrimonialistic one) adopts an analytical and atomistic view: the *azienda* is the sum of several elements, every item of wealth is likely an independent atom with its own value and it has to be valuated independently from the other ones.

Wealth is the object of Besta's accounting system, the so-called "patrimonial system" (an equity-based accounting system), based on rigorous application of double-entry bookkeeping method, i.e. a record-keeping system aimed at knowledge and measurement of the *azienda*'s wealth. Significantly, Besta is the first scholar to draw a strict distinction between accounting system and method, two concepts that had hitherto been improperly conflated (Besta 1920: p. 276).

With respect to wealth, the complex object of this system, we can highlight two aspects: first, the "real aspect", relating to the various real elements it is composed of (money, debts, credits, properties, etc.); and second an "ideal aspect", inherent in wealth as a whole and every value ascribable to variations resulting from *azienda*'s operations (equity and its variations for income and loss).

The assets and liabilities variations (real or original changes) determine the corresponding changes in equity (ideal or derivative changes). One series of accounts was kept for real elements (assets and liabilities) and another one for ideal elements, derived from the fund's variable total sum. The sum of individual changes in assets and liabilities occurring in a certain period yields the income measure: periodic income is a specific change in equity. In fact, in Besta's view, the balance sheet is the financial statement's principal document, whereas the profit and loss account is a kind of addition, given that income is the accounting measurement for wealth variation.

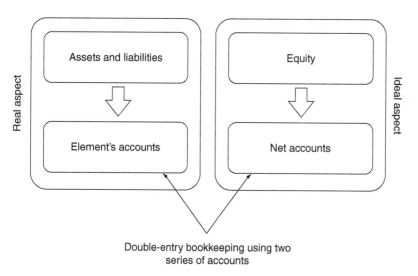

Figure 2.1 Fabio Besta's equity-based accounting system.

3 Financial valuations in Besta's accounting theory

3.1 General principles

Besta's contributions to valuation of an *azienda*'s operational capital is undoubtedly critical for its:

- detailed and specific explanations for every item to be valued;
- coherent and rigorous scientific approach, used for the first time.

As noted earlier, economic control – that is, accounting – the stronghold of the equity-based accounting system becomes the unifying analytical concept. Besta applies it uniformly and with uniform tools across all kinds of *aziende*. Thus, control includes an accounting system based on the "value-based accounting theory". Value, understood as the monetary expression of assets,[1] had allowed Besta's peers and their predecessors to imagine accounts that worked better within these unifying parameters. Besta completes his theory by identifying a single complex object, formed from individual accounts/elements of wealth of all *aziende*. The valuation concept is ever-present, operation by operation and movement after movement, even if the unifying thread (the general principle) is that of first establishing the analytical result of each operation and then the general result of all operations relating to the relevant period.

What is being valued? What are the elements comprising this entire body of wealth being studied?

According to Besta, we can identify the wealth's elements (and thus arrive at its monetary measure or valuation) by combining two criteria:

1 Possession: the wealth element's value is linked to single, simple availability, that is, to ownership of the asset or rights and responsibilities. In Besta's view, simple possession, the passage of time, and changing environmental (market) conditions could impact the subject element's intrinsic value.
2 Use: the wealth element's value is linked to its role in the *azienda*'s functioning.

Besta is one of the first Italian accounting scholars to make a serious and systematic study of valuation theory based on the work of several economists of that period, such as F. Ferrara and M. Pantaleoni, from whom he borrowed some value concepts, such as the use value (*valor d'uso*), that is a subjective value; the production cost value or replacement cost value (*valore di costo* or *costo di riproduzione*), based on real facts; and the exchange value (*valore di cambio*), the price at which an exchange is made.

Besta identifies the exchange value as representing the only real value (*valore vero o reale*): the best criterion to accurately value the *azienda*'s wealth at a specific moment of its life cycle. Similarly, Besta clearly states, "there can be no doubt that, if we seek true precision in determining wealth at a given moment, we have to determine the exchange value of each of its component elements for which such values are known" (Besta 1909b: p. 417). Moreover, many passages highlight that exchange value is the building block of the *azienda*'s wealth: "wealth means every asset that can be exchanged for another, that therefore can be purchased, or, if you will, an exchange value" (Besta, 1909b: p. 2).

This approach is consistent with Besta's positivist approach, according to which theoretical development must be based on observation of actual facts: transactions are actual facts, and their monetary value can be considered an objective value.

Does a valid financial valuation principle exist for every element of wealth? To Besta the answer is affirmative: it is real value (*valore reale*) or the real price (*prezzo reale*). Here it bears mention that this clean and concise statement reflects the writers' own deliberation and conclusion. The term "real value" has the same meaning as other synonyms Besta uses, which more precisely indicate value on a case-by-case basis.

Besta differentiates between price, the monetary expression of an asset at the moment of its purchase or sale, and value, the sum of money at the moment of valuation and exchange, at which latter point it changes to price, even if these are frequently identical.

Following is a glossary of terms Besta employs, relating back to the concept of "real value":

- "true value" (*valore vero*) or "trade value" (*valore di scambio*), an estimate of the amount of money necessary to buy the same type of asset one is valuing, or with minor differences but having the same utility, using active markets as a frame of reference;
- "current price" (*prezzo corrente*) and "current value" (*valore corrente*) when parties agree to purchase or sell, or negotiate, the amount of money required to obtain the same kind of assets one is valuing, or a slightly different asset having the same utility, using values from an active market as a frame of reference;
- "normal or common price" (*prezzo normale* or *comune*) and "normal or common value" (*valore normale* or *comune*): prices or values that are between a *minimum* "current price" (or current value) and a *maximum* current price (or current value), with terms as defined above;
- "reproduction value" (*valore di riproduzione*) an estimate of the amount of money necessary to physically reconstruct the same asset one is valuing (with internal physical reproduction data) or build a different asset that can offer the same utility (with internal economic reproduction information);
- "actual value" (*valore attuale*) using an asset's income (rent, interest, profit, etc.) as a basis for valuation using its discounting calculation (capitalization).

Besta's preference for "real value" over "cost" does not mean that he fails to elucidate or use the concept of cost in its various meanings, but rather that in the value estimation, as with every other judgment relating to sufficiency, the human mind is not moved by the contemplations of the past, but by the ones of the present and the future; rather, we think about the past only in order to reason about the present and predict the future with greater accuracy. Knowing the actual cost of given assets, especially if they were recently manufactured, can influence the assessment of their value, as it is a clue about the current cost and the future of identical assets.

(Besta 1909b: p. 231)

Given the foregoing general principles, we turn now to an assessment of his valuation process for a few positive and negative elements of the *azienda*'s wealth. To aid the reader, the following is a logical analysis of Besta's work:

- first, we will explain the theoretical/ideal financial valuation criteria the author describes and proposes as optimal;
- we will then set forth the possible problems in concrete application of these rules (*problems of application*);
- finally we offer solutions to problems posed by the author (*practical solutions*).

3.2 Inventories

In Besta's time, the main category of wealth was definitely "assets in stock or circulating capital" (*beni che appartengono alla scorta o al capitale circolante*). The diffusion of commercial companies and non-automated manufacturing firms with high numbers of labourers demonstrates that assets in inventory were one of the main components of wealth.

The general principle of valuation of inventory is that of normal price or repurchase price (*prezzo normale, comune,* or *ricompera*), also identified in various other parts of Besta's work as "exchange value" or also "current price."

We note first that as a general inventory valuation principle Besta prefers the value expressed by the market at the moment of its valuation. For Besta, inventory, apart from the moment of its purchase, or from its current and future use, has a market-driven, negotiable value, and it is in that market where one must gather current pricing information.

Besta is, however, fully aware that it is not always possible or convenient to gather such information. We've therefore chosen two of the main situations Besta used to illustrate some of the problems relating to application of the general rule of current price:

1   it does not apply for goods that are not purchased frequently or for goods that have very volatile prices;
2   it does not apply for semi-finished goods and goods that are works-in-progress, as they are not objects of trade and there are no market references.

These two cases are not entirely marginal, especially the second relating to manufacturing companies, which finally spread to Italy in the second half of the nineteenth century; as a solution Besta proposes substituting "current price" (*prezzo corrente*) with "effective cost (*costo effettivo*) or "nominal value" (*valore nominale*), which could be consistent with "purchase price" (*costo d'acquisto*) in case 1 above and "cost of production" (*costo di produzione*) in case 2.

To summarize, Besta thought it more accurate that wealth – in the case of inventory – has current value in line with its reference markets; the current value (*valore corrente*) is preferable as it follows general rules relating to an asset's intrinsic value (the rule of possession) and then its use (asset use for operations).

Pragmatically speaking, Besta is willing to change principles only if "current price" cannot be recouped, and he advises using internal information, from asset purchase to production documentation.

3.3 Fixed assets

During Besta's time agricultural holdings are still a principle component of the Italian economy, in fact the fixed assets of *aziende* are mainly land, as well as material capital or equipment goods. Besta devotes many pages to the classification of these aspects of production: "goods that currently belong to the *azienda*" (Besta 1909b: p. 83), divided mainly into real property or fixed assets and personal property; these last are today grouped together and broadly defined as tangible fixed assets, that is, land, buildings, and capital or equipment goods.

For Besta, the valuation principle for fixed assets is no different from the general principle we've already described for inventory. However, he employs an additional specific term: "actual exchange value" (*valore di cambio attuale*) to indicate that real estate is not frequently bought or sold. Nonetheless, compared to certain markets where inventory is negotiated (consumer goods), markets in which fixed assets are exchanged function well and it is to them one must turn to ascertain the actual value of one's assets, i.e. the "current price".

Notwithstanding such observations, the difficulties of determining the exchange value of rural and urban assets were clear to Besta: values contained in balance sheets are temporally distant from actual market value and, therefore, he is fully aware that as a general rule one could assign values that are indicia of their purchase price, that is "the portion that has not been amortized" (Besta 1909b: p. 266). He emphasizes though, that exchange value – i.e. market value – "must never be lost sight of", as it is the maximum amount that can be reasonably assigned to those assets in determining net wealth. Besta suggests the use of valuation criteria implemented by the *Istituto di credito fondiario* when taking fixed assets as security for loans.

The goal of the valuation of fixed assets is to find its exchange value. To determine this one uses recommended specific methods:

1   direct method in markets: a) summary; b) detailed;
2   indirect method on valuation data: a) summary; b) detailed;

1a) *direct method/summary*: can be determined without too much uncertainty as one studies market transactions with the knowledge (i.e. conscious of the issues) that contracts unfold slowly and that assets subject to valuation are seldom homogenous;

1b) *direct method/detailed*: identification of positive and negative components of net income derived from fixed assets and discounted to arrive at the capital value of those fixed assets, knowing that income is not constant over time;

2a) *indirect method/summary*: one could consult a land register in order to use the relationship between "typical land value" and "typical income from land"; this indicator is considered constant across all lands and can be used to discount taxable income from goods to be valued, so as to assess their value;

2b) *indirect method/detailed*: assets to be valued are classified based on their extent and other quali-quantitative characteristics; one can examine available estimates for "types of land" and then calculate net income; finally, for individual categories one applies the discount calculation. Notwithstanding the choice of principle and availability of alternative methods to determine exchange value, Besta spends numerous pages on valuation based on costs of fixed assets (Besta 1909b: pp. 238–257).

Excluding land[2] from the issue of amortization and loss of value, all other fixed assets are not exempt, and therefore, initial value is certainly a general problem to be resolved, but not as much for Besta. He maintains that the depreciation calculation corresponds proportionally to the determination of profits to be restarted from the end of each financial period[3] as well as the interests that would mature on amounts so calculated;[4] every amortized portion is subtracted from the profits from the same year without, however, this operation being considered "reserve profits" (*utili posti in serbo*) (Besta 1909b: p. 251), but rather as a negative or loss component of the final net profit.

Besta then organizes the calculation of the depreciation amount, that is the decrease in the asset's original cost, by classifying the fixed assets according to three categories:

1   owned real property (buildings, machines, tools, furniture, etc.);
2   licensed real property (aqueducts, lighting systems, etc.);
3   capitalized costs (enterprise organization costs, client acquisition, start-up costs for specific undertakings, etc.).

With respect to the first category, he specifically notes that their deterioration can never be complete (Besta 1909b: p. 241). Moreover, the amount of depreciation is expressed as the difference between cost and the price that is attainable at the moment of their divestment. He also notes that it is impossible to determine the economically useful lifespan in numbers of years for many reasons, such as:

its use for different purposes (more or less active use), the *azienda*'s condition, new necessities, habits, new uses, future progress or discoveries.

As for the second and third categories of assets, the depreciation calculation is more simple because it is linked to time: the annual amounts must be able to cover the entire cost based on when they were granted/acquired in the case of fixed assets it contains, based on the lifespan of the *azienda*, or its transactions for capitalized costs, etc.

For Besta, valuation of assets of the *azienda* having long lifespans is therefore complex, and, using a practical approach, he looks for specific solutions to many problems posed by the different asset classes, which we will briefly address.

As he specifies in one chapter's title, the purchase price – summary and detailed valuations – should be used, especially for rural and urban fixed assets. Specifically, in the case of public administration (as well as individual non-commercial businesses where profit distribution is unnecessary) fixed assets keep the same value, i.e. cost, or purchase price, old estimates, or summary valuations, for long periods in the company records. He reiterates that this is all unacceptable for companies that must, for financial period after financial period, distribute profits and losses among partners; therefore, he hopes for a non-arbitrary measure of fixed assets, but in fact achieves, once again, cost valuation while hoping it is correct, accurate and complete in the records, so that the asset cost is the amount to take into consideration and subject to depreciation (Besta 1909b: p. 303).

The desired valuation at a more correct "current price" is not always easy to achieve, given the intrinsic and varied characteristics of such assets, especially because, from an accounting perspective, there is increased complexity. Moreover, the following coexist: purchase price; the asset's incremental cost; costs that must take total progression of the business into account (production of profits or losses), and interest rate trends that amounts invested in such goods might yield; actual exchange value (on the market) apart from the functions performed by the assets within the *azienda*. Besta therefore accepts both criteria: the adoption of the cost criterion seems, nonetheless, more a possibility than a stringent necessity (Gonnella 2012: p. 543).

3.4 Types of credit and debt. Securities

For these categories of wealth, it is easier to apply the preferred valuation criteria, namely, their "actual value" (*valore attuale*):

• amounts relating to rights to receive payments on account of debts from third parties, to the net amount of estimated losses, marked up by applicable interest receivable, accrued for the longer periods for repayment that the *azienda* grants its debtors;
• amounts relating to debts owed to third parties, marked up by applicable interest payable, accrued for any longer period for repayment the *azienda*'s creditors grant the *azienda*;
• the most recent quotation in the market where the securities are negotiated.

However, even in these cases Besta finds significant problems for the general valuation rule. Specifically:

1   not all debts or credits are easily discounted;
2   credit instruments, particularly shares, are not always available on the markets.

Besta's solution to the problem of lack of application of current value due to discounting is "nominal value" (*valore nominale*) which has two meanings:

1   it corresponds "in a certain, fixed way" to the amount of money measuring the rise in the debt or credit;
2   it is the historic cost of purchase – or issue – of a "fixed nominal value" (*valore nominale fermo*).

For the first meaning, nominal values, for Besta, "are not values in the true sense of the word, because they cannot be valued against assets that are identical in type and shape" (Besta 1909b: p. 257), but they are important and can be safely and consistently estimated. In this sense, he cites the nominal value of public and private credit instruments, but also the promissory notes and bonds issued by companies.

   With respect to the second meaning, on the other hand, nominal values are "real values, even if roughly estimated, and remind one somehow of the *nominal prices* that appear in stock exchanges" (Besta 1909b: p. 258); they are equally important, but cannot be definitively determined, given that they are based on: old estimates that were never updated/modified; summary and arbitrary estimates; historical costs.

   Ultimately, it would be necessary to discount the nominal value to arrive at current value if it is impossible to determine nominal value within the original meaning.

4 The real value of wealth elements: the accrual and prudence principles

In Section 3.1, we described Besta's clear preference for "real value" in the area of wealth valuation. In theory, this should be used to measure all wealth elements as well as their modifications:

- internal management operations determine physical variations that could increase real value for example in the case of materials that are transformed to semi-finished products;
- external management operations determine physical variations that can increase real value for example in the case of the sale of products.

From a practical perspective, as we've observed in the preceding sections, Besta highlights that it is not always possible to increase "real value", for example in the case of semi-finished products. We have therefore queried whether this "real value" is always "current value". The answer is not clear:

- yes, if current value is reliably determined or determinable by the existence of a functional exchange market;
- no, if the uncertainty of realizing current value justifies adoption of "effective cost" or "nominal value" criteria.

The "real value" equals the "current value", as Besta hoped, if the final current value of a wealth element is different from its initial current value, insofar as a holding gain or loss can be determined. This is therefore a valuation that systematically and periodically takes wealth revaluation into account (higher final current value of initial current value) or wealth devaluation (lower final current value of initial current value) and therefore the value of a single wealth element is included in the income calculation not only based on its use for management, but also for its intrinsic value. This procedure for valuation of wealth elements can be deemed:

- correct if the real value is reliable;
- underestimation or overestimation of income (lack of prudency) if valuation is not reliable.

However, such a holding gain or loss can also derive from changes in valuation criteria. If an asset increases and decreases as a result of changes in valuation criteria, Besta proposes an asymmetric accounting treatment. In fact, if a change in a valuation criterion causes an increase of wealth at the end of period, the higher value cannot be considered a component of income but must be included in a special reserve (*fondi di riserva speciali* or *masse di rispetto*). If, on the other hand, a change in a valuation criterion causes wealth to decrease at the end of the period, we may not automatically use the special reserve; rather, in specific circumstances, it is proper to consider the lower value as a component of loss (Alexander *et al.* 2010: p. 4).

Is value then, according to Besta, an absolute or relative concept? He would appear to think that value is relative when he states that "different criteria and procedures must be followed according to the causes and different purposes arising with inventory drafting" (Besta, 1920: p. 11):

- Liquidation of the firm: if exchange value is correctly used, then it is advisable to sell products/goods at prices lower than current ones (Besta 1920: pp. 11–12).
- Sale of the firm: this is not a dissolution of the firm, thus goodwill must be calculated (future profits exceeding normal ones characterizing firms of the same kind/sector (Besta 1920: p. 12).
- Year-end financial statement (going-concern business): it would be incorrect to use exchange value, because it would imply a liquidation (disaggregation of wealth), which is not the case.

In the end, even if Besta identifies real value as the best criterion, is real value used to measure all kinds of wealth elements and their modifications? According to him, in theory, yes. In practice – as we saw in relation to different elements of the *azienda*'s wealth – no, given that problems arise when Besta moves from theory to practice (for example to assess the exchange value of an asset when there is no real exchange, which leads to an estimate, not an objective value). So Besta adopts the historical cost (a second choice of sorts, an accommodation criterion) as the standard criterion for the valuation of wealth's elements in order to meet two main priorities:

- he wants to reduce the discretion of those who prepare financial statements to the greatest extent possible, even as it is an instrument of control of their work;
- following the prudence principle, he wants to "prevent by all means any incorrect calculation of any profit that is not based on reality" (Besta 1909b: p. 264).

These two reasons are so compelling that they lead Besta to surrender to an (ideally) correct assessment of the *azienda*'s wealth – one that should be obtained using exchange value. He writes that "in preparing financial statements, rather than an exact assessment of single elements, it is important to obtain a prudent, and not arbitrary, determination of net profit" (Besta 1909b: p. 265). We must also consider that the conditions for price stability and the trend of perfect competition characterizing the second half of the nineteenth and the early twentieth century lead to only minor differences between assessments made at cost and assessments made at normal price (*de minimis* error, which is justified by the above need).

Therefore, from a reading of Besta's work, the accrual principle emerges as the salient principle. In fact, as he writes, "any change in value ... is gain or loss ... future changes will increase, decrease, or eradicate that gain or loss, but they cannot change what has happened" (Besta 1909b: p. 264). Thus, transactions and other events are linked to the periods to which they relate, regardless of when cash or its equivalent is exchanged, and causes of changes in the asset's value compared to its initial value can either be business transactions in that period or belong to the firm's wealth.

The prudence principle may be considered a residual principle. Besta writes that it needs to not exceed in financial valuations to avoid a wrong income measurement; this seems more an administrative prudence that an estimative one, and it suggests that valuations should be reliable.

Besta states that the firm should not consider profits as realized, but that it must record a loss that has already occurred in order to avoid subjecting itself to failures and losses (Besta 1909b: p. 264). However, he is critical of a strong prudence principle if it leads to undervaluation of assets in such a way that the owner may be induced to sell them at a low price. Besta states that each firm should be ready for liquidation:

well-ordered firms should always be ready for an orderly liquidation ...,
they must keep their accounting records and prepare their annual financial
statements so that, if the liquidation occurs, wealth appears in its original
measure and therefore does not appear diminished.

(Besta 1909b: p. 423)

This sentence is significant for Besta's concept of prudence as a "secondary"
principle.

Notes

1 "With respect to accounting the sole determinant and enunciation of value through
money has true importance. In all procedures for economic control the values express
themselves as numbers referable to the adopted currency" (Besta 1909b: p. 219).
2 Apart from land, he notes:

> some works of art and some monuments, [stating that] time, within certain limits,
> adds rather than subtracts value; and that rationally cultivated farms can sustain
> their fertility level indefinitely. Even these assets can maintain their cost for signi-
> ficant periods, as indicative of the role they play in any given *azienda*.
>
> (Besta 1909b: p. 239)

3   Individual amounts of depreciation must be periodically revised, whenever the
preparation of a balance sheet requires that an asset be assigned a value, to which
the depreciation cost is being attributed. Given that normally profits are proportional to the quantity of products, it seems to me that there should be a correlation
between subsequent depreciations relating to an asset's cost and the profits attributable to the assets in the accounting period, for which that cost has been consequently sustained.

(Besta 1909b: p. 242)

4   In achieving profits and calculating the amounts of depreciation in different
and subsequent periods, in the determination of constant relationships, one must
pay attention to interest corresponding to the time periods, which separate the
periods in which the individual amounts (constituting the endpoints) appear
available.

(Besta 1909b: p. 242)

References

Alexander, D., Fiondella, C. and Maffei, M. (2010), "The conservatism principle in the
history of Italian accounting theory. The influences of domestic economy, legalism and
regulation, accounting profession and standards setters", paper presented at the 6th
Workshop on European Financial Reporting, University of Stirling (UK).

Anselmi, L. (ed.) (2006), *Modelli economico-patrimoniali per il bilancio e la contabilità
di Stato*, Milan: Giuffrè.

Antoni, T. (1970), *Fabio Besta. Contributo alla conoscenza degli studi aziendali*, Pisa:
Colombo Cursi.

Besta, F. (1880), *La ragioneria: prolusione letta nella solenne apertura degli studii per
l'anno scolastico 1880–81 alla R. Scuola Superiore di Commercio in Venezia*, Venice:
Tipografia dell'Istituto Coletti.

Besta, F. (1909a), *Sulle riforme proposte ai nostri istituti di contabilità di Stato. Prolusione letta nella solenne apertura degli studi per l'anno scolastico 1908–1909*, Venice: Istituto veneto di arti grafiche.

Besta, F. (1909b), *La ragioneria. Parte prima. Ragioneria generale. Volume I, seconda edizione riveduta ed ampliata col concorso dei professori Vittorio Alfieri, Carlo Ghidiglia, Pietro Rigobon*, Milan: Vallardi.

Besta, F. (1920), *La ragioneria. Parte prima. Ragioneria generale. Volume II, seconda edizione riveduta ed ampliata col concorso dei professori Vittorio Alfieri, Carlo Ghidiglia, Pietro Rigobon*, Milan: Vallardi (reprinting).

Catturi, G. (1997), *Teorie contabili e scenari economico-aziendali, seconda edizione*, Padua: Cedam.

Ceriani, G. (2006), "Il sistema contabile patrimoniale nell'impostazione di Fabio Besta, nella variante corrente e nella variante anglo-americana", *Contabilità e Cultura Aziendale*, 6(2), 33–62.

Coronella, S. (2007), *La ragioneria in Italia nella seconda metà del XIX secolo. Profili teorici e proposte applicative*, Milan: Giuffrè.

Ferraris Franceschi, R. (1994), *Il percorso scientifico dell'economia aziendale. Saggi di analisi storica e dottrinale*, Turin: Giappichelli.

Giannessi, E. (1980), *I precursori in economia aziendale*, 4th edition, Milan: Giuffrè.

Gonnella, E. (2012), "Fabio Besta sulle valutazioni di bilancio. breve analisi critico-interpretativa", in Rossi, C., Rusconi, G. and Servalli, S. (eds), *Saggi di storia delle discipline aziendali e delle dottrine economiche. Scritti in onore di Antonio Amaduzzi professore emerito*, Rome: RIREA, 539–561.

Melis, F. (1950), *Storia della ragioneria. Contributo alla conoscenza e interpretazione delle fonti più significative della storia economica*, Bologna: Zuffi.

Paolini, A. (1990), *La rilevazione e il controllo economico. Riflessioni sull'impostazione dottrinale di Fabio Besta*, Lucca: Pacini Fazzi.

Sargiacomo, M., Servalli, S. and Andrei, P. (2012), "Fabio Besta: accounting thinker and accounting history pioneer", *Accounting History Review*, 22(3), 249–267.

Zan, L. (1994), "Toward a history of accounting histories", *European Accounting Review*, 3(2), 255–307.

3 Financial valuations in the Italian patrimonialist tradition

Stefano Coronella

1 Introduction

This chapter intends to point out the contribution of Italian patrimonialists relating to the issue of financial valuations.

It is generally thought that they essentially share the same vision on this subject and that this point of view is basically aligned to Fabio Besta's thought.

Actually, we will notice that, although supporters of the patrimonialist logic haven't examined in depth the issue of valuations, some scholars have anyway provided an original and relevant contribution to the development of the matter, turning away somehow significantly from Besta's vision of the phenomenon.

After having clarified what is meant by the term "patrimonialist", we have analysed the contents of Fabio Basta's first and second generation of academics' works and those of "independent" scholars who have followed the patrimonialist approach anyway.

First of all, this has allowed us to recognize the authors who have provided added value to the issue of financial valuations comparing to Fabio Besta's approach. After, we have analysed in depth the thought of those authors in order to raise the innovative impact of their visions on the issue.

2 The Italian patrimonialist: a framework

The term "patrimonialist" refers to a group of scholars who have kept on using the patrimonialist system created by Fabio Besta at the end of nineteenth century, even after the ensuing invention of the income system by Gino Zappa in the first decades of the twentieth century. As is generally known, the second system has gradually spread and established itself all over Italy. The income logic, even under more or less significant variations (D'Alessio 2011: pp. 85ff.; Coronella 2014: pp. 403ff.), is used nowadays in almost all the accounting entries.

However, beside this common thread, the term "patrimonialist" identifies a group of scholars who have different points of view, even structural differences. For this reason, it is worth outlining the bounds of this definition.

Fabio Besta was a great innovator in accounting in Italy. He is granted several ideas and fundamental contributions to the growth of the subject (Giannessi

1980: p. 117ff.). From a technical point of view, the most important concerns undoubtedly lie on the invention of the "patrimonialist system" and the related "value theory" and from an academic point of view, on the formulation of the "scientific accounting" (Zan 1994: pp. 286–288; Sargiacomo *et al.* 2012).

Fabio Besta had some "first generation" scholars who can be defined as "orthodox" as they kept on pursuing, devoid of relevant modifications, the Master's binomial structure "patrimonialist system – scientific accounting". They belong to Fabio Besta's School, also known as the "Venetian School" (Melis 1950: pp. 772ff.; Masi 1997: pp. 329ff.; Serra 1999: pp. 265ff.; Amaduzzi 2004: pp. 210ff.; Siboni 2005: pp. 65ff.; Coronella 2014: pp. 274ff.). The best known are Vittorio Alfieri, Carlo Ghidiglia, Vincenzo Vianello, Francesco De Gobbis and Pietro D'Alvise. Among the old scholars of Fabio Besta's first generation, there is also Benedetto Lorusso, who however has portrayed an ambiguous attitude: on one hand, he showed interest in Gino Zappa's thesis, on the other hand he sought to defend Besta's structure.

We also have to consider Fabio Besta's younger (those of the second-generation) direct and indirect scholars, as well as the "independent" ones still tied up to Besta's approach who have forwarded some of the Master's points of view – even after Gino Zappa's ideas of "Economia Aziendale" and the income system. Although they followed Fabio Besta's approach, some of them personalized their own scientific path.

Among them, Francesco della Penna, Vittorio Alfieri's scholar and Angelo Chianale, Vincenzo Vianello's scholar (both Fabio Besta's indirect scholars), faithfully applied Besta's approach. Vincenzo Masi too, Fabio Besta's direct scholar, pursued Besta's approach, trying to strengthen his Master's thought since he interpreted accounting as "Science of the equity".

The "independent" scholars Ubaldo De Dominicis and Edoardo Petix were partially distanced from Besta's paradigm. Indeed, they were convinced patrimonialists but they developed a particular vision about accounting from a doctrinal point of view (Giannessi 1954: pp. 313ff.; Costa 2001: pp. 157ff.; Coronella 2014: pp. 394ff.).

To be thorough, some of Besta's direct scholars (the "old" ones, those of the first generation) developed independent paths that created new schools and currents of thoughts, divorcing from the Master's approach – after a period of faithful acceptance. These scholars are Gino Zappa, founder of the "Bocconi School" and Alberto Ceccherelli, founder of the "Tuscan School" (Costa 2001: p. 63; Siboni 2005: pp. 79ff.; Coronella 2014: pp. 365ff.).

This is the reason why, even if they were Fabio Besta's scholars, we can consider them "patrimonialists" only in their youth period, that is before changing their point of view. The concern is relevant since Gino Zappa's young-age vision of patrimonialist valuations introduces original and modern hints.

3 Insights about Italian patrimonialists

In order to understand the patrimonialist approach, the introduction of Fabio Besta's direct and indirect followers and "independent" scholars – that is those who applied the patrimonialist system to the double-entry method – is followed by an insight about all of them. The aim is to supply useful information about each scholar and to single out those who provided an added value about valuations regarding Besta's approach.

3.1 Vittorio Alfieri

Vittorio Alfieri (1863–1930) was undoubtedly the most distinguished among Besta's "orthodox" scholars. First, he taught in Ticino Canton, then in the Technical High Schools in Chieti, Perugia (where he was absent to get the degree at the "Regia Scuola Superiore di Commercio di Venezia" – Business School of Venezia) and in Roma, where in 1907 he became Full Professor at the "Regio Istituto Superiore Coloniale" (Business School of Roma).

He was author of excellent historical (Alfieri V. 1891, 1892–1893, 1896) and institutional (Alfieri V. 1902, 1907) essays about accounting, in which he sought to develop his Master's thought and, in particular, referring to accounting as the science of economic control. He devoted himself to the organizational study as well (Alfieri V. 1921a, 1921b, 1924) and to the financial valuation for the accounting period (Alfieri V. 1908, 1925), for which he was particularly praised.

He might have opened accounting to new horizons but unfortunately he died relatively young, on 19 July 1930, eight years after his Master's death. So he didn't have time to make any proposal about it.

Indeed, many years after his death, his daughter Tommasa told that her father was preparing a remarkable essay on accounting. On the edge of death, he ordered her to destroy the 300 handwritten pages elaborated till then, because the essay was unfinished (Alfieri T. 1997: pp. 238–239). As his notes didn't express the full idea of his thought and needed a further reflection, he suspected they could be misunderstood. According to Masi those pages contained the new ways of investigation about accounting probably asserting again the centrality of Besta's approach compared to Gino Zappa's new doctrine called "Economia Aziendale" (Masi 1997: pp. 343–344). Since no proof of this essay exists, the truth will never be known.

3.2 Carlo Ghidiglia

After the diploma in accounting, Carlo Ghidiglia (1870–1913) attended the "Regia Scuola Superiore di Commercio" (Business School) in Venezia, where he ended his studies in summer, 1893.

He consecrated his life to teaching, studying and researching with an extreme passion and devotion. He taught at the Technical High Schools in Assisi, Melfi, Foggia and Roma, where he took the lecturing post of State accounting at the "Regio Istituto di Studi Commerciali, Coloniali ed Attuariali" (Business School).

In 1911–1912 academic year, when he was still a young man, he asked to be placed on leave of absence due to a degenerative illness. Unfortunately, he didn't teach any more.

Carlo Ghidiglia was praised as a great teacher and a great scholar referring to his studies in the Italian scientific field between the nineteenth and twentieth century, when our branch of knowledge reached its climax.

At the age of 25, he was already known and appreciated as an excellent researcher, having already published several papers and booklets, held conferences and prepared a textbook on accounting for the students of Assisi Technical High School.

He was among the best and most promising of Fabio Besta's scholars; he was sensitive and diligent, endowed with a particular talent.

His many and worthy essays include general and theoretical accounting, applied accounting, State accounting and history of accounting. In almost 20 years of lively scientific activity he published articles in several important journals, such as *Rivista Italiana di Ragioneria* and numerous monographs. Among them, we can highlight the huge work on applied accounting in two volumes with more than 1,200 pages (Ghidiglia 1906). There he applied Besta's approach to the different categories of private and public companies, besides his interest in professional accounting.

He took part in congresses and conventions, writing papers whose influence in the formative process of accounting and on his academic path is remarkable, since he was among the most passionate boosters of the need to advance accounting as a subject in the course of study in law (Ghidiglia 1909, 1910, 1911).

3.3 Vincenzo Vianello

After the diploma at the Business School in Venezia, Vincenzo Vianello (1866–1935) taught in Cividale del Friuli, Casale Monferrato, Messina, Napoli, Roma and Padova (where he was assigned the lecturing post on State accounting) before gaining the title of Full Professor in accounting at the "Regio Istituto Superiore di Scienze Economiche e Commerciali" (Business School) in Torino. There he taught from 1907 to 1930, when he moved back to Roma to get the chair in accounting at the Business School after the death of Vittorio Alfieri.

As with many of Besta's scholars, he can boast several historical studies above all when he was young (Vianello 1891, 1893, 1895, 1896, 1898). He also wrote about State accounting, agricultural accounting and maritime accounting (for captains), but his best-known work (it had eight editions till the year of Vianello's death) is *Ragioneria generale* volume, published for the first time in 1907 (Vianello 1907) where he clearly retraced and summarized his Master's vision on accounting.

3.4 Francesco De Gobbis

After the Business School diploma in Venezia in 1884, Francesco De Gobbis (1863–1942) started to teach in Asti and then moved to Reggio Calabria, Foggia, L'Aquila, Cremona, Bergamo, back to Cremona, Firenze, Torino and finally to Roma, where he got the chair at the famous "Leonardo da Vinci" Technical High School. Then, he taught at the Business School of Trieste and then in Torino. In 51 years of teaching (he retired in 1935) he reached 12 locations.

Differently from most other famous Besta's followers, De Gobbis hasn't authored important historical studies. Anyway, he was among the most active of the Master's supporters of the Venetian School "paradigm". In 1934 he took a famous lecture at the Business School in Torino, where he heavily attacked Zappa's approach accusing him to have destroyed on purpose what had come before him. He accused him that he hadn't been the first to analyse the strict connections among management and operations, organizations and accounting (the three tenets of "Economia Aziendale"), than he made comparisons with Giuseppe Cerboni's thought, judging it as anticipating Zappa's future reflections (De Gobbis 1934).

Concerning the scientific production, he is famous for his most appreciated volumes on "general accounting" (De Gobbis 1889) – which had 21 editions up to 1939 – and on the "applied accounting to private companies" (De Gobbis 1916) – which had 13 editions until 1936 – in addition to excellent studies on financial statements of limited liability companies (De Gobbis 1925).

All his works follow in Besta's wake, except some attempts of innovation especially with reference to the notion of firm.

According to an objective analysis, De Gobbis's works on accounting are considered inferior to those of other Besta's followers, even if his essays on the subject had a wide diffusion and successful printing, due to the simple and clear quality of the syntax rather than the quality of their contents (Giannessi 1980: pp. 165ff.). Otherwise, his works on financial statements are so interesting and original to be considered as a point of reference in accounting studies.

3.5 Pietro D'Alvise

After the Business School diploma in Venezia, Pietro D'Alvise (1860–1943) started to teach in 1882 in Pordenone, then moved to Spoleto, Teramo and Padova, which was the main location for his activity of teacher and expert, finally to Genova and Venezia.

Like De Gobbis, Pietro D'Alvise was among the most active of Besta's followers to defend his Master's studies, first against Giuseppe Cerboni (D'Alvise 1901), later against Gino Zappa (D'Alvise 1933, 1934, 1937, 1940a).

After his first history studies (D'Alvise 1889, 1891), he focused on general accounting (D'Alvise 1892, 1920), State accounting (D'Alvise 1900, 1940b) and professional accounting (D'Alvise 1924).

His well-known volume is undoubtedly *Principi e precetti di ragioneria* (D'Alvise 1932). It is a rational, wise theoretical work of 600 pages, maybe the best written by one of Besta's followers after the rise of "Economia Aziendale".

Other information deserves to be mentioned to get a full list of his long academic and professional activities: in 1904 in Padova he founded the journal *Rivista dei Ragionieri*, which he chaired for 25 years. It is one of the most known and important journals of our discipline (Coronella 2007a: p. 109).

In the same year, Fabio Besta claimed his assistance when he was assigned the task to arrange a project on the reintegration of the double-entry method in State accounting following the bad logismography experience (Coronella 2014: p. 282). It is noteworthy to remember that in 1918 Fabio Besta left the chair at Ca' Foscari and the same Pietro D'Alvise followed as substitute until 1921, when Gino Zappa definitively took his place.

3.6 Benedetto Lorusso

Benedetto Lorusso (1869–1839) attended the Business School in Venezia and, before qualifying, he began to work in a private company and then in a small savings bank.

He started teaching in 1894 as Professor of accounting at "Regia Scuola Superiore di Commercio" (Business School) in Bari, taking the place of Professor Emanuele Pisani who had asked for a temporary layoff from work. The next year, he taught at "Regia Scuola Tecnico-Commerciale Italiana" (Technical High School) in Alessandria d'Egitto, later to Lecce and then back to Bari, where since 1901 he gained the teaching at the "Regia Scuola Superiore di Commercio" (Business School) chairing it from 1921 to 1924.

The distinctive feature about Lorusso lies in the fact that, in more than 40 years as a teacher, he mastered several subjects: business arithmetic, general and applied accounting, State accounting, commercial and banking management and operations.

He published works about accounting and many other subjects too (Lorusso 1894, 1896, 1905, 1911, 1919, 1923, 1931).

From a theoretical point of view, although he was neglected by many historians of accounting, his essays had some relevance (Giannessi 1980: pp. 226ff.). From his essays, over time, the question about some key issues "ambiguity" rises. Indeed, among Besta's "orthodox" scholars, he was the one who was subjugated by Zappa's theory. He neither embraced it nor rejected it as others did. This process of "incomplete conversion" comes out from some of his papers, the first of which dates back to 1926. In the above-mentioned essay, the income system and the contact points between it and the patrimonialist one are highlighted, recognizing the advantages of the former from the latter. Thus the income has become the core on behalf of accounting entries (Lorusso 1926).

Lorusso didn't totally reject Zappa's theory concerning the three connected disciplines of accounting – organizations, management and operations.

Notwithstanding, he ended up accepting their synergistic bound, still singling out each of them as autonomous sciences (Lorusso 1931, 1932).

In a few words, Lorusso deserves attention because he identifies the period of transition from Besta's theories to those supported by Zappa and his followers (Giannessi 1980: p. 227).

3.7 Francesco della Penna

Francesco della Penna (1886–1976), Vittorio Alfieri's scholar, deeply felt his sense of membership to Besta's School. So, when "Economia Aziendale" rose, he strongly argued with all its supporters.

On 21 November 1936, he held the first lecture at the Faculty of Economics and Commerce of the University of Roma and in his course of General and Applied Accounting he quarreled against what he defined as the degeneration of the accounting thought whose outcomes, over a ten-year period, have marked a "total set-back in the accounting studies, the worst disorientation of young scholars in our field" (Informazioni e notizie varie 1937: p. 47).

Soon after, della Penna himself stated (and instigated) one of the longest and most famous theoretical debates about the discipline, published in the *Rivista Italiana di ragioneria* journal (Bertini 2012; Aprile and Nicoliello 2015). The trigger was the changing of name from "Corso magistrale di ragioneria" ("Accounting course") at Ca' Foscari University in Venezia to "Corso di magistero in Economia Aziendale" ("Economia Aziendale course"), implying a loss of relevance of the accounting teaching at the Venetian University. Thus, a long debate arose, above all with Alberto Ceccherelli, who was accused by della Penna to be a traitor because of his rejection of their Master Fabio Besta's thought in order to espouse Zappa's one.

As Fabio Besta's scholar (although indirect), della Penna was so strongly involved in the historic concern of accounting and its insights that he held the first course of historic lectures of accounting in Italy (later turned into a proper course of history of accounting) and opened, within his Institute, a department dedicated to the studies of history of accounting.

His devotion to historical research can be appreciated reading his most famous work *Le istituzioni contabili*, which is mostly dedicated to the history of accounting (della Penna 1946–1950).

Among his works, those dedicated to the institution of accounting (della Penna 1931, 1946–1950) and to the different types of corporations stand out (della Penna 1938), analysed under the technical–bookkeeping point of view. His thought is aligned with that of Fabio Besta and that of his direct Master Vittorio Alfieri.

3.8 Vincenzo Masi

Vincenzo Masi (1893–1977) was Fabio Besta's scholar in Venezia just before the First World War. He was first lecturer and then appointed in accounting at

Bologna University. From 1960 to September 1966 he was also appointed as editor in chief of *Rivista Italiana di Ragioneria* journal.

In 1917 he conceived the "agendologia" – meant as "science of company life" – standing as an older sister of accounting (Masi 1917: pp. 306ff.). In relation to this issue he devoted his degree thesis entitled "L'Agendologia come dottrina della costituzione, della vita e dell'organizzazione delle aziende" (the Agendology as doctrine of the enterprise building, life and organization) (Masi 1997: p. 353). However, his cognitive effort, which could be somewhat intended as a pioneer of "Economia Aziendale" (at least for the juxtaposition of the different disciplines) was unheard and consequently forgotten.

Faithful to Besta, he wrote several monographs and hundreds of papers nearly always dedicated to reassert the scientific core and the high cultural significance of accounting, which he defined as "Science of equity" (Masi 1927), while he denied the existence of Zappa's "Economia Aziendale".

Masi remained among the few supporters even after the success of "Economia Aziendale". After his active participation to the quarrel between Besta's and Zappa's supporters, since the 1920s (Coronella 2013: pp. 80ff.), like a "voice crying in the wilderness", Masi kept on publishing papers with a hectic rhythm in order to contrast the dominance of "Economia Aziendale" comparing to the "counters", to question the scientific issue of their approach, to reaffirm the leadership of accounting as a patrimonialist science and to blame them for having damaged the discipline.

His later works against "Economia Aziendale", since the 1950s, even if asserting a "rearguard" position, can be considered reliable (Masi 1951, 1959, 1960, 1962b).

3.9 Ubaldo De Dominicis

Once having begun his studies in Bari, Ubaldo De Dominicis (1913–1998) moved to Venezia where he attended Fabio Besta's lectures. As a patrimonialist supporter, he considered Benedetto Lorusso, Pietro D'Alvise, Francesco De Gobbis and Angelo Chianale as his Masters.

He began his career as teacher at the Technical High School of Cuneo to upgrade to University: Trieste, Cagliari, Aquila, Bologna and finally Genova University where he retired in 1987.

His theoretical position is completely independent and in countertrend regarding the development of "Economia Aziendale".

Indeed, he totally refused the idea of business–economic science and sought to defend the integrity of accounting, paving the way to an "anti-Zappa" or "post-Besta" scenario. Some other scholars shared his remarks on "Economia Aziendale" rejection, but De Dominicis distinguished himself by a specific concept of accounting thanks to which he made very original contributions.

If "anti-Zappa" and "post-Besta" supporters – in different shades – tended to cast accounting as a science, he denied this attribution while prompting *economic policy* as a science with reference to accounting. According to De Dominicis, the task of economic policy is to identify the general laws that have to direct management decisions, while accounting is meant as a technical code entrusted with duties about economic calculations that are the basis of business decisions.

Among his several witty and incisive works, it is worth noting the huge work in five volumes on general accounting (De Dominicis 1963, 1964, 1965, 1966a, 1966b), which had numerous editions and reprintings, besides the essay on technical assets (De Dominicis 1956).

3.10 Angelo Chianale

Angelo Chianale (1896–1974), Vincenzo Vianello's scholar, worked in a group with Francesco De Gobbis for some years. He taught in Torino and Trieste. He was faithful to Besta's teaching and he openly queried the existence of "Economia Aziendale" and claimed the need to bring the studies on accounting back to their proper context, that is the accounting methodology, to avoid accounting being contaminated by useless awkward philosophical reflections.

Besides theoretical issues (Chianale 1931a) and accounting (Chianale 1956), he employed a long time in business arithmetic (Chianale 1935a, 1955) which he considered to be preparatory to accounting and to management and banking operations, while the broad consensus was in favour of considering it an independent discipline (Giannessi 1954: p. 315).

Chianale took State accounting (Chianale 1926, 1931b, 1934, 1935b) in serious consideration, judging it a discipline in itself even though it was connected to accounting (Giannessi 1954: p. 317).

3.11 Edoardo Petix

After having graduated in Messina, Edoardo Petix (1899–1982) taught for several years at the Technical High School in Catania, before deserving the chair at Palermo University, and then moving to University of Torino. The following year he asked for a period of discharge and shortly after he was appointed Professor of bank and professional technique at the University of Messina.

His publications, above all the first ones, mainly concentrated on accounting (Petix 1936, 1942, 1946), a subject of special interest for him, as inferred by his theoretical volume about it (Petix 1949).

If on one hand he rejected the existence of "Economia Aziendale", on the other hand he went beyond Besta's theory of accounting as the science of business control, giving it the task to formulate laws about asset balances in all kinds of economic units, that is production and supply business concerns. Moreover, he denied the existence of management theory and didn't acknowledge dignity to organizational studies, ending up with the achievement that both discipline theories belong to the investigative scope of accounting (Giannessi 1954: pp. 331–332).

3.12 Gino Zappa (young period)

Gino Zappa (1879–1960) attended the Business School in Venezia and became Besta's scholar. He taught in Genova from 1906 to 1921 when he went back to Venezia and took his Master's chair in accounting. In 1920 he gained the role at Bocconi University in Milan, wherein he held lectures from 1920 to 1951 in addition to Ca'Foscari University in Venezia, being a commuter between the two cities.

In 1926 he definitively divorced from his Master's vision giving rise to a new discipline: "Economia Aziendale". As widely acknowledged, thanks to his famous first lecture in Venezia entitled "Tendenze nuove negli studi di ragioneria" (new trends in accounting studies) he launched "Economia Aziendale" which absorbed accounting, management and operations and business organization (Zappa 1927).

Even if Gino Zappa is considered a wrecker of Besta's scientific accounting and the father of "Economia Aziendale" (Zan 1994: pp. 288–291; Viganò 1998; Serra 1999: p. 274; Antonelli 2012), it's beyond doubt that in his youth he was one of Besta's cleverest followers and a convinced "patrimonialist" (Biondi 2002: pp. 29–35).

His early and relevant works show patrimonialist roots (Zappa 1910; Zappa 1920). For our purposes, among them, it is worth noting the 1910 volume, which is Zappa's first scientific work thoroughly on financial statements.

3.13 Alberto Ceccherelli (young period)

Alberto Ceccherelli (1885–1958) attended the Business School in Venezia and was Fabio Besta's scholar.

He was Professor at the "Regio Istituto Superiore di Scienze Economiche e Commerciali" (Business School) in Firenze. He appeared on the national scientific scene thanks to a little historic monograph (Ceccherelli 1910) later on followed by a wide and qualified academic production which stretched from history of accounting to general and applied accounting, from financial statements to bank management, from business arithmetic to "Economia Aziendale", from cost accounting to forecasting (Coronella 2014: pp. 390–391).

His most relevant work is undoubtedly *Il linguaggio dei bilanci* (Ceccherelli 1939) (the language of financial statements), which has been reprinted several times in over 40 years.

He is well known as the founder of the "Tuscan School" of "Economia Aziendale" but, at least until the mid-1930s, he was a loyal scholar and follower of Fabio Besta, as well as a supporter of his theories (Coronella 2014: p. 390). Until that period, he is to be considered a proper "patrimonialist". Indeed his monograph on bank financial statements is based on patrimonialist roots (Ceccherelli 1921), wherein a wide survey on credit institutions appraisal – according to Besta's traditional approach – is carried out.

4 Italian patrimonialists and valuation concerns

4.1 Introductory remarks

As acknowledged at the outset, the many patrimonialists reviewed concentrated above all on theoretical focus (Accounting vs "Economia Aziendale"), institutional focus (contents of study) and technical focus (accounting entries, budgeting, financial statements, and professional focus).

Nearly all of them questioned about valuation concerns. However except for Zappa (1910), Alfieri (1925) and De Gobbis (1925), the others discussed the above-mentioned focuses (valuation) within their works on general accounting (De Gobbis 1889; Alfieri 1907; Vianello 1907; Lorusso 1919; D'Alvise 1920; Masi 1926; della Penna 1931; Petix 1942; Chianale 1956; De Dominicis 1965), hence from a merely technical–practical point of view.

Furthermore, the subject of valuations was developed – both approach and contents – along the lines of Besta's work (Besta 1891, 1909) and so they kept on using the Master's vision. Sometimes Besta's "indirect" scholars – for instance, della Penna – have drawn on their previous Master in the role of Besta's scholar (specifically, Vittorio Alfieri).

It is worthy of note that before Besta, valuation concerns had been neglected by almost all the accounting authors. The only one who took it into account (although not in a clever form) was Francesco Villa (Villa 1850), thus he can be considered a forerunner.

Indeed, until the publishing of Besta's work, valuations were deemed irrelevant to the accounting. Even the most important authors had only focused on the technical mechanisms of accounting trying to identify the basic theories that underwent the functioning of the accounts (Coronella 2007b: pp. 119ff.).

Fabio Besta was the first author to systematically and analytically analyse valuations according to both general accounting principles and to specific accounting items (Besta 1891).

To do so, he introduced principles and estimative concepts drawn from economic policy, real estate valuation, financial and actuarial mathematics, mercantile and bank calculation, all the disciplines concerning "values" and "valuations" as well. Obviously, he was trying to employ the connected regulations to our specific discipline and to the target purposes (valuation of the accounting values in order to draw up financial statements).

Moreover, worth noting is the fact that, thanks to Fabio Besta's intellectual effort, he stated the principle that the issue of patrimonialist valuation had to be part of accounting duties. So, although his scholars and fellows hadn't portrayed innovative concepts and contents, their works had spread and strengthened this principle (for instance, see Zappa 1910: p. 24). Thus, the matter that valuation principles of accounting items commonly belong to the accounting field is owed to patrimonialist authors.

Having said this, among the many patrimonialists, the only ones who deviated from Fabio Besta's approach showing original remarks to valuation issues are Vittorio Alfieri, Gino Zappa (young period) and Francesco De Gobbis.

Following, we will illustrate their contribution to the topic of financial valuations.

4.2 Vittorio Alfieri

Vittorio Alfieri's contribution about financial valuations, in terms of added value in comparison with Fabio Besta's work, rises from three works: his paper about goodwill (Alfieri V. 1908), the fourth edition of his volume about general accounting (Alfieri V. 1921c) and his paper about year-end financial valuations (Alfieri V. 1925).

In the last two (1921 and 1925), it is worth noting the effort he made to trace a kind of "general theory of valuation" (della Penna 1931: p. 178), that is to provide an overall framework on the phenomenon of asset evaluations. Furthermore he believed that valuations must be subordinated to the aim we want to reach through them (Alfieri V. 1921c: p. 58).

Alfieri's vision about a general theory of valuation can be traced in his 1925 paper wherein he distinguished two typologies of estimations: the "real" estimates (as well as "actual" or "true" estimates) and the "apparent" estimates (as well as "accounting" or "pseudo-estimates").

"Real" estimates occur to the sale price that can be realized within a given time. Thus it takes place devoid of any complementary relationship to the firm ("breakdown estimate"). These valuations have to be taken into account at the liquidation phase (when the productive coordination of the economic units winds up). However, according to Alfieri, real estimates can be employed under specific conditions even in working concerns (Alfieri V. 1925: p. 394).

It is apparent that this kind of valuation can be applied only on assets having a marketplace. Moreover, the reliability of estimates varies according to the exact time when the transaction is expected or to the time-lag of the forward sale/purchase regarding to which the valuation is done (Alfieri V. 1925: p. 393).

"Apparent" estimates can be traced to the asset's value in relation to their complementary relationship with the firm ("composition estimate"). They typically occur to the going concern, so they can be considered as "persistent estimates" of the economic subject over a period of time expecting the income registration for the accounting year (della Penna 1931: p. 179).

"Apparent" estimates can be further divided into three categories (Alfieri V. 1925: pp. 397–400):

- estimates based on the market prices of things to be estimated;
- estimates based on the fruits the things to be estimated are capable of bearing;
- estimates based on the costs related to the above-mentioned things.

"Market-price-based valuations" can be also qualified as "indirect" or "for comparison" and refer to the valuation of goods by reference to the current price that is set by the market for virtually identical goods (or to the arithmetic average of the range of prices which refers to the same items). Among the "apparent estimates", market-price-based valuations are certainly the less aleatory ones.

"Estimates on the fruits" refer to the valuation of the present value expected from the future revenues that the things bear. Nevertheless, under the present circumstances, two elements of uncertainty have to be assessed: the necessity of estimating an appropriate discount rate and the possibility that future and expected revenues should not be realized.

"Cost-based valuations", also defined as "direct estimates", refer to the "stratification" of value of a product that can be obtained within the firm, thus through the identification of the diverse configurations of costs (prime cost, industrial cost, technical–economic cost, etc.). These kinds of estimates are the most uncertain ones, since they are affected by many uncertain factors introduced, for instance, by the fixed cost splitting-up on the overall cost of the product.

It is worth noting that Alfieri was the first scholar to stress the nature of estimates as unilateral acts, that is as a valuation without the exchange of goods. Indeed, the author highlights that the lack of a counterpart or of an effective exchange impinges the objectivity of the value to the thing to be evaluated (Siboni 2005: p. 77).

Vittorio Alfieri's thoughts about estimates are different from Fabio Besta, thus introducing the hallmark of originality as well as a high level of detail.

First of all, Alfieri runs counter to the principle of the uniqueness of the valuation criterion within the same financial statement, which is against the principle of constant uniformity of valuations which was enshrined in Besta's works, as well as in Zappa's early works (Besta 1891: p. 11; Zappa 1910: p. 29). Therefore, Alfieri considers the above-mentioned principle not to be always applicable, just because the elements (which constitute the capital of a firm and have to be valued) generally present different natures, different origins and different uses (Alfieri V. 1921c: p. 58, 1925: p. 402).

Stating that he advocates the application of different valuation criteria in one financial statement (taking into account the specific characteristics of the asset concerned), he distances himself from his Master's thought and, thereby, from the approach that was generally accepted back then. So, Alfieri has proved to be rather more innovative and radical in his argument than the dominant position on the issue was (Anselmi 1978: pp. 370–371).

In addition, a new element emerges compared to Besta's approach: the denial of the traditional "historical cost" criterion which was broadly accepted by the dominant thought (even by Fabio Besta) and by the accounting practice at that time. According to Alfieri, the "historical cost" criterion is inconsistent with the principle of complementarity among all the elements within assets and liabilities relating to the enterprise which can be conceived as a unitary concern. Furthermore, the historical cost criterion leads costs' significance to become lost, insofar as the costs can be atomistically singled or ruled out from the whole encompassing items (Anselmi 1978: p. 369). However, Alfieri welcomes the application of the most appropriate valuation rule, that is the case-by-case criterion required by each asset. It depends on the different element to be valued and on the different purposes to be pursued. In case of any aleatory in valuations, Alfieri appeals for a plurality of valuation criteria to be held simultaneously (among the above-mentioned three: market-price estimates, estimates on the fruits, cost estimates) and, subsequently, for an average value to be expressed. Alternatively, it is also possible to select one criterion and close its existing inadequacies through further estimates on the grounds set out by other requirements (Anselmi 1978: p. 372). It is worth noting that, in evaluative processes, any exaggeration has to be rejected, as well as wisdom shall be claimed (Alfieri V. 1925: p. 403).

This argument takes into account another original insight by Alfieri, which is that all assets and liabilities relating to the enterprise shall bear a clearly visible acknowledgement to their relevant bounds of complementarity. This contribution seems to deserve special attention, because it leads to estimates of "composition" and also to valuations that rely on the endurance of the entity over time (Palumbo 2003: pp. 115–126). This sends us back to the "goodwill" concept, which had already been widely investigated by the scholar (Alfieri V. 1908).

Indeed, according to Alfieri, single assets have to be valued in such conditions that their sum does point out the future expected revenue which might be assumed following their overall sale, by ensuring both the assumptions of going concern and working perspective (Alfieri V. 1908: p. 156). So, Alfieri's "goodwill" concept leads to encompass both assets and intangibles, termed by Alfieri as "fattori di potenza economica" ("economic strength factors"). The latter are marked by an untouchable nature that is supportive of the enterprise and, therefore, belongs to the goodwill (Alfieri V. 1921c: p. 8).

Whereas the approach to both financial valuations and goodwill has evolved over the years to perceive Gino Zappa's insights, it is worth noting that, back to Alfieri's time, the above-mentioned assessments and assumptions dazzled in their originality, and do so even today (Cinquini 1991: pp. 506–509).

4.3 Gino Zappa (young period)

Gino Zappa's contribution about financial valuations from a patrimonialist perspective is written down in his book on financial statements (Zappa 1910). This work was reissued in 1927 and deserves special attention for different reasons.

First of all, thanks to it, Gino Zappa set a record among accountants, as he was the first to investigate the issue of financial statements by means of a specific monograph, while generally only papers or chapters of books dealt with topics about it.

Second, Zappa's work is entirely devoted to evaluative concerns, except for its first introductory part.

Third, his book, which is enhanced by some relevant and clever points, set a benchmark for a long time, especially since it allowed the further framework on financial reporting disclosure to develop.

However, Zappa has not exactly distinguished himself as an innovator, since he largely took inspiration from prior technical contributions, as well as from the best practices of anonymous companies. Nevertheless, thanks to his book, Zappa deserves credit for his in-depth analysis and evaluative concerns on systematization, which had been only partially examined until then.

Furthermore, his work prompted a crucial contribution to the debate about the reform of the Commercial Code (with regard to the financial statements): the debate had begun at the end of the eighteenth century but it spiced up again after the first two decades of the twentieth century. Many innovations introduced by the 1942 Italian Civil Code basically comply with the scholar's recommendations, whereas some of his proposals have been transposed in Legislative Decree No. 127/91 and in Legislative Decree No. 6/2003 (Coronella 2008).

Finally, what is most interesting is that Zappa's work provides a particular insight about the valuation of "goodwill", which is quite similar to the International Accounting Standards (IAS)–International Financial Reporting Standards (IFRS) principles.

Zappa discussed valuations in the second part of his volume (Zappa 1910: pp. 23–117) on assessment in general, that is about various competing "basic criteria" of valuation: market prices, estimated exchange-values, stand-alone value, present price of future revenues, nominal values and costs. In the third part of the volume, the scholar takes stock of the different criteria that address the issue of single asset valuation, highlighting pros and cons as previously done. From his thorough analysis, Zappa therefore gathers a proposal to amend the Italian legislation on financial statements and on its valuation criteria, which he quotes in the fourth and last part of his work (Zappa 1910: pp. 119–220).

However, compared to Besta's approach, little originality emerges. There are still differences, although they seem to be modest (for the opposite view, see Gonnella 2008: pp. 23–28). Certainly, Zappa's work deserves special attention towards the excellent systematization of the subject and its clear presentation.

As above-written, Zappa's particular insight on goodwill to be entered in balance sheet is worth noting, because, in recent times, his dazzling 1910 statements have turned into a very topical question through the IAS–IFRS.

Differently from the common practice at that time, according to which goodwill expenses have to be amortized over the shortest time, Zappa stated that goodwill,

> if it were to proceed in a rational way, it would be entered in the balance sheet inversely proportional to the amount of the realized extra profits; in the event that extra profits were not gained, the cost of goodwill should be deleted from assets and counted as a loss.[1]
>
> (Zappa 1910: p. 174)

If a constant stream of extra profits occurs, Zappa suggests, therefore, to retain goodwill registered in the asset side of balance sheet and to leave it unamortized, since in this case goodwill should not suffer any impairment loss.

Whereas if goodwill decreases its flow of future economic benefits, Zappa suggests to amortize it according to its loss of expected future extra profits, as far as to delete it from accounting when goodwill is deemed entirely impaired, by allocating the relative cost to profit and loss account.

It is apparent how Zappa's vision is very similar to that currently laid down by the IAS, in particular regarding IAS 38. In fact, IAS 38 states that the amortization of goodwill is prohibited and it is required to follow an impairment regime on an annual basis and, in case of detecting a devaluation amount, the amount to charge to the profit and loss account shall be consequently undertaken.

Therefore, the only structural difference between Zappa's insight and that of IAS–IFRS standards, lay in the fact that the former dealt with amortization as a technical tool to reduce the carrying amount of goodwill allocated in the balance sheet for the accounting period. Nevertheless, as already stated, it is also possible to charge the amount for write-down to the profit and loss account when a total impairment loss of goodwill is recognized. Another difference is that the impairment test must be carried out not only at the end of the accounting period, but whenever impairment loss is expected.

We don't acknowledge these differences to be decisive. Notwithstanding the issue about terminological discrepancies, it is remarked that the IAS 38 approach is practically adherent to that of Zappa's. However, at the beginning of the twentieth century, this particularly innovative and daring "vision" would never have been welcomed by the other scholars. Indeed, it clashed with the principle of prudence to which both Italian thought and practice had in-depth bonds. The principle of prudence obliged to amortize goodwill in a short time regardless of its future economic benefits.

One soon realizes why the young scholar Zappa ceased to hold his own vision and, soon after its utterance, he stated that: "the doctrine suggests the fast amortization of goodwill and it is highly recommended by me, too"[2] (Zappa 1910: p. 144).

Then, looking for a compromise between the two approaches, Zappa soon after remarks that: "goodwill doesn't necessarily decrease as time passes. Actually, it can increase its possible market value".[3] Consequently, Zappa suggests that:

> goodwill shall not be amortized in accordance with the dominant methods, but a reserve of the equal amount should be allocated in the balance sheet. Reserve has to be used as a means to compensate for any losses of goodwill.[4]
>
> (Zappa 1910: p. 144).

Zappa's vision of the issue doesn't decrease its significance; even if he renounced his first proposal, he clearly commented on it. Otherwise, the intellectual background at Zappa's time was utterly different from the present one; his young age prevented him to maintain his non-conformist thought, which would have been surely interpreted as an "accounting heresy", thus forcing him to recant it.

However, it is clear that his contribution about the valuation of goodwill has an amazing modernity.

4.4 *Francesco De Gobbis*

Besides the young Gino Zappa, the only other patrimonialist to deal with financial statements by the means of a specific monograph was Francesco De Gobbis. His work had two editions (De Gobbis 1925, 1931), but the second one has been widely enlarged compared to the previous one.

De Gobbis's insights about financial statements have an economic–juridical frame (Giannessi 1980: p. 168). The author often comments on legal provisions in whose boundaries he steered his reflections.

De Gobbis didn't provide several original cues about financial valuations. His contribution on reporting has a "general" approach, that is, it concerns the format, the content, the process of drawing-up the financial statement, while from the evaluative perspective, he addresses the valuation of specific items without any originality.

It is worth noting that De Gobbis shared many of Alfieri's insights. He particularly agreed with the concept that the choice of evaluative criteria was conditional on the aim the evaluation needed to achieve (De Gobbis 1925: pp. 121–123). He also agreed with the plurality of evaluative criteria to be applied within the single set of financial statements (De Gobbis 1925: pp. 126–129). As Alfieri did, he maintained that the valuation of each item should not be individually carried out, but it should encompass each item as belonging to the whole enterprise, thus introducing correlations among other items (De Gobbis 1925: pp. 122–123).

However, the scholar achieved an original interpretation at that time through an in-depth analysis of the evaluative concerns, even if his approach on the assessment was basically juridical and was aligned to that of Besta and Alfieri, and although his thought was tied up to already developed and well-known criteria and evaluations.

De Gobbis steered his insights toward the aspect that, in limited liability companies, shareholders pressure the Board of Directors to gain a high profit distribution, while this kind of pressure doesn't exist in the sole proprietorship (De Gobbis 1925: p. 122).

De Gobbis dedicated particular attention to portray a guideline of "precautionary" nature (Amodeo 1955: pp. 20–25; Gonnella 2008: pp. 36–37) to avoid that financial valuations leave room for arbitrariness thus leading to exaggerated and less prudential estimates. They would lead to diluted stock and, therefore, to the risk of both sham earnings distribution and of depressing a firm's life, perhaps to endanger the firm itself in its entirety. Indeed, he stated that the year-end assessment has to be carried out in order to prevent undue earning distributions thus undermining equity. This is because the integrity of equity represents both a condition for the existence of an on-going concern and a guarantee for creditors (De Gobbis 1925: p. 129). These concepts have been explained by the author also in another volume (De Gobbis 1926: pp. 289–292).

Basically, De Gobbis was the first to verbalize a prior principle of "stock integrity safeguard" which supplies a guide of behaviour and warning for management when drawing up the financial statements.

Summarizing, the author upgrades "prudenza amministrativa" ("stewardship prudence") as a real "general clause" of behaviour (De Gobbis 1925: p. 128), which is essential to grant rationality to valuations (Giannetti 1998: p. 391), as well as objectivity and to ensure unimpaired stock. This approach leads to the operating principle suggested by the author and which identifies the cost as "maximum threshold" entered in a balance sheet (De Gobbis 1925: pp. 131–132).

This contribution can be interpreted as a relevant upgrade of the evaluative matter from a technical–normative level to a theoretical level of accounting (Gonnella 2008: p. 37).

Moreover, it is remarkable that, at a later stage, other (no longer patrimonialist) scholars have summarized De Gobbis's precautionary idea to safeguard stock capital thus following its content but varying its exposition (De Minico 1935: pp. 291–292; Onida 1935: pp. 56–57).

5 Concluding remarks

Italian patrimonialists' contributions about financial valuations widely follow Fabio Besta's approach. However, it is required to specify that those who are generically termed "patrimonialists" have such remarkable differences from a theoretical point of view even if they all share the patrimonialist approach and its accounting system.

On the other hand, among the patrimonialists, Besta's first and second-generation followers, as well as the indirect ones and independent scholars, are included. We also need to consider that some Besta supporters (namely Gino Zappa and Alberto Ceccherelli) supported their Master, as well as the patrimonialist approach, but only up to a certain time. Indeed, later on, they developed their own insights, even in contradiction to those of Besta. So, their contribution has to, at least, be considered among those of the patrimonialists but only concerning the youth period essays.

That said, no significant difference of insights about financial valuation can be detected among patrimonialists. From this perspective, the majority (including those who were not Fabio Besta's direct or indirect fellows) tends to conform to the Master's thought.

However, having examined each scholar's thought, three followers of "the first generation" – with particular interest to Vittorio Alfieri, Gino Zappa (youth period) and Francesco De Gobbis – provided very original insights on valuations, breaking away from Besta's approach or, even better, turning it into something different from their Master's vision.

Thanks to the three above-mentioned authors, relevant innovations occur. Among the important ones, we quote a general theory on valuations set up, the requirements of a plurality of evaluative criteria within one financial statement which have to be chosen depending on the purposes to achieve, in a teleological way, the forecast of guidelines of "precautionary" nature to guarantee the integrity of the capital, the complementarily bounds between all the firm items and the relative role of goodwill, goodwill valuation according to logics and contemporary rules enlightened by IAS–IFRS.

From this point of view, the patrimonialist contribution proves to be original, improved in relation to Besta's approach and above all very important from a theoretical perspective. Thanks to these authors' efforts, concerns surrounding financial valuations have begun to separate from a merely technical–professional characterization to upgrade to a scientific subject of investigation.

Notes

1 Original text:

> se si procedesse razionalmente, dovrebbe essere inserito in bilancio in ragione inversamente proporzionale all'ammontare dei soprareddditi realizzati; nel caso poi in cui non si conseguissero extra-profitti il costo dell'avviamento dovrebbe essere depennato dagli elementi patrimoniali attivi ed essere conteggiato come una perdita.

2 Original text: "la dottrina consiglia il rapido ammortamento dell'avviamento e ciò è ritenuto opportuno anche da me".
3 Original text: "l'avviamento non deperisce necessariamente per effetto del trascorrere del tempo. Anzi, esso può assumere progressivamente un eventuale maggior valore di scambio."
4 Original text: "di non ammortizzarlo secondo i metodi consueti, ma di costituire una riserva di ammontare uguale al costo che appare in attivo, tale quindi da poter ovviare alle conseguenze di ogni possibile deprezzamento dell'avviamento".

References

Alfieri, T. (1997), "Una testimonianza su Vittorio Alfieri", in *Atti del primo convegno nazionale di storia della ragioneria*, Siena, 20–21 Dicembre 1991, reprint, Siena: Tipografia Senese, 235–239.
Alfieri, V. (1891), *La partita doppia applicata alle scritture delle antiche aziende mercantili veneziane*, Torino–Roma–Milano–Firenze–Napoli: Ditta G.B. Paravia e Comp.
Alfieri, V. (1892–1893), "Le registrazioni per le associazioni in partecipazione spiegate da Alvise Casanova", *Il Ragioniere. Rivista di Contabilità*, VIII (24), 381–383; IX (1), 5–11; IX (2), 27–31.
Alfieri, V. (1896), *L'amministrazione economica dell'antico comune di Perugia*, Perugia: Unione Tipografica Cooperativa.
Alfieri, V. (1902), *Metodi di registrazione a partita doppia*, Perugia: Unione Tipografica Cooperativa.
Alfieri, V. (1907), *Ragioneria Generale*, Roma–Milano: Società Editrice Dante Alighieri.
Alfieri, V. (1908), "La valutazione dell'avviamento", *Rivista Italiana di Ragioneria*, VIII (4), 155–166.
Alfieri, V. (1921a), "Le norme di organizzazione del lavoro", *Rivista Italiana di Ragioneria*, XIV (7), 153–165.
Alfieri, V. (1921b), "L'organizzazione aziendale", *Rivista Italiana di Ragioneria*, XIV (8–9), 205–218.
Alfieri, V. (1921c), *Ragioneria Generale*, 4th edn, Milano–Roma–Napoli: Società Editrice Dante Alighieri.

Alfieri, V. (1924), "L'organizzazione aziendale nei riguardi delle rilevazioni amministrative", *Rivista Italiana di Ragioneria*, XVII (12), 613–620.

Alfieri, V. (1925), "Osservazioni intorno alle stime", *Rivista Italiana di Ragioneria*, XVIII (9), 393–403.

Amaduzzi, A. (2004), *Storia della ragioneria. Percorsi di ricerca tra aziende e contabilità, dottrine e professioni*, Milano: Giuffrè.

Amodeo, D. (1955), *Intorno alla teoria generale del bilancio di esercizio delle imprese*, Napoli: Giannini.

Anselmi, L. (1978), "Vittorio Alfieri e il problema valutativo", *Rivista Italiana di Ragioneria e di Economia Aziendale*, LXXVIII (11), 367–374.

Antonelli, V. (2012), *Ragioneria ed economia aziendale. Osservazioni in prospettiva storico-dottrinale sulle controversie in tema di posizionamento*, Roma: Rirea.

Aprile, R. and Nicoliello, M. (2015), "Gli albori dell'Economia Aziendale nel dibattito sulla Rivista Italiana di Ragioneria", *Contabilità e Cultura Aziendale*, XV (1), 121–143.

Bertini, U. (2012), "Francesco della Penna, Alberto Ceccherelli e l'Economia aziendale", *Contabilità e Cultura Aziendale*, XII (1), 5–25.

Besta, F. (1891), *Corso di ragioneria professato alla classe di magistero nella R. Scuola Superiore di Commercio in Venezia, Parte prima, Ragioneria Generale*, Volume I, Venezia: Coi tipi dei Fratelli Visentini.

Besta, F. (1909), *La ragioneria, Parte Prima, Ragioneria generale*, Volume I, 2nd edn, Milano: Casa Editrice Dottor Francesco Vallardi.

Biondi, Y. (2002), *Gino Zappa e la rivoluzione del reddito. Azienda, moneta e contabilità nella nascente economia aziendale*, Padova: Cedam.

Ceccherelli, A. (1910), *Le scritture commerciali nelle antiche aziende fiorentine*, Firenze: Tip. R. Lastrucci.

Ceccherelli, A. (1921), *La tecnica del bilancio con speciale riguardo alle aziende bancarie*, Milano: Vallardi.

Ceccherelli, A. (1939), *Il linguaggio dei bilanci. Formazione e interpretazione dei bilanci commerciali*, Firenze: Le Monnier.

Chianale, A. (1926), *I Bilanci dello Stato Pontificio alla vigilia della Rivoluzione Romana*, Torino: Mercurio.

Chianale, A. (1931a), *Saggio su alcuni problemi di ragioneria*, Torino: Giappichelli.

Chianale, A. (1931b), *Contabilità di Stato*, Torino: Giappichelli.

Chianale, A. (1934), *I beni patrimoniali degli enti pubblici*, Torino: Giappichelli.

Chianale, A. (1935a), *Computisteria*, Torino: Coop. Libri Del Gruppo Universitario Fascista.

Chianale, A. (1935b), *Il patrimonio degli enti pubblici nei conti e nei bilanci*, Torino: Giappichelli.

Chianale, A. (1955), *Calcolo mercantile e bancario*, Torino: Libreria Editrice Universitaria Levrotto & Bella.

Chianale, A. (1956), *Ragioneria generale*, Torino: Libreria Editrice Universitaria Levrotto & Bella.

Cinquini, L. (1991), "Le 'stime' nel pensiero di Vittorio Alfieri: aspetti di attualità per la valutazione dei beni immateriali", *Rivista Italiana di Ragioneria e di Economia Aziendale*, XCI (9–10), 496–509.

Coronella, S. (2007a), "Gli strumenti di diffusione della conoscenza nel periodo 'aureo' della ragioneria italiana: trattati, dizionari, enciclopedie, riviste e collane", *Rivista Italiana di Ragioneria e di Economia Aziendale*, CVII (1–2), 101–113.

Coronella, S. (2007b), *La ragioneria in Italia nella seconda metà del XIX secolo. Profili teorici e proposte applicative*, Milano: Giuffrè.

Coronella, S. (2008), "Il bilancio di esercizio nella prima concezione di Gino Zappa. Spunti di attualità a distanza di un secolo", *Rivista dei Dottori Commercialisti*, 59 (6), 1057–1098.

Coronella, S. (2013), *Cerboniani, bestani e zappiani a confronto. I dibattiti scientifici nella Rivista Italiana di Ragioneria (1901–1950)*, Roma: Rirea.

Coronella, S. (2014), *Storia della ragioneria italiana. Epoche, uomini e idee*, Milano: FrancoAngeli.

Costa, M. (2001), *Le concezioni della ragioneria nella dottrina italiana. Profili storici e storiografici nella sistematica delle discipline aziendali*, Torino: Giappichelli.

D'Alessio, R. (2011), *Ascesa e declino del sistema del reddito. Modelli, polemiche e degradazioni*, Roma: Rirea.

D'Alvise, P. (1889), "La teorica dei conti nel passato e nel presente", *Il Ragioniere. Rivista di Contabilità*, V (2), 17–21; V (3), 33–36.

D'Alvise, P. (1891), "Il mastro a partita doppia a scacchi prima dell'anno 1865", *Il Ragioniere. Rivista di Contabilità*, VII (6), 87–91.

D'Alvise, P. (1892), *Nozioni di Ragioneria razionale per gli studiosi di scienze amministrative. Introduzione e Ragioneria generale con varie applicazioni*, Milano: Giovanni Massa Editore.

D'Alvise, P. (1900), *Nozioni teorico-pratiche di Contabilità di Stato*, Firenze: G. Barbèra Editore.

D'Alvise, P. (1901), "Sull'articolo 18 della legge di contabilità dello Stato", *Rivista di Ragioneria*, I (3), 4–7.

D'Alvise, P. (1920), *Nozioni fondamentali di ragioneria. Vol. I. Nel mondo delle Aziende economiche. – Organizzazione amministrativa delle Aziende. – Stato della materia aziendale. – Inventariazione*, Padova: Stab. Tip. Del Messaggiero.

D'Alvise, P. (1924), *Monografie di ragioneria professionale. Graduatorie, eredità, liquidazioni, fallimenti, concordati, con applicazioni reali secondo il corso di lezioni 1922–23 al R. Istituto superiore di scienze economiche e commerciali di Genova*, Padova: R. Zannoni.

D'Alvise, P. (1932), *Principi e precetti di ragioneria per l'amministrazione economica delle aziende*, Padova: Cedam.

D'Alvise, P. (1933), "Reminiscenze ed attualità nel campo degli studi ragioneristici", *Rivista Italiana di Ragioneria*, XXVI (3–4), 101–109.

D'Alvise, P. (1934), "Sull'impotenza dei soli conti a valori nella determinazione del reddito", *Rivista Italiana di Ragioneria*, XXVII (9), 365–366.

D'Alvise, P. (1937), "Concetti e voci fondamentali in ragioneria", *Rivista Italiana di Ragioneria*, XXX (5), 177–188.

D'Alvise, P. (1940a), "Esumazioni contro esumazioni intorno ad una 'scienza unitaria'", *Rivista Italiana di Ragioneria*, XXXIII (5), 113–118.

D'Alvise, P. (1940b), *Studio sintetico di Ragioneria Statale Italiana in regime fascista, ossia Contabilità generale dello Stato (Regno, Egeo, Libia, Africa orientale italiana) secondo le ultime disposizioni*, Padova: R. Zannoni.

De Dominicis, U. (1950), *La ragioneria quale tecnica dell'economia politica*, Cuneo: Ghibaudo.

De Dominicis, U. (1956), *Le immobilizzazioni tecniche nei problemi d'impresa*, Cuneo: Ghibaudo.

De Dominicis, U. (1963), *Lezioni di ragioneria generale, Volume secondo, Nozioni preliminari*, Bologna: Sab.

De Dominicis, U. (1964), *Lezioni di ragioneria generale, Volume terzo, Capitale, costi, ricavi e reddito*, Parte I, 2nd edn, Bologna: Azzoguidi.

De Dominicis, U. (1965), *Lezioni di ragioneria generale, Volume quarto, Capitale, costi, ricavi e reddito*, Parte II, Bologna: Azzoguidi.

De Dominicis, U. (1966a), *Lezioni di ragioneria generale, Volume primo, Introduzione allo studio della ragioneria*, Bologna: Azzoguidi.

De Dominicis, U. (1966b), *Lezioni di ragioneria generale, Volume quinto, La contabilità generale e la contabilità analitica d'esercizio nelle imprese*, Bologna: Sab.

De Gobbis, F. (1889), *Ragioneria generale. Corso teorico-pratico ad uso degli alunni degli istituti tecnici e degli istituti commerciali*, Treviso: L. Zoppelli.

De Gobbis, F. (1916), *Ragioneria privata, con una appendice sulle funzioni speciali del ragioniere*, Milano–Roma–Napoli: Società Editrice Dante Alighieri.

De Gobbis, F. (1925), *Il bilancio delle società anonime*, Milano–Roma–Napoli: Società Editrice Dante Alighieri.

De Gobbis, F. (1926), "La integrità del capitale e la solidarietà degli esercizi", *Rivista Italiana di Ragioneria*, XIX (7–8), 289–292.

De Gobbis, F. (1931), *Il bilancio delle società anonime*, 2nd edn, Milano–Genova–Roma–Napoli: Società Editrice Dante Alighieri.

De Gobbis, F. (1934), "Tendenze nuove negli studi di ragioneria?", *Rivista Italiana di Ragioneria*, XXVII (3), 129–137.

De Minico, L. (1935), *Elasticità e relazioni dinamiche dei costi nelle imprese industriali*, Napoli: Rondinella.

della Penna, F. (1922), *Il contenuto scientifico e la partizione della Ragioneria teorica*, Città di Castello: Unioni Arti Grafiche.

della Penna, F. (1931), *I fondamenti della ragioneria*, Roma: Casa Editrice Castellani.

della Penna, F. (1938), *Le forme aziendali*, Catania: Vincenzo Muglia Editore.

della Penna, F. (1946–1950), *Le istituzioni contabili, parte prima – parte seconda*, Roma: Casa Editrice Castellani.

Ghidiglia, C. (1906), *Corso di ragioneria applicata, Volume primo e Volume secondo*, Roma-Milano: Società editrice Dante Alighieri.

Ghidiglia, C. (1909), "L'avvenire degli studi di ragioneria", *Rivista Italiana di Ragioneria*, II (3), 109–116.

Ghidiglia, C. (1910), "L'insegnamento superiore nel progresso degli studi di ragioneria", *Rivista Italiana di Ragioneria*, III (9), 416–417.

Ghidiglia, C. (1911), "L'insegnamento della Ragioneria nelle Università", *Giornale degli Economisti e Rivista di Statistica*, 28 (7), 67–85.

Giannessi, E. (1954), *Attuali tendenze delle dottrine economico-tecniche italiane*, Pisa: Colombo Cursi Editore.

Giannessi, E. (1980), *I precursori in economia aziendale*, 4th edn, Milano: Giuffrè.

Giannetti, R. (1998), "Il bilancio d'esercizio nel pensiero di Francesco De Gobbis", *Rivista Italiana di Ragioneria e di Economia Aziendale*, XCVIII (7–8), 389–400.

Gonnella, E. (2008), *Osservazioni sul problema delle valutazioni di bilancio nella dottrina italiana. Dal "valore di scambio" al "valore funzionale"*, Roma: Rirea.

Informazioni e notizie varie (1937), "Nella R. Università di Roma – La prelezione del prof. della Penna", *Rivista Italiana di Ragioneria*, XXX (1), 47.

Lorusso, B. (1894), *La contabilità delle aziende comunali in conformità del r. Decreto 6 Luglio 1890*, Venezia: Tip. M. S. Fra Compositori Tipografi.

Lorusso, B. (1896), *La partita doppia applicata al commercio ed alla banca, secondo il nuovo programma delle R. Scuole italiane di commercio all'estero*, Torino: Ditta G.B. Paravia e C. Edit.

Lorusso, B. (1905), *Nozioni di computisteria per le scuole tecnico-commerciali e per le scuole tecniche a tipo comune secondo i vigenti programmi governativi*, Torino: Stamp. Reale Della Ditta G.B. Paravia e C. Edit.

Lorusso, B. (1911), *Calcolo e documenti commerciali, ad uso degli alunni delle scuole medie di commercio, degli istituti tecnici (Sezione di Ragioneria e commercio) e delle R. scuole di commercio all'estero*, Torino: G.B. Paravia e C.

Lorusso, B. (1919), *Ragioneria generale basata sul sistema delle funzioni di controllo economico*, Bari: Accolti.

Lorusso, B. (1923), *Nozioni di computisteria per le scuole complementari e Istituti tecnici*, Torino: G.B. Paravia e C.

Lorusso, B. (1926), "La partita doppia nel sistema del reddito", *Rivista Italiana di Ragioneria*, XIX (10), 401–408.

Lorusso, B. (1931), "La Ragioneria quale scienza che studia la ricchezza, o il patrimonio delle aziende? (A proposito della polemica Masi-Spinedi)", *Rivista Italiana di Ragioneria*, XXIV (10), 297–299.

Lorusso, B. (1931), *Commercio d'importazione e di esportazione. Nozioni di tecnica e di ragioneria commerciale*, Bari: Laterza.

Lorusso, B. (1932), "I capisaldi della teorica del Besta (Obbiettivo della Ragioneria)", *Rivista Italiana di Ragioneria*, XXV (10–11–12), 312–316.

Masi, V. (1917), "Studi logismologici e guerra", *Rivista dei Ragionieri*, XIII (6), 306–313.

Masi, V. (1926), *Ragioneria Generale*, Bologna: Cappelli.

Masi, V. (1927), *La ragioneria come scienza del patrimonio*, Bologna: Cappelli.

Masi, V. (1951), "Per la Difesa e l'Autonomia Scientifica della Ragioneria (Tempo di edificare)", *Rivista Italiana di Ragioneria*, XLIV (5–6), 85–99.

Masi, V. (1959), "La Ragioneria è morta! Viva la Ragioneria!", *Rivista Italiana di Ragioneria*, LVIII (5–6), 110–114.

Masi, V. (1960), "La ragioneria di Cà Foscari gettata in Canal Grande", *Rivista Italiana di Ragioneria*, LIX (11–12), 275–277.

Masi, V. (1962a), "Gino Zappa e la caduta della ragioneria nel suo insegnamento universitario", *Rivista Italiana di Ragioneria*, LXI (1–2), 3–10.

Masi, V. (1962b), "J'accuse", *Rivista Italiana di Ragioneria*, LXI (5–6), 111–125.

Masi, V. (1997), *La ragioneria nell'età moderna e contemporanea, testo riveduto e completato da Carlo Antinori*, Milano: Giuffrè.

Melis, F. (1950), *Storia della ragioneria. Contributo alla conoscenza e interpretazione delle fonti più significative della storia economica*, Bologna: Dott. Cesare Zuffi.

Onida, P. (1935), *Il bilancio delle aziende commerciali. La determinazione del capitale di bilancio*, Milano: Giuffrè.

Palumbo, R. (2003), *Profili della teoria del valore negli studi di ragioneria. Dall'affermazione del paradigma bestano alla definizione delle "tendenze nuove"*, Torino: Giappichelli.

Petix, E. (1936), *La gestione e la rilevazione contabile nelle aziende di erogazione*, Catania: Studio Ed. Moderno.

Petix, E. (1942), *Lezioni di ragioneria generale. La rilevazione contabile*, Padova: Cedam.

Petix, E. (1946), *Ragioneria applicata alle aziende divise. Associazioni in partecipazione*, Catania: Muglia.

Petix, E. (1949), *Gli orizzonti della ragioneria*, Milano: Pirola.

Sargiacomo, M., Servalli, S. and Andrei, P. (2012), "Fabio Besta. Accounting thinker and accounting history pioneer", *Accounting History Review*, 22 (3), 249–267.

Serra, L. (1999), *Storia della ragioneria italiana*, Milano: Giuffrè.

Siboni, B. (2005), *Introduzione allo studio di storia della ragioneria attraverso il pensiero e le opere dei suoi maestri*, Milano: FrancoAngeli.

Vianello, V. (1891), "Dell'Universal trattato di libri doppi di Giovanni Antonio Moschetti", *Rivista di Amministrazione e Contabilità*, XI, 34–37; XI, 58–59; XI, 70–72.

Vianello, V. (1893), "Bibliografia di opere antiche", *Rivista di Amministrazione e Contabilità*, XIII, 13; XIII, 22–23; XIII, 30–31; XIII, 38–39.

Vianello, V. (1895), "Antichi codici e libri di computisteria e di scrittura doppia", *Rivista di Amministrazione e Contabilità*, XV, 37–39.

Vianello, V. (1896), *Luca Paciolo nella storia della ragioneria, con documenti inediti*, Messina: Libreria Internazionale Ant. Trimarchi.

Vianello, V. (1898), "La partita doppia nello Stato italiano prima del 1869", *Rivista di Amministrazione e Contabilità*, XIII, 33–34; XVIII, 42–45; XVIII, 49–53; XVIII, 57.

Vianello, V. (1907), *Istituzioni di ragioneria generale*, Napoli: Luigi Pierro, Editore.

Viganò, E. (1998), "Accounting and business economics tradition in Italy", *The European Accounting Review*, 7 (3), 381–403.

Villa, F. (1850), *Elementi di amministrazione e contabilità*, Pavia: Bizzoni.

Zan, L. (1994), "Toward a History of Accounting Histories", *European Accounting Review*, 3 (2), 255–310.

Zappa, G. (1910), *Le valutazioni di bilancio con particolare riguardo ai bilanci delle società per azioni*, Milano: Società Editrice Libraria.

Zappa, G. (1920), *La determinazione del reddito nelle imprese commerciali. I valori di conto in relazione alla formazione dei bilanci, Prima puntata*, Roma: Anonima Libraria Italiana.

Zappa, G. (1927), *Tendenze nuove negli studi di ragioneria. Discorso inaugurale dell'Anno Accademico. 1926–27 nel R. Istituto Superiore di Scienze economiche e Commerciali di Venezia*, Milano: S.A. Istituto Editoriale Scientifico.

4 Income measurement and asset valuation under Zappa's theory

David Alexander, Roberta Fasiello and Francesco Giaccari*

Anche la ragioneria se vuol vivere feconda, ... deve rinunciare alla presunzione di aver compiuto opera definitiva ... anche la nostra scienza è contingente ed in perpetua via di compimento.

If accounting wishes to develop productively, ... it must renounce all presumptions to have produced definite results ... since our science is contingent, and in a state of perpetual searching for conclusions.

(Zappa, 1927: p. 15)

1 Asset valuation in Zappa (1910)

1.1 Gino Zappa: an academic profile

Zappa (1879–1960) attended Fabio Besta's courses at Ca' Foscari in Venice in the academic years 1903–1904 and 1904–1905. In 1905 he earned the teaching qualification in Accounting and since 1906, under the leading figure of Fabio Besta, he started to teach in Genova, as assistant before and as appointed teacher after. In 1921 Zappa won a competition for a tenure in Accounting in Venice, and in 1929 he moved to Milan in Bocconi where he was tenure, but he continued to teach in Venice too. In 1910, when he was only 31 years old, he wrote his first scientific book, *Le valutazioni di bilancio con particolare riguardo ai bilanci delle società per azioni*, where the influence of the patrimonialist school of Fabio Besta shines through. In the following years Gino Zappa grew up and developed his income system theory, distancing himself from the previous positions. This theory was published for the first time in two booklets in 1920 and in 1929 (*La determinazione del reddito nelle imprese commerciali – I valori di conto in relazione alla formazione dei bilanci*) and in 1926 he proclaimed his new theoretical approach during the inauguration of the academic year at Ca' Foscari in Venice with the well-known lecture *Tendenze nuove negli studi di Ragioneria*. The income system was brought to completion in 1937 and in 1950 with the publishing of the book *Il reddito di impresa. Scritture doppie. Conti e bilanci di aziende commerciali*. In 1951 Gino Zappa gave up the academic tenure because he was already blind and in 1955 was named Emeritus Professor.

His blindness did not prevent him from continuing scientific studies and publishing in 1956 *Le produzioni nell'economia delle imprese* in three books.

1.2 Financial valuations in the first work of Gino Zappa (1910) under the influence of the patrimonialist school of Fabio Besta

In the book *Le valutazioni di bilancio* published in 1910, Gino Zappa introduces an early theoretical thought in most part, even if not in total, corresponding to the main assumptions of the patrimonialistic school of Fabio Besta. In this work, he takes positions in contrast with ones argued by some economists of the time (first of all Maffeo Pantaleoni), but in the following books he changed ideas on some of them. After, even Zappa admitted that the book *Le valutazioni di bilancio* is the result of a strong influence of Fabio Besta's thought (and Onida (1961: p. 7) remembered that Zappa defined this book as inspired to "a scarce independence in thought") and Zappa devalued its importance considering its contents as "elementary revelations" (Zappa 1920–1929: p. 328).

A first issue on which Zappa (1910) dwelt is the relationship between valuation criteria and financial statement purpose, highlighting that the valuation criteria to be adopted were dependent on the financial statement's aim and that these criteria had a meaning only when defined according to the financial statement purpose. Indeed, in this regard, Zappa clarifies "the values recorded in the inventory ... must be defined only with respect to the purpose for which the same inventory is composed" (1910: p. 27), as

> regardless of this purpose those values couldn't be even defined, and whereas they were defined no useful precept could be obtained from them. Then, several valuation criteria must be followed in the formation of inventories with different purposes, so much that the same combination of elements, forming the property of a business, must be valued with different measures if, for example, the business is in ordinary conditions or in abnormal ones of its life
>
> (1910: pp. 29–31)

and with reference to this he referred to the different criteria required by a statement of realization and liquidation compared with an ordinary asset and liability statement. These observations are the same as Fabio Besta ("Different criteria and different procedures must be followed according to the causes and to the several purposes arousing the inventory drafting", 1909: p. 11) and as Maffeo Pantaleoni ("the value attribution must be made in a rigorous matching with the financial statement purpose", 1909: p. 88) (see earlier chapters) and they propose as an example just the statements of realization and liquidation.

However, unlike Maffeo Pantaleoni (1909: p. 98, p. 132), Zappa (1910) asserts the uniqueness of the valuation criteria for the financial statements having the same purpose ("it is not possible to understand how ... we couldn't have a single guidance principle that could be used to assess the values in those inventories drafted to achieve the same purposes", "non si può davvero capire come mai ... non possa sussistere un unico principio direttivo, che serva di guida nell'assegnazione dei valori in quegli inventari che per raggiungere scopi identici si erigono" 1910: p. 27), suggesting the uniformity of the values not only in terms of money, but also in terms of criteria (Zappa 1910: pp. 27–28) as Fabio Besta had already suggested (1909: p. 11). Zappa's position, in this regard, radically changed in his income theory, where in accordance to what Pantaleoni asserted (1909: pp. 98–99), Zappa recognized the impossibility to identify *ex ante* the valuation criteria. Indeed, as shown below in Section 2, Zappa highlighted that the valuation criteria couldn't be identified on the basis of general rules, but that they could be "defined only in the specific case in relation to the various and changeable circumstances of the business and of the market" (1939: p. 641).

Zappa clarifies the main purposes in relation to the financial statements of a stock company limited by shares (in this case, he refers to different sub-purposes for the same type of financial statement, that is the annual asset and liability statement):

- to indicate the financial and economic condition of the company (Zappa 1910: p. 32), even if he is aware that "as a matter of fact the financial statements are not able to supply all the needed elements for arriving to a sure and complete judgement of the economic condition of a business" (pp. 32–33);
- to assess profits and dividends (Zappa 1910: p. 36) that the shareholders could collect in the measure they are really realized (the article 176 of the 1882 Commerce Code declaims "profits really realized and suffered losses");
- as a tool for prior and subsequent control (Zappa 1910: p. 44);
- as the basis for the income tax assessment (Zappa 1910: p. 44).

When the financial statement purpose is identified as the assessment of profits and dividends, Zappa observes that profits really realized and losses really suffered could be determined only at the end of the business life, with the dissolution of a company, but he observes that the determination of these magnitudes is needed in practice by companies (Zappa 1910: pp. 39–40). In relation to this purpose, Zappa is looking for the more appropriate criterion among the several possible ones (current prices, estimated discounted exchange values, individual values, future revenue prices, nominal values, costs) being aware that the financial statements drafted in order to assess the distributable profits are not able to supply a correct judgement on the economic condition of the company (Zappa 1910: p. 47).

Reviewing and criticizing the various valuation criteria, Zappa takes a different position to that of Fabio Besta's regarding several issues.

First, Zappa (1910) criticizes the terms actual values, real values, true values on which Fabio Besta's approach is based. In this regard, Zappa observes

the expressions actual values, real values, true values, right prices, fair prices are frequently used in the works attaining the inventory valuations …
but they are meaningless in logic and they are related to an economic utopia of former times.

(Zappa 1910: p. 54)

Second, even if both Zappa and Besta suggest the adoption of the cost as valuation criterion, they start from different assumptions. Indeed, we remember Besta suggests the valore reale (actual value), that is the exchange value as valuation criterion, using, if some conditions exist, the replacement cost as a proxy, and these values are the ideal values in Besta's approach and only in practice and for prudence reasons, that is in order to reduce the administrator discretion, should we adopt the historical cost (Alexander and Fasiello 2014, 2016).

Zappa too chooses a general valuation criterion "inspired to prudence principles" (1910: p. 42) and for this reason he suggests the cost criterion as

it is the criterion that leaves the lesser latitude to the more or less enlightened, but always interested, judgements of the administrators to whom the determination of the financial values is delegated. This is the *only* criterion that is based in the most part on real data, and is often difficult to distort; in conclusion this is the only criterion that, cramping in a limited space what is necessarily arbitrary for the same nature of the valuation, is of use for an as far as possible correct determination of contingent profits to be distributed.

(Zappa 1910: p. 110, emphasis added)

It is important to note the different position of Zappa and Besta on this issue, as even if they converge on cost adoption, in Zappa's (1910) approach the cost represents the only adoptable value; instead, in Besta's approach the cost assumes a petty role (Gonnella 2008: pp. 23–24), as it is a makeshift choice, an accommodation criterion.

Entering into the merits of the application of the cost criterion to each asset, according to the approach adopted by Zappa (1910):

* *Fixed assets* must be valued at a value that can never be higher than cost (1910: p. 75) and they must be depreciated computing appropriate depreciation expenses considering not only the physical depreciation, but also the economic one. Zappa highlights the menace of the undervaluation of the depreciation expenses that could imply the distribution of sham dividends, but also the menace of the overvaluation of depreciation expenses that could imply illegal profit provisions (1910: pp. 79–81). In both cases the depreciation would be not rational (1910: p. 82) and depreciation cannot be overestimated to cover future losses or be determined on the basis of the amount of profits (1910: p. 80, pp. 92–93) in order to create hidden reserves, to avoid also because they leave space to possible speculations by the administrators (1910: p. 215).

- *Assets to be sold* valued at the lower between the cost and the discounted estimated revenue price at the time of the balance sheet (1910: p. 109). So, Zappa suggests as reference for comparing with the cost, not the current price suggested by Besta (1909: p. 265) but a subjective value and, as such, incoherent with the purpose of economic control in Fabio Besta's theory and subscribed by Zappa (Palumbo 2003: pp. 109–113).

Zappa's early work, even if it follows the patrimonialistic approach of Fabio Besta and even if it is based on some observations that will be completely repudiated by Zappa in his future works (like the adoption of general valuation rules and of the cost, as easily determinable value, prudent and founded on real data), contains some topical and relevant issues for the future development of the doctrine. First, Zappa's initial suggestion not to depreciate the goodwill if the business is able to produce an additional profit (1910: p. 144) in compliance with the International Accounting Standards (IAS) 38 approach, and which Zappa doesn't consider introducing in the proposal for law amendment as too much in contrast with the doctrine and the practice of the age pegged to the prudence principle (Coronella 2008: p. 1083).

Second, the priority, in respect to the shareholders' interests, attributed to the business and to its continuity considered at the time of assessing the valuation criterion in order to determine the distributable profit (with movement from a subjective interest to an objective one, Palumbo 2003: p. 112). Indeed, Zappa asserts: "before considering the interests of the present shareholders we must consider, even in the stock companies, the right of each entity to preserve its existence" (1910: p. 116), so, "the dividend right of the shareholder must, in practice, be mitigated considering that the dividend distribution does not cause damage to the company" (1910: p. 42). Now, the importance of this observation in the view of prudence and capital maintenance needs to be considered (see Section 4), even if Zappa is already aware that the cost criterion "is not able to avoid the menace of the distribution of sham profits" (1910: p. 116).

2 Zappa (1937) and his theories

As outlined in Section 1, Zappa, acting in his capacity as Besta's "star" pupil, produced a major text (Zappa 1910) which broadly followed and built on the theoretical work of his "Maestro", and strongly supported the practical use (as a "safe" expedient, accepted as not close to the theoretical ideal of "valore reale" (Alexander and Fasiello 2014, for an in-depth analysis see Chapter 2 of this book)) of historical cost as the central valuation basis. We discuss in more detail in Section 4 below the major arguments for this, related to prudence, the removal of management discretion and an almost pathological fear of the dangers of distributing unrealized profits.

But over time Zappa's views changed. They can be traced through the notes taken by the young student Aldo Amaduzzi from Zappa's 1923–1924 "corso critico alla dottrina prevalente" and notably by the famous "Tendenze nuove" inaugural lecture of 1926, published the following year (Zappa 1927). We do not trace these changes through time here, but by the time of his major work (Zappa 1937; 2nd edition 1946) his ideas were fully formed. To follow our convenient shorthand labels, Zappa 2 significantly rejected Zappa 1.

The doctrine propounded in Zappa 2 is universally regarded as the basis, still widely accepted today in its theoretical essentials, of Economia Aziendale. The name represents an excellent summation. Accounting is regarded as an entirely economics-related discipline and it is to be applied with its focus very much on the azienda, or business entity. In fact there are two major elements to Economia Aziendale, first the various but always coordinated aspects of managing the azienda, and second the question of valuation bases and performance measurement and reporting.

To outline the former, Zappa's key contribution consists of the development of a theory of the company intended as an economic institution. The enterprise/institution is represented by a set of elements that make up the structure, coordinated in order to achieve the conditions for a balanced performance of the production activity in the long run. According to this perspective, the elements making up the enterprise/institution become evident:

- the continuity in the long run;
- a multi-faceted structure composed of different elements;
- the dynamic coordination of the elements through management.

Economia Aziendale studies the processes of financial circulation and economic transformation considered jointly both to the business system and the assessment techniques of the management operations in a systemic and joint perspective.

In Economia Aziendale, therefore, the value is linked to:

- the study of the logical assumptions and the application criteria for the assessment of the enterprise resources (assets) and the management results (income);
- the analysis of the measurements to supervise and facilitate decision-making processes;
- the enterprise perceived as a unitary and dynamic system aimed at economic production.

Alexander and Servalli (2011: p. 292) summarize the position clearly.

The economic aspect is central in Zappa's theorisation, as the factor which unifies each kind of manifestation of the Azienda's life. It is the common denominator of all activities within the Azienda and, as a consequence, of all disciplines that study them: operations (gestione), organisation (organizzazione) and accounting (controllo) (Zappa 1927).

The above described features of the azienda, in Zappa's notion, involve a change in accounting theory that, in the light of the dynamism of the economic unit, can't be centred on net worth, i.e. a static dimension as in previous theorizations (Besta 1922), but must be focused on a dynamic notion of wealth, as income is. In particular, Zappa elaborates an accounting system, named income based accounting system (sistema contabile del reddito), whose aim is to determine income.

His accounting system, whose values are ordered on the basis of a scheme that defines homogeneous values in relation to their link with income, singles out monetary values, income values (costs and revenues) and capital values. On the basis of this accounting theory, in the light of the aim of income measurement, i.e. of the wealth linked to the dynamism which characterized the Azienda's activity in a context of monetary exchanges, income determination comes from flows that, by the exchange, lead to the creation of wealth.

The above quotation neatly links the two key elements of Economia Aziendale thinking. The rejection of a focus on "net worth" and its replacement by a focus on income and the long-term maintenance of income is seen to necessarily follow from a properly rational analysis of the enterprise as a unitary and dynamic system aimed at economic production (Alexander and Fasiello 2014).

The key quotation from Zappa himself may be given as:

> Income available for consumption, or which is available for taxation or distribution, must not only not reduce the initial capital, but it shouldn't even damage the capacity of the capital to provide an income: income is essentially a surplus value, whose making leaves unimpaired the value which is the mechanism for its creation.

> (Il reddito devoluto al consumo, o che si può prelevare o distribuire, non solo dunque deve essere tale da non diminuire il capitale iniziale, ma nemmeno dovrebbe intaccare l'attitudine del capitale a fornire un reddito: il reddito è essenzialmente un valore eccedente, che nel determinarsi lascia integro il valore che è mezzo di sua rilevazione.)

> (Zappa 1946: p. 267)

This is long-run capital maintenance. It is exactly consistent with the famous "income number 3 definition" of Hicks (1946): "the maximum amount of money which the individual can spend this week, and still expect to be able to spend the same amount in real terms in each ensuing week". It is about, and theoretically ensures, the capacity of the business (azienda) to continue to operate for the indefinite future.

Consider the simplest of examples, discussed also in Alexander and Fasiello (2016). An enterprise has a business model to buy and sell one item at a time. Capital is 100. Buy for 20 (historical "actual/factual" cost). Buying price rises to 40. Sell for 50. Maximize distribution to owners. Replace for 40 and repeat the process to infinity. How much can be distributed?

Applying the Besta conservative model using historical cost, supported by Italian law, we have revenue of 50 and cost of 20. After the sale is made the difference of 30 is realized, so can safely be distributed. So cash, originally 100, becomes $100-20+50-30-40=60$. So the opening "patrimonio" when the business is first operational, of 80 plus physical sellable item, becomes closing patrimonio of 60 plus physical sellable item. So the business is contracting and will eventually, if the process, the cost trend, and the accounting policy continue, become bankrupt. The conclusion is very simple: conservatism fails to conserve! Note that the problem is nothing to do with realization: the sales proceeds (revenues in the IASB sense) of 50, are indeed realized.

More formally, our little example ensures the maintenance of financial capital in nominal terms. The original 100, before purchase of the first unit, remains as 100, before the purchase of the second unit. But the net cash inflow from the first unit, of $50-20$, which under historical cost accounting is also the net income of revenues less expenses, of $50-20$, needs to be regarded as two elements: the holding gain of 20 ($40-20$) and the operating gain of ten ($50-40$). The holding gain of 20 needs to be retained ("permanently held") and is not available for distribution.

Note also that the point, economically, operationally, and in terms of basic business common sense, is not that the income of 30 needs to be split into two parts. Zappa, quite correctly, disagrees with the "Business Income" concept of Edwards and Bell (1961), which takes the "Business Income" to be the 30. The point is that the income, Zappa's reddito according to his own definition, is only ten in the first place. The above quotation (Zappa 1946: p. 267) makes this absolutely clear.

In a way, we can expose the required accounting and valuation treatment by taking the logic backwards. The "answer" is that profit (reddito) is ten. What are the assumptions and workings necessary to arrive at this answer? The key point is that the expense to be associated (matched) with the revenue of today's sale is the expense of tomorrow's (replacement) purchase, not of yesterday's (historical) purchase. In other words, in the general case, a forward-looking replacement expense figure needs to be incorporated into the income calculation, not the historical purchase or production cost.

The final point to emphasise is that realization is not relevant. If the cash from the sale of 50 has not come in, then 40 is not distributable. And if the cash from the sale of 50 has come in then 40, not 20, of that cash is not distributable. The operating cash surplus from these events, of ten, is the maximum distributable, whether or not the sales proceeds are realized.

In fact Zappa rather generalizes his valuation recommendations. He very explicitly rejects the doctrinaire usage of historical costs, but he would certainly also regard our logical recommendations for obligatory usage of operational replacement costs as excessively doctrinaire as well. He believes in a flexible valuation approach, specific to time and place, i.e. focused always on the particular azienda in its particular economic and operational circumstances, and at a specific time. In other words, Zappa thought that assessments must consider the conditions peculiar to each enterprise and the contextual situations of the market. In fact, he maintained that:

- rigid assessment criteria had to be replaced with "procedures for discretionary evaluation" ("procedimenti di valutazione discretiva");
- values become reasoned values, based on operational conditions and market trends;
- estimated values are entered in a systemic and unified vision in order to protect the profitability of future years;
- the consistency of the income has to be assessed by comparing the capital with the future outcome of current operations.

The choice of the reasoned values grows out of two of Zappa's fundamental issues:

- it is not possible to match specific costs and specific revenues due to the continuous flow of all costs and all revenues. Costs and revenues are linked together in a blurred and fuzzy way (Zappa 1939: p. 614);
- cost is not an actual measurement criterion because the elements allocated may be changeable, and mostly appraised by subjective methods (Zappa 1939: p. 634).

Founded on these arguments, Zappa contends that suitable evaluation principles are supposed to be consistent with the specific surrounding conditions of the enterprise and the markets in a forward-looking philosophy, as follows.

Inventories: the evaluation is appropriate in a range of values whose limits are the actual costs and the estimated revenues (Zappa 1939: p. 641). When it is difficult to estimate future revenues and one can rationally appreciate the actual cost then the latter is an admissible criterion. In the matter of raw material and work-in-progress inventories not saleable, the range of values is determined on the one hand by the actual cost and on the other hand by the estimated future replacement costs (Zappa 1939: p. 642). In this way, Zappa acknowledges the anticipation of the future revenues, though one must assess the real conditions relating to the enterprise and the markets and when the assessment is suitable.

Tangible assets: the evaluation of tangible assets is put into effect by means of reductions. The calculations take into account not technical issues but economic ones relating to the enterprise and the market conditions (Zappa 1939: p. 662). This means that reduction is not only linked with the expected future profits, but we have to take in account the future capability of the enterprise to produce profits in the following accounting period (Zappa 1939: p. 666). Anyway to implement the comprehensive effects on the income it is necessary to allocate in each period provisions related to preventive maintenance and to the replacement of the assets.

In other words, the entire process is forward-looking and prospective.

A number of criticisms of exchange values have been proposed by Zappa, such as the following:

- irrationality of the atomistic view of the assets;
- inadmissibility of the exchange value for items not subject to self-transferability;
- irrationality in the case of items not intended for sale;
- excessive subjectivity;
- risk to distribute unrealized gains.

The fourth is a value judgement. It is certainly true that there is a considerable increase in subjectivity as compared with historical cost-based numbers (although there is significant subjectivity with them too). There is also a considerable increase in economic meaning and managerial relevance. Management has the opportunity, and accountants have the obligation, to focus the financial numbers on the specific entity and its operations, thereby sharply increasing the usefulness and relevance of the reported numbers. Such relevant flexibility may well also increase opportunity for manipulation of the numbers towards the interests of management. The arguments here are two-sided.

But the other four suggested criticisms are all more or less invalid. For the first, the benefits of asset usage are indeed derived through "dynamic coordination", and consideration of the assets as a single coordinated and inter-related set. But individual assets have to be replaced at the prevailing replacement price at the date of replacement. For the second, the need is not to be able to replace the asset, whether or not it is separately "transferable". The need is to be able to replace the input or service that the original asset provides. Such replacement may, in certain circumstances, involve significant managerial and operational/technical change, which is likely to increase uncertainty of estimation. But the replacement still has to be undertaken, and its implications still have to be planned for, and reported on for appraisal purposes.

Whether or not the item is intended for sale is just irrelevant. The item, if its holding was rational in the first place, is intended to be used in some way in the operations of the business. It therefore either gets sold or gets used up, and it is irrelevant which. In both cases, it will need replacing, and the above arguments again apply in full. The final point concerns the danger of distribution of unrealized gains. It is important here to distinguish economic arguments and requirements and legal ones. Economically, much the greatest danger, as we have illustrated above, is to distribute *realized* gains when they are not surplus to the retentions necessary to ensure that the business "leaves unimpaired the value which is the mechanism for its creation (lascia integro il valore che è mezzo di sua rilevazione)".

Economically the business can borrow cash against reliable (but unreceived) revenue flows to pay dividends early. This lacks prudence to some degree, and the law may, and in Italy usually does, prevent such a distribution. So this can be prevented by statute, but note that Italian statute is sufficiently stupid to *allow* distribution of the replacement cost increase (the additional 20 in our earlier example) after realization, which fails to achieve the fundamental and rational and, paradoxically, prudent objective of long-run operational capital maintenance and therefore long-run entity survival.

The overall conclusion is very simple: Economia Aziendale as developed by "Zappa 2" makes economic and managerial sense. For reporting purposes it theoretically makes complete sense too – indeed it must do, because the job of external reporting is to give a transparent reflection of the economics of the azienda and its relations with other economic players. In operational terms there is some trade-off between relevance and reliability.

3 Relevance to today

We can be brief here, first because the arguments are to us obvious, and second because they are elaborated with greater rigour and depth in Alexander and Fasiello (2016). Financial reporting requires a true and fair view, fair presentation, quadro fedele, in modo veritiero e corretto *of the entity*. Belatedly, the entity-specific implications of this seem to be recently recognized by the sudden explosion of interest in the "business model". In the context of a discussion which tries, rather laboriously, to draw a distinction between "management intent" and "business model" EFRAG (2013 para. B43) states as follows:

> An important similarity between the two notions is that they are both entity-specific, i.e., the financial statements reflecting the business model and management intent both present what actually happened and how the entity made or lost money…. The resulting information … has … predictive value.

So our first proposition is absolutely clear: relevant financial reporting requires a focus on the entity (or azienda). The entire Economia Aziendale tradition, not only Zappa but his precursors and successors, provides exactly this focus. It is worth underlining that fair value, as defined and operationalized in International Financial Reporting Standard (IFRS) 13, goes out of its way to emphasize that it is market-specific, and not entity-specific!

Our second proposition is that Zappa 2 gets his theory right (as Zappa 1 so very clearly failed to do). The emphasis on long-term survival and long-term performance, together with the clear understanding that historical cost so visibly fails to achieve this, is exactly what is needed as a standard (not necessarily perfectly achievable of course) against which second and third-rate "conveniences" (accommodation criteria; criteria di comodo; (Ferrero 1976: p. 426)) can and should be judged. The reddito definition given in this chapter, and its working out in the context of each specific azienda, provides a rational basis for appraising, reporting and predicting the economic performance, over time, of a business entity. Relevant to today it certainly is.

4 Prudence and the legal tradition

The adoption of historical cost and the concept of prudence in Italian accounting doctrine: implications for capital maintenance

First, it should be underlined that in the Italian accounting tradition the historical cost is generally introduced as an accommodation criterion (criterio di comodo). The historical cost is not considered a criterion able to express the economic utility of the goods considered in their unity and complementarity with the entire business unit, as it is a past value of a single good. Only values able to represent the economic utility of goods considering their complementarity to all the factors of production can be considered universal and, hence, rational.

Therefore, the historical cost does not represent a rational criterion, but only an accommodation criterion (Ferrero 1976: p. 426) introduced by the Italian accounting theory since:

- it is able to reduce the managers' subjectivity in financial statement valuations and the consequent drawbacks. It is based on real transactions that can be verified, so it represents a criterion generally considered more reliable and more verifiable than others;
- it is generally considered easy to apply and, therefore, able to reduce time and efforts in drawing up accounts (the adoption, in this case, is justified by reasons of efficiency).

In the approach proposed by Fabio Besta, the historical cost does not represent the best value to adopt, that is the ideal value, but it represents an accommodation criterion whose use is justified by reasons of prudence for its greater reliability compared with the other criteria (Besta 1909, I: p. 238, p. 264).[1] Indeed, for prudence, Besta asserts that the historical cost can be considered acceptable only after a rationality check of this criterion: this check requires the comparison with the exchange values, that is with the selling prices identified as a maximum limit not to be exceeded (Besta 1909, I: p. 264; II: p. 14; for the valuation criteria suggested by Besta in his theory refer to Chapter 2 of this book).[2]

In substance, Besta proposes the adoption of the historical cost as accommodation criterion for:

- the greater reliability of this value in comparison with others in the valuation of the business assets;
- removing the assessment of the gains and losses of the accounting period from the free will of managers (Besta 1909, II: p. 14);[3]
- simplifying the estimating procedures (the determination of the exchange value could require time and costs that the adoption of historical cost generally allows to avoid) (Besta 1909, II: p. 12).

However, Besta believes that the historical cost (costi effettivi) adoption is appropriate only if the costs, considered as aggregate, are not greater than exchange values "fino a quando non risulti che i costi, cumulativamente consid-erati, soverchiano i valori di cambio" (Besta 1909, I: p. 238). Indeed, according to Besta, the adoption of the historical cost in this case would be "irrational and dangerous too" (Besta 1909, II: p. 14). In the viewpoint of the prudence prin-ciple, then, Besta stresses that, for the purpose of going concern, the business could not consider profits realized, but in order to avoid to "lay itself open to failures and losses" it must record "an already happened loss" (Besta 1909, I: p. 264).

In his first work of 1910 Zappa too agrees with Besta's observations because he believes that "in comparison with the others, the historical cost criterion allows the lesser space to the managers' assessments, more or less learned (illu-minati) as they are, but always self-interested" and "it is the only criterion whose adoption takes in not a little part its foundation in real facts, that it can be often difficult to alter" (Zappa, 1910: p. 110).

In the perspective of reliability of the financial statement values, the historical cost, used to assess the value of each asset considered as a single good, repres-ents the criterion more convenient because it allows an ex post checking of its value (it is verifiable). Therefore, it is an accommodation criterion that in order to be rational needs to be compatible with the prudential limit values.

Zappa too (1910) suggests adopting inventory values lower than costs and, hence, he recommends opting for the lower value between historical cost and "the discounted estimated revenue price" (Zappa 1910: p. 105), this for the prudence principle in order to protect the original capital (capitale sociale). It should be observed that according to Zappa the historical cost should not be compared with the current price, but with the actual future revenue price discounted to the time of the drawing up of the financial statements (pp. 108–109).

Finally, therefore, the main reason for the adoption of the historical cost is the interest to reduce the managers' subjectivity in order to avoid that managers could represent a too optimistic profile of the company financial position (Lee 1986 (1994 Italian edition: p. 69)). In substance, through the adoption of the historical cost and the asymmetrical application of the realization principle (which implies the consideration of the losses not realized, and the exclusion of the not realized profits), caution in appraisal and in the income determination is performed as required by the prudence principle. Lee asserts that the prudence principle is widely accepted insomuch as the literature does not seem to look to explain its relevance and validity in the income determination (p. 69), consider-ing this principle more as a mental attitude than a principle expressible in stand-ardized rules. In this regard, it seems necessary to define the concept of prudence and its interpretations.

According to De Dominicis (1984, III: p. 479) the prudence principle is implemented though compliance with the following practical rules:

• "never overcome the maximum limit that can be reasonably attributed to each asset and the minimum limit attributable to each liability";

- "keep below the maximum in the estimation of assets and over the minimum in those of liabilities". But this good rule must not justify the adoption of assets' values lower than rational minimum and liabilities' values greater than rational maximum in order to avoid the creation of hidden reserves, which Zappa (1910: p. 215) too deems dangerous.

With regards to the first rule, the prudential maximum limit for assets is the estimated direct or indirect realizable value and with regards to liabilities it is the estimated extinction of financial obligations. These prudential limits allow the analytic determination of each element, even by the adoption of accommodation values.

In order to come to an aggregate estimate of the capital that could be considered compatible with these prudential value limits, the second rule concerning the principle of administrative prudence occurs. This administrative prudence "dominates all the appraisal process in all moments or phases of the valuation of the operating assets and its related income determination" (Ferrero 1995: p. 149) and it involves the prudential estimation of the net worth and of the yielded income. Thus, the net operating income, not including unrealized profits, but comprising the expected losses, and the net worth neither overstated nor underestimated, are considered prudential values (Ferrero 1995: p. 156). Thus, the administrative prudence entails the compliance with a rational process of valuation, the result of a sound and conscious management, and it can be identified in a rule of conduct to be observed in every moment of the business management, including that concerning the decision about the amount of distributable profits.

The determination of the operating income according to Besta is not made mainly to assess the distributable profits, even if this issue is not entirely lacking in Besta's observations (Besta 1909, I: p. 240).[4]

Moreover, the early Zappa is conscious that the historical cost cannot avoid the risk of distributing sham profits (Zappa 1910: p. 116) and as observed by Maffeo Pantaleoni with reference to the Léautey system (Pantaleoni 1909: p. 115, and see Chapter 1 in this volume) in the viewpoint of profit distribution it is more prudent to not adopt the historical cost, but to enter goods at their realizable prices highlighting the surplus value on the costs in order to allow the recording of this surplus value on the credit side of the balance sheet as a reserve (for surplus or lower value) of undistributable profits (Zappa 1910: p. 107). But this Léautey system is criticized by both Zappa (1910: p. 108) and Pantaleoni (1909: p. 114) because it does not consider how this surplus value has to be identified.

In relation to this, the adoption of the historical cost by the Italian accounting doctrine is not made in order to assess the amount of the distributable profits, the problem of which comes after the determination of the operating income.

Thus, the concept of prudence needs to be interpreted on the basis of the information needs of the financial statements, because the interpretation changes if the aim is the determination of the distributable profit, instead of the yielded income (reddito prodotto) in the accounting period.

The historical cost, as well as the other accommodation criteria (criteri di comodo), allows a particular configuration of income named yielded income (reddito prodotto) to be assessed and this configuration is not an adequate basis for the estimation of the distributable profits, even if the prudence principle is rigorously observed (Ferrero 1976: p. 434). The adoption of the historical cost entails a separate assets valuation for assessing each item in the value of the operating resources (Capitale di Funzionamento), since the historical cost disregards the conditions for the future profitability of the business management, and without the consideration of these conditions it is not possible to come to a conscious profits distribution in the viewpoint of the preservation of the going concern (Ferrero 1976: p. 435).

In the perspective of the distributable profit determination, in such a measure to come to a profit estimation that does not damage the profitability prospects of the business in the future and consequently its going concern ability, the prudence principle applies in the economic capital maintenance (Rossi 2006: p. 131). Therefore, in this case, the prudential limits identified for the compliance with the prudence principle are the direct or indirect estimated realizable value, as maximum value for the assets, and the estimated extinction value, as minimum value for liabilities (Ferrero 1995: p. 60).

In substance, the compliance with the principle of administrative prudence in order to come to the determination of the yielded income definitely entails a minimization of the estimation risk implying the existence of overstatements in the business assets, but it is not able to cancel the risk affecting the maintenance of the economic integrity of the capital and the operating ability of the business in the future.

In effect, the adoption of the lower value between the historical cost and the market value (estimated realizable value on the market) allows the recording of not realized gains (due to the assets valuation at historical costs) to be excluded, but it also implies the prudential recording of the estimated losses (because of the lower value rule).

There is much confusion in the literature about the origins, and usage over time and place, of the "lower of cost and market value" rule. For example Transacc (2001: p. 1225) and Richard (2013: p. 258) both confirm that the rule was only introduced in Germany, supposedly the ultimate in a permanent and extreme adherence to prudence and the imparitätsprinzip, in 1884, replacing something that appears remarkably close to fair value!

Richard (2013: p. 255) shows with reference to, and quotation from, the famous Savary book (Savary 1675) that his explicit proposal was for the lower of historical cost and replacement cost, *not* the lower of historical cost and net realizable value. Chatfield (1977: p. 72) writing in English, and Perrone (1997: p. 272), writing in Italian, both get this quite wrong, and both seem widely accepted in their respective language circles. The rationale, and here we can validly quote Perrone, is that the basis of historical cost can be used "because the adoption of this criterion allows to consider a gain in the accounting periods in which the sale of the goods really occurs, but also to limit its maximum measure" (Perrone 1997: p. 273). Note that this statement is only true if unrealized possible losses due to falls in market selling price are *not* recorded! The issue is peripheral to our purposes here, and we do not give the full quotations (all available via our references). But the important point made inter alia by Zappa and in this chapter, that value principles and practical usages are a unique function of time and place, is well illustrated.

Indeed, the configuration of the yielded income based on the historical cost adoption allows the exclusion of the gains not realized and only expected, but this, on the one hand, reduces the risk to distribute not yet realized profits, but on the other hand, it does not guard against the possibility to distribute all the gains of the accounting period, even if they are realized. In this regard, first, it is important to clarify that the distinction between realized and not realized profits, as observed by Onida, is improper as even a realized profit cannot be considered actual because it is obtained through estimations.[5] Second, it is commonly known that the distribution of the realized profits does not guarantee a prudential behaviour in the capital maintenance perspective. Indeed, the generalized distribution of the profits, even if limited to the realized ones, can jeopardize the future profitability of the business, as shown in Section 3. In this sense, the historical cost adoption allows the maintenance of the financial capital in nominal terms (and, therefore, of the "social capital") being, consequently, only a minimum guarantee for creditors, not sufficient to preserve the conditions for the future profitability and, therefore, the economic integrity of the capital, and of the entity itself.

In order to achieve this purpose, that is able to safeguard the entire business and at the same time all the stakeholders (creditors included), it is necessary to also adopt prudential behaviour on the occasion of the profits distribution. This behaviour, identified by Ferrero (1995: p. 188) with the "decision prudence" (prudenza decisionale) is expressed in the identification of an appropriate policy of income adjustment. This income stabilization can be applied through the estimations at the end of the accounting period with the creation of income reserves to be used for the setting-off of the additional costs (for example for the replacement of goods) that could occur in the following accounting periods, in consideration of the economic relationships being between costs and revenues of an accounting period compared with the previous and following accounting periods (the concept of economic time, Onida 1975: p. 17).

This need found different solutions in the Italian accounting tradition. Indeed, the Italian accounting doctrine faced both the problem of capital maintenance in terms of preservation of the business's profitability in the future and of the unsuitableness of replacement costs of resources used in the past by the business. About this, we can identify two different stances in the twentieth- century Italian doctrine:[6]

- The problem of the capital maintenance has to be considered not at the moment of the annual profit assessing or the assets' valuation, but at the moment of the allocation of profit. Therefore, when we allocate profits we have to verify how large is the profit we can distribute and, on the other hand, how large is the portion of profit that we have to retain for the greater costs incurred for the resources renewal (this quantification will be calculated considering the replacement costs and the values inferable by the expected plans of the business management).[7]

• The profit assessment has to be carried out on the basis of what we can rationally expect in the near future. So we have to assess the value of the not concluded operations at the end of the accounting period (essentially inventory estimates) based on the business planning, i.e. considering the renewal resources prospects of the business (the planned productive combinations, the future business management processes, etc.). Therefore, a systematic adoption of replacement costs isn't sufficient because we need to consider the specific business conditions and the business renewal policy planned for the future, appraising the future prospects of direct and indirect realization values. In order to do this, it's necessary to consider the greater costs incurred for the resources renewal, obtained comparing the future replacement costs with the future realization values. Nevertheless, the advocates of this position are conscious of the difficulty in estimating the future replacement costs as they are based on the future prospects, but they think that this cannot be a convincing reason to refuse to look ahead and to preserve a normal (*normale*) working of the business over the long term.

Comparing the "two different stances" which we describe above, their similarities are much more significant than their differences. The essential difference is that the first calculates "profit" and then restricts this, as a second and distinct stage, to the (usually smaller) "distributable profit". The second regards "profit" as automatically meaning "(economically) distributable profit", and in effect jumps straight to the second stage. In terms of our earlier example, the first goes for the 30 and then restricts it to ten, whereas the second defines the "reddito" as ten in the first place.

But the key point is the essential similarity, indeed identicality, which is that the "resources renewal" to allow the permanent continued operation of the entity, in cognisance of the specific plans of the specific management at the specific time and in the specific place, must be ensured. "Profit", using the word now in the general economic sense, is what has become available as a result of the activities of the reporting period *after* achieving this position.

This last conclusion is essentially what "prudence" means under the Economia Aziendale tradition, as created by the later Zappa and further refined by a series of desciples. Under this conceptualization, the authors of this Chapter are firm supporters of the prudence principle. But this prudence principle is far removed from that of IASB, that of traditional "Continental" accounting, and that of current Italian practice. The issue of legal/lawyer thinking versus economic/Zapparian thinking very much remains on the table.

5 Quo vadis?

As indicated, there are two key elements to Economia Aziendale as developed by Gino Zappa (2!). The first continues earlier traditions, and emphasizes the coordinated and unitary nature of the azienda and of its management and activities, and therefore its reporting. The second, more innovative at the time in the Italian scenario, relates to income measurement and asset valuation. Here the focus is firmly on income (reddito), in the context (as it logically must be, but often is not) of capital maintenance, focusing here on the long-run sustainability of the azienda as an integrated whole. This then leads in turn to asset considerations, logically as a derivative rather than as a focus in themselves.

Essentially we suggest each of these elements should be considered separately, in relation to the following questions.

1   Has the theoretical argument stood the test of time from the viewpoint of later Italian theorists?
2   Has the theoretical argument influenced Italian practice?
3   Has the theoretical argument had influence on international thinking?
4   Has the theoretical argument had influence on international practice?

This represents eight questions in all and for the replies to this question the chapters contained in this book and representing the evolution of Italian accounting doctrine and its today's relevance could give appropriate and pertinent responses.

Notes

*   This work was developed jointly by the authors. Nevertheless primary attribution can be suggested as: Section 1.1 Francesco Giaccari; Sections 1.2, 2 (but with minor material from David publications) and 4 Roberta Fasiello; Section 3 David Alexander and Section 5 David Alexander and Francesco Giaccari.
1   The motivation that suggests to value products and goods at their costs doesn't consist in the precise estimation of the profit/loss already gained/occurred, but rather in avoiding arbitrary calculations and, above all, overestimations of the profits because the profit overestimation leads the enterprise to hard disillusions. If the real goods value could always be exactly and with absolute certainty valorized with no difficulties, we couldn't have estimations based on the cost. Only motives of prudence and the need to avoid an erroneous assessment of the net profits (considering not realized ones) can justify an estimation based on the cost.
(Besta 1909, I: p. 264)

However,

the goods valuation on the basis of the actual cost has the advantage to not be dependent on the valuations made by the estimator because it is based on real data. Therefore, this estimation isn't arbitrary and it is especially convenient for the company's profits and losses assessment in the following years unless the costs, considered as aggregate, go over the exchange values.
(Besta 1909, I: p. 238)

2   It remains to be seen whether, and till when, the criterion of historical cost could be rationally applied in the estimation of products and goods. First it is needed that the determination of this cost could be made, without overwork; then, it is necessary

the actual cost would be not greater than the goods' value and above all than the price to which these goods are sold.

(Besta 1909, I: p. 264)

3 Now, it is not always indifferent to leave to the free will of managers the determination of the income and of the loss in a given measure rather than to another one. In joint-stock companies, for example, nothing is more important for the credit stability than to remove every doubt and every free will in declaring dividends.

(Besta 1909, vol. II: p. 14)

4 The determination of the percentage depreciation is particularly important for companies, because this is related to the determination of the profits to be distributed at the end of each business period with a positive result; these profits must be assessed in a proper measure in order to avoid the destruction of the corporate capital and lead one to estimate it more or less than its value. But, in displaying the evaluation method it is needed to consider above all the enterprises and their needs.

(Besta 1909, I: p. 240)

5 "The operating income could be considered yielded and real only in a relative sense; to the same degree in which could be considered yielded and real a result based also on estimated values, obtained through suppositions and expectations" (Onida 1945: p. 38).
6 For an in-depth analysis on these doctrinal stances and for the relevant bibliography, including also the most recent references on the subject: Fasiello 2010: pp. 42–49 and pp. 56–57.
7 Among the advocates of this position, in addition to P. D'Alvise, there is another patrimonialist academic, Ubaldo De Dominicis (De Dominicis 1960: pp. 131–160).

References

Alexander, D. and Fasiello, R. (2014) "Valore reale, fair value and the business model: was Besta best after all?" In *International Conference on Accounting and Management Information Systems* AMIS, Bucharest.

Alexander, D. and Fasiello, R. (2016) "Besta and Zappa are alive and well: historical contributions to 21st Century problems"; paper presented at *7th Workshop on Accounting and Regulation*; Siena, July.

Alexander, D. and Servalli, S. (2011) "Economia Aziendale and financial valuations in Italy: some contradictions and insights", *Accounting History*, vol. 16, no. 3: 291–312.

Besta, F. (1909) *La ragioneria*, vol. I, second ed., Milano: Vallardi Editore.

Besta, F. (1932) *La ragioneria*, vol. II, second ed., Milano: Vallardi Editore.

Chatfield, M. (1977) *A history of accounting thought*, New York: Krieger.

Coronella, S. (2008) "Il bilancio di esercizio nella prima concezione di Gino Zappa. Spunti di attualità a distanza di un secolo", *Rivista dei Dottori Commercialisti*, vol. 59, no. 6: 1057–1098.

De Dominicis, U. (1960) "L'integrità economica del capitale nel tempo", in *Scritti di Ragioneria e tecnica economica in onore del Prof. Alberto Ceccherelli*, Firenze: Le Monnier.

De Dominicis, U. (1984) *Lezioni di Ragioneria Generale. Capitale, Costi, Ricavi e Reddito*, vol. III. Part I, Bologna: Azzoguidi.

Edwards E.O. and Bell P.W. (1961) *The Theory and Measurement of Business Income*, Berkeley: University of California.

EFRAG (2013) *The role of the business model in financial statements*, research paper, December, Brussels: EFRAG.

88   *D. Alexander* et al.

Fasiello, R. (2010) *Il capitale e la conservazione della sua integrità*, QMR no. 90, Roma: Rirea.

Ferrero, G. (1976) "I limiti del costo come "criterio base" nelle valutazioni di bilancio", *Rivista dei Dottori Commercialisti*, Milano: Giuffrè.

Ferrero, G. (1995) *La valutazione del capitale di bilancio*, updated edition, Milano: Giuffrè.

Gonnella, E. (2008) *Osservazioni sul problema delle valutazioni di bilancio nella dottrina italiana. Dal "valore di scambio" al "valore funzionale"*, 66, Roma: Rirea.

Hicks J.R. (1946) *Value and Capital*, Oxford: Clarendon Press.

Lee, T.A. (1986) *Income and value measurement: theory and practice*, edizione tradotta in italiano del 1994, Milano: Egea.

Onida, P. (1945) *Il bilancio d'esercizio nelle imprese. Significato economico del bilancio. Problemi di valutazione*, Milano: Giuffrè.

Onida, P. (1961) *Gino Zappa. Il Maestro*, Milano: Giuffrè.

Onida, P. (1975) Natura e limiti della politica di bilancio, in Aa.Vv. *Scritti in onore di Ugo Caprara*, Milano: Giuffrè.

Palumbo, R. (2003) *Profili della teoria del valore negli studi di ragioneria. Dall'affermazione del paradigma bestano alla definizione delle "tendenze nuove"*, Torino: Giappichelli.

Pantaleoni, M. (1909) *Alcune osservazioni sulle attribuzioni di valori in assenza di formazione di prezzi di mercato, in Scritti varii di economia*, second series, Milano: Remo Sandron.

Perrone, E. (1997) *La ragioneria e i paradigmi contabili*, Padova: Cedam.

Richard, J. (2013) "The three main schools of the French financial accounting doctrine. A historical survey", in Biondi, Y. And Zambon, S., *Accounting and business economics*, Routledge Studies in Accounting, New York: Routledge.

Rossi, G. (2006) *Il principio di prudenza nel bilancio di esercizio*, Roma: Aracne.

Savary, J. (1675) *Le parfait négociant ou instruction générale pour ce qui regarde le commerce ... et l'application des ordonnances; chez louis Billaire; avec le privilège du ROY*. Reproduction en fac similé de la 1ère edition par Klassiker der National ökonomie, 1993, Deutschland.

Transacc: transnational accounting (2001), edited by Dieter Ordelheide and KPMG, London: MacMillan.

Zappa, G. (1910) *Le valutazioni di bilancio con particolare riguardo ai bilanci delle società per azioni*, Milano: Società Editrice Libraria.

Zappa, G. (1920–1929) *La determinazione del reddito nelle imprese commerciali – I valori di conto in relazione alla formazione dei bilanci*, Roma: Anonima Libraria Italiana.

Zappa, G. (1927) *Tendenze nuove negli studi di ragioneria. Discorso inaugurale dell'anno accademico 1926–27 nel R. Istituto Superiore di Scienze Economiche e Commerciali di Venezia*, Milano.

Zappa, G. (1937) *Il reddito di impresa. Scritture doppie. Conti e bilanci di aziende commerciali*, Milano: Giuffrè.

Zappa, G. (1939) *Il reddito di impresa. Scritture doppie. Conti e bilanci di aziende commerciali*, Milano: Giuffrè.

Zappa, G. (1946) *Il reddito di impresa. Scritture doppie. Conti e bilanci di aziende commerciali*, Milano: Giuffrè.

5 The "functional value" (valore funzionale) in the Tuscan School of "Economia Aziendale"

The contribution of Alberto Ceccherelli and Egidio Giannessi to financial valuation theory

Enrico Gonnella[1]

1 Introduction

A "school of thought" is usually defined as a group of scholars who share a common scientific vision. But to be really defined as such, a school of thought must meet at least two requirements: the logical consistency of the key ideas developed by its members and simultaneously their capacity to be distinguished from other traditions of thought (Negru 2013: p. 984). Usually, a school of thought is formed around a first core of innovative and original concepts developed by a person who will be later recognized as the "founding father" of that school, to be further developed and reinforced with the contributions of the ideas of his disciples in order to investigate its subject matter more and more effectively.

This is also the case of the school commenced in Italy by Alberto Ceccherelli (1885–1958) and further developed by his direct disciples Alberto Riparbelli (1907–1971), Egidio Giannessi (1908–1982) and Guido Ponzanelli (1910–1984).[2] Defined by Giannessi himself as one of the "modern schools" of Italian accounting, and initially called by him *Scuola Fiorentina di Ragioneria* (1954a: p. 409) probably referring to the origin of its leader and to the place where he conducted his activity, the University of Florence. It has since become known as *Scuola Toscana di Economia Aziendale* (see Bandettini *et al.* 1996).

The economy of this chapter does not allow for an in-depth critical examination of the various theoretical constructs posited by the School and the scientific production of each of its members. The analysis will be limited to the thought of Alberto Ceccherelli and Egidio Giannessi, the two scholars who, in the School, studied in depth the problem of financial statement valuations and developed their own theories about such topic, which are among the most innovative and original in the Italian doctrine.

2 Short biographies of the two authors

2.1 Alberto Ceccherelli

Alberto Ceccherelli was born in Florence on 22 March 1885. In his birth town, he attended the *Istituto Commerciale di Firenze* (Business Secondary School), named at that time *Scuola di Commercio "Leon Battista Alberti"*, until 1902, when he obtained his high school diploma. In that same year, he enrolled at *Scuola Superiore di Commercio di Venezia "Ca' Foscari"* (Higher School of Commerce), the first Italian business school and among the oldest in the world (Kaplan 2014: p. 530). There he studied with Fabio Besta, who had been teaching accounting in that school since 1872, and had the opportunity to meet with Gino Zappa (1879–1960). He obtained his degree in advanced accounting in November 1906 and eventually graduated in July 1908 with Professor Fabio Besta, being therefore qualified to teach accounting in the business high schools of the Kingdom of Italy (Riparbelli 1960: p. 8; Antoni 1979: p. 78).

Having completed his studies, Ceccherelli started teaching, with various assignments in several Florentine secondary schools. In 1915, when the First World War broke out (1915–1918), Ceccherelli had to interrupt his teaching activity as he was called to arms; then resumed his job after discharge in April 1919, when he was appointed as Lecturer in "Trading and Banking" at the business school *Istituto Commerciale Duca d'Aosta*, where he was awarded the Chair of Accounting in 1921, after passing a public competitive examination to become Full Professor. He would remain in that school until 1932 (Riparbelli 1960: pp. 8–9).

Meanwhile, with the birth of the *Regio Istituto Superiore di Scienze Economiche e Commerciali* (Royal Institute of Economic and Trade Sciences) of the University of Florence, in 1926, Ceccherelli became a Lecturer in "Accounting and Calculation", with a Chair that was awarded to him on 1 December 1932 after a public competition. Since then, Ceccherelli would teach Accounting, Banking and Forensic Accounting at that institute, which would become the Faculty of Economics and Trade of the University of Florence since the academic year 1936–1937. He retired in 1955, as he reached pension age, and died in Florence on 28 January 1958.

The scientific activity of Ceccherelli covered a time span of almost 50 years, from 1910 to 1958, starting therefore at a time when Italian accounting was strongly linked to the fundamental work of Besta, to later develop in the period of the birth and spreading of the new trends of Gino Zappa's thought (Antoni 1979: pp. 81–82). Ceccherelli's scientific production includes 24 books, two essays, 18 articles and a contribution in a volume (see Riparbelli 1960: pp. 26–29; Pezzoli 1996: pp. 27–30). Table 5.1 lists the most significant works of the scholar.

The scientific production of Ceccherelli includes various topics in the fields of accounting history, accounting and *Economia Aziendale*.

The scientific research of Ceccherelli started with some publications of accounting history (see Antonelli 2014; Antonelli and Sargiacomo 2015),

Table 5.1 Main publications of Alberto Ceccherelli (first editions)

Year	Original title	English translation
1915	*La logismologia*	The logismology
1921	*La tecnica del bilancio con speciale riguardo alle aziende bancarie*	The financial statement technique with special reference to banking companies
1922	*L'indirizzo teorico degli studi di ragioneria*	The theoretical orientation of accounting studies
1923	*L'introduzione allo studio della ragioneria generale*	Introduction to the study of general accounting
1930	*Istituzioni di ragioneria*	Accounting basics
1931	*Le prospettive economiche e finanziarie nelle aziende commerciali*	Economic and financial forecasts in firms
1936	*Il problema dei costi nelle prospettive economiche e finanziarie delle imprese*	Costing in the economic and financial forecasts of firms
1939	*Il linguaggio dei bilanci. Formazione e interpretazione dei bilanci commerciali*	The language of financial statements. preparation and interpretation of business financial statements
1948	*L'Economia Aziendale e amministrazione delle imprese*	Economia Aziendale and business management
1951	*El lenguaje del balance. Traducción de la cuarta edición italiana*	The language of financial statements. Translation of the fourth Italian edition
1964	*Problemi di Economia Aziendale*	Problems in Economia Aziendale

according to the address indicated to him by his teacher Fabio Besta (1960, III: p. 322). In this research domain, the scholar took an interest in two big themes, essentially: the accounting practices of Medieval Florentine firms (Ceccherelli 1910, 1913a, 1913b), with a special focus on the origins of the balance sheet (Ceccherelli 1914a, 1914b, 1914c), and the history of accounting theories from ancient times to the nineteenth century (Ceccherelli 1915), works for which he was recognized among the greatest Italian accounting history experts (Mattessich 2003: p. 149).

The main pillar of Ceccherelli's scientific production was in the field of accounting. His preferred subjects, in this field, concerned doctrinal matters, such as the definition of the scope and method adopted for the study of accounting (Ceccherelli 1922, 1934), with insights and suggestions capable of significantly influencing the scholars of the time (Mariani 1968: p. 232). However, Ceccherelli did not only deal with the big underlying issues of accounting, as he also wrote monographs. Inspired, *inter alia*, by the "Business Forecasting" debated at that time in the United States (Ceccherelli 1931: p. 16, no. 1), in 1931 he dealt with a new theme for the Italian scientific community, i.e. investigations on the future, and advocated the need to introduce in the study of accounting the prospective interpretation of financial statement information and the internal statistical data of the *azienda* (Ceccherelli 1931: pp. V–VI). Ceccherelli demonstrated in many instances a peculiar interest for the general theory of the financial statements (Ceccherelli 1921, 1928, 1933, 1939a) and paid particular attention to the problem of financial valuation (Ceccherelli 1928, 1939b, 1949).

But Ceccherelli also studied *Economia Aziendale*. In this discipline, he not only proposed his personal interpretation – which differed from Zappa's – concerning the scope, study methodology and relationships with the other branches of knowledge regarding for-profit and not-for-profit organizations (accounting, i.e. *ragioneria*, organization, and management), primarily accounting (Ceccherelli 1948), but devoted most of his time to the development of a general theory of the *azienda* (Ceccherelli 1923, 1948, 1964). In particular, he identified the specific subject of research of *Economia Aziendale* in the phenomenon of the *azienda* (Ceccherelli 1964: p. 13). His texts on *Economia Aziendale* also include works on production costs (Ceccherelli 1936a and 1936b), where Ceccherelli primarily examined how the costing should change with respect to the different phases of the economic cycle (Ceccherelli 1936a: p. 93).

It is worthwhile mentioning the most significant scientific contributions of Ceccherelli for the purpose of our studies, with no claim of being exhaustive: the idea of elevating accounting to the status of science by developing the doctrinal part of the subject matter (Ceccherelli 1922: pp. 6 and 11–12); the notion of accounting as an interpretative discipline of operations, to be expressed in numbers (*ex ante* interpretation), and of figures, from which operating dynamics should be inferred (ex post interpretation), aimed at providing "a thorough knowledge of the activity of the *azienda*" (Ceccherelli 1934: p. 122); a theory of financial statements that, *inter alia*, requires a clear distinction between the preparation and the interpretation of the document (Ceccherelli 1939a: pp. 18–23); the introduction in Italian *Economia Aziendale* of the prospective investigation of the dynamics and results of the *azienda*, to highlight its importance for the purpose of conducting its operations (Ceccherelli 1931); the idea that *Economia Aziendale* stems from a spontaneous evolution of the studies of the *azienda* and, most of all, of accounting (Ceccherelli 1948: pp. 5 and 14); the notion of *Economia Aziendale* as a preparatory subject that serves as an introduction to studies of accounting, management and organization (see Ceccherelli 1948: pp. 13–14), consisting of an "organic set of general principles" (Ceccherelli 1948: p. 12); the idea that the general theory of the *azienda* is the core of *Economia Aziendale* (Ceccherelli 1948: p. 15; 1964: pp. 18–27); the development of a personal general theory of the *azienda*, based on an organicistic interpretation, where the *azienda* is a phenomenon that includes the explanation of an objective component (operation processes, economic and financial turnover, capital, costs, revenues, profits) (Ceccherelli 1948: p. 16) and a subjective component (decision-making activity) (Ceccherelli 1964); the idea of calculating costs with different criteria depending on the different stages of the economic cycle, so as to align, as much as possible, cost trends with variable revenue trends (Ceccherelli 1936a: p. 156), and the formulation of a new notion of reserve, connected with the notion of average income, naturally grounded in the average cost criterion (Riparbelli 1960: p. 16). And finally, among the most significant theoretical contributions of Ceccherelli is the theory of financial statement valuation, which is the main scope of our investigation and will be described hereinafter.

This short overview reveals the multifaceted nature of our author, which reveals three "souls": in fact, he was an enthusiast of the accounting history, a researcher in contemporary accounting and an economist of the *azienda* in a broader sense. But most times he tackled research with a very personal approach, as he said himself (Ceccherelli 1959: p. 2).

During his years of work at the university, Ceccherelli entertained intense relationships and cooperated with some Italian scientific reviews. He wrote a text on the fundamentals of accounting that was used at secondary schools and at the university (1930), which has reached its eleventh publication, as well as a professional manual for accountants (1952), which was also re-published several times.

He took part actively in the academic life of the University of Florence as member of the Faculty Advisory Board of the *Facoltà di Economia e Commercio* (Faculty of Economics and Trade) and in the government of the University as member of the Board of Directors (Riparbelli 1968: pp. 22–23).

But, probably, one of his most important scientific credits is that he created a school of thought that would later be identified as the "Tuscan School of Economia Aziendale" (Bandettini *et al.* 1996).

2.2 Egidio Giannessi

Egidio Giannessi was born in Pisa on 28 July 1908. In 1932 he graduated *magna cum laude* in *Tecnica Industriale* (Management) working with Professor Teodoro D'Ippolito at the *Regio Istituto Superiore di Scienze Economiche e Commerciali* of Florence. After the degree, he worked actively for a few years as volunteer assistant of D'Ippolito in Milan, where he met Gino Zappa and Ugo Caprara, all three professors at the Bocconi University in those years (Giannessi 1971: p. 3).

In 1936, when D'Ippolito passed to the Palermo University and Ugo Caprara went to the University of Turin, Giannessi left the Milan scene and went back to Tuscany to teach in secondary school, which was a natural passage at that time in Italy – a sort of "test bench" before the university career (Giannessi 1971: p. 3). That same year he obtained a teaching qualification in Accounting and Calculations (Corticelli 1982: p. 488). Still in 1936, his colleague Alberto Riparbelli introduced him to Professor Ceccherelli, who invited him to become his assistant (Giannessi 1971: p. 4). So it was that, from the 1930s to the 1950s, he worked as Adjunct Assistant Professor in the Chair of Accounting and Calculations, teaching courses in Management of Industrial Firms and Management of Farms and Mining Firms at the University of Florence (Miolo Vitali and Gonnella 2006: p. 577). Over that period Giannessi continued as Adjunct Assistant Professor in Florence and also worked in Pisa, where he had obtained the Chair of Accounting at the *Istituto Tecnico Commerciale* (Business Secondary School).

Furthermore, since the 1940s, he also held teaching posts at the University of Pisa for courses in Economia Aziendale at the *Scuola di Perfezionamento nelle Discipline Corporative* (Postgraduate School in Corporative Disciplines), in Business Statistics at *Istituto di Studi per la Riforma Sociale* (Institute of Studies for Social Reform) of the Faculty of Law, in Calculations, General and Applied Accounting in the detached section of the University of Florence at the aforesaid University of Pisa (Miolo Vitali and Gonnella 2006: p. 577).

In 1956, Giannessi won the public competition organized by the University of Parma. After one year in Parma, in 1957, he moved to the University of Pisa, where he had already been teaching since the academic year 1955–1956 as Lecturer, when the Faculty of Economics and Trade was opened. Since 1957, he held the Chair of General and Applied Accounting in Pisa, where he became Full Professor. He also held a post as teacher of Industrial and Trade Management. In May 1978, he held the conclusive lecture of his courses on the theme: "La conoscenza" [Knowledge] (Corticelli 1982: p. 488). Giannessi died in Pisa on 13 July 1982.

Giannessi's publications span over a period going from 1935 to 1981, without considering his posthumous work (Giannessi 1992). His scientific production consists of 19 books, 20 articles, three essays, five among conference papers and speeches, 11 writings in honour of colleagues, one translation and other minor writings, prevalently in Italian, but also in German, English and Portuguese. His most significant works are listed in Table 5.2 below.

Giannessi's works deal with many themes: from production costs, financial accounting and the accounting history to organization, research methodology and, most of all, *Economia Aziendale*. However, we should point out that his works are often difficult to categorize because they combine themes belonging to multiple scientific areas, such as *Economia Aziendale* and accounting, with an approach that reveals the true nature of Giannessi, who was an "all-round business economist" (Bertini 1994: p. 101).

Among his main works, it is worthwhile mentioning those on production costs, the initial subject of his research. His first two monographs are devoted to costing methods in industrial firms (Giannessi 1935 and 1943) with the precise purpose of supplementing and deeply investigating the previous research studies developed by his Master Ceccherelli (Giannessi 1954a: p. 422). Subsequently, he published an essay that is very well known in Italy and abroad, where he essentially examined the circular relationship between costs, production volumes and economic results – the "Kreislauf" (Giannessi 1958a, 1958b and 1982a), as well as the various uncertainties of the calculation of costs and revenues, with the purpose of figuring out the impossibility to apply said data as exclusive basis for sales decisions, and conversely the need to refer them to a wider range of elements of judgement (Giannessi 1982a: pp. 46ff).

Then there are significant works on accounting history, the field of research he always preferred, perhaps because inspired by his Master. Among these works, we should first mention a book (Giannessi 1954a) originated from the idea of disseminating, particularly abroad, the status of the Italian doctrines

Table 5.2 Main publications of Egidio Giannessi (first editions)

Year	Original title	English translation
1935	*I costi di produzione nelle imprese tessili cotoniere*	Production costs in cotton textile firms
1943	*Costi e prezzi-tipo nelle aziende industriali*	Standard costs and prices in industrial firms
1954	*Attuali tendenze delle dottrine economico-tecniche italiane*	Current trends in italian economic-technical doctrines
1954	*Die Finanzbedarfsgleichung im Produktionsbetrieb und die Möglichkeit ihrer Darstellung*	The financial needs equation in firm and the possibility of its representation
1955	*L'equazione del fabbisogno di finanziamento nelle aziende di produzione e le possibili vie della sua soluzione*	The financing needs equation in firms and possible ways of its solutions
1962	*A Equação do Financiamento nas Empresas (Possível Vias da Sua Solução)*	
1956	*Il piano finanziario nel sistema dei piani d'azienda*	The financial plan in the business planning system
1958	*Der Kreislauf zwischen Kosten und Preisen als bestimmender Faktor der Gleichgewichtsbedingungen im System der Unternehmung*	The "circularity" between costs and prices as a determinant of firm's equilibrium
1958	*Il Kreislauf tra costi e prezzi come elemento determinante delle condizioni di equilibrio del sistema d'azienda*	
1960	*Le aziende di produzione originaria, Vol. I, Le aziende agricole*	The primary activities firms, vol. I, the farms
1961	*Interpretazione del concetto di azienda pubblica*	Interpretation of the concept of public economic unit
1964	*I precursori in Economia Aziendale*	The forerunners of economia aziendale
1969	*Considerazioni critiche intorno al concetto di azienda*	Critical considerations on the notion of azienda
1970	*Appunti di Economia Aziendale con particolare riferimento alle aziende agricole*	Notes on economia aziendale, with particular reference to farms
1981	*Possibilità e limiti della programmazione*	Possibilities and limitations of planning
1992	*Considerazioni introduttive sul metodo storico*	Introductory considerations on the historical method

regarding the *azienda* (Giannessi 1954a: p. XI). In this volume, Giannessi describes, on the one hand, the status of the university and post-university teaching of *azienda*-related disciplines, and the various projects for the reform of the Faculties of Economics and Trade; on the other hand, both the Italian "historical schools" (the Lombard School, Giuseppe Cerboni's approach and the Fabio Besta School) and the scientific trends of his time, defined as "modern schools" by the author (Giannessi 1954a). Then, the part dedicated to historical schools will be developed in a second monograph pertaining to the history of Italian accounting thinking, published in multiple editions (Giannessi 1980). His historical works also include studies on the thought of Harrington Emerson (1966) and Frederich Winslow Taylor (1970), where the scholar examined the contributions given by these two authors to the development of management.

Giannessi was also particularly attracted by the financial issues of firms, and specifically by the theme of calculation and coverage of financing needs. He devoted two important texts to this subject, one with a more theoretical perspective (Giannessi 1954b, 1955, 1962 and 1982b) and the other with a more operational approach (Giannessi 1956).

One theme that is particularly highlighted in Giannessi's thought is the general theory of the *azienda*, which he investigated on several occasions: first in his main work (Giannessi 1960) and then in two subsequent monographs (Giannessi 1961 and 1969).

The above-mentioned work, dated 1960 and entitled *Le aziende di produzione originaria – Vol. I – Le aziende agricole*, deserves some specific comments. In this large 838-page volume, which provides a sort of *summa* of his thought, the scholar dealt with many subjects regarding both business economics (e.g. the general theory of the *azienda*, the notion of *Economia Aziendale*, the nature of relationships between *Economia Aziendale*, accounting and similar disciplines, the decision-making issue and its related risks in the different life stages of the *azienda*), and accounting (development trends in accounting, business planning, valuation, bookkeeping and financial statements), according to a very rigorous theoretical approach characterized by a considerable depth of thought. It is particularly in this wide-spanning work that, in our opinion, we can see the figure of Giannessi fully emerge as that of a scholar of *azienda*-related subject matters. The volume would be subsequently published even in a reduced and very successful version (Giannessi 1970 and 1979).

But Giannessi also took an interest in research methodologies, particularly with a posthumous monograph (Giannessi 1992). This text, which should have been only the first chapter of a much larger work in the author's mind, presents the basic theme of the objectivity and neutrality of scientific research (Ferraris Franceschi 1992: pp. XXV and XXVI).

Although much in harmony with those of Master Ceccherelli, Giannessi's theoretical conceptions appear to be particularly innovative, as one may infer from this short, and not necessarily exhaustive, list: the unitary conception of the *azienda* as a phenomenon, beyond the different function performed by each individual entity (Giannessi 1961: pp. 13–14); the development of a general theory of the *azienda*, according to a systemic, dynamic and probabilistic perspective (Giannessi 1956: p. 103) where the notion of a threefold order stands out – combinatory, systematic and of composition[3] – together with that of the durable economic equilibrium as the only aim of any kind of for-profit and non-profit entities (see Giannessi 1960: pp. 39–107, 1961, 1969); the vision of accounting as a "science that studies the conversion of *azienda*'s dynamics into numbers and the reconversion of these numbers into economic trends" (Giannessi 1960: p. 22); the notion of the financial statements as a historical–probabilistic document (Giannessi 1960: p. 815), with the purpose of "determining an appropriate result to identify the balance positions of the *azienda* and the nature of their related motion" (Giannessi 1960: p. 805); the impossibility to ground economic judgements exclusively on accounting data (e.g. costs, prices and revenues) having a more or less uncertain nature and, more generally, to rely on the "application of rigid mathematical rules" to solve the problems of the *azienda*, in the awareness that it is instead necessary to evaluate "all the historical, current and future elements making up the judgement" (Giannessi 1982a: pp. 56 and 63); the idea that historical research is essential not only in itself, but also for scientific research, as it allows researchers to identify the evolution of a given phenomenon (Giannessi 1980: pp. XI–VII). Then we should separately mention the financial valuation theory developed by Giannessi, which we will examine more in depth hereinafter.

Giannessi had a long and intense cooperation with several Italian scientific reviews and also foreign scientific journals. He attended a high number of conferences as speaker both in Italy and abroad (Corticelli 1982: p. 489).

To fully outline the scientific profile of our scholar, we should also analyse the bibliographic material stored in his personal scientific library, called *Dono Giannessi*, donated by him to the then Institute of Accounting of the University of Pisa, today preserved in the homonymous room of the Department of Economics and Management of the University of Pisa (see Miolo Vitali and Gonnella 2006). The high number of texts in foreign languages clearly shows how Giannessi carefully followed the vibrant international debate on the matters of his interest, particularly in the period after World War II, and not as a simple spectator but as a veritable protagonist (see also Ferraris Franceschi 2013). In fact, as a scholar, he took active part in the activities of the scientific community of his time, not only at national level, but also internationally. This is proved by the high number of books and excerpts taken from magazines and various foreign publications we found, mainly German and South American, accompanied by *"ex-donis"* or authors' presentation cards, as we find for Italian publications. These inscriptions are the direct testimony of the network of relationships established by Giannessi in Italy and abroad. Furthermore, the presence of texts of economics, law, statistics and appraisal seems to demonstrate the scholar's tendency to expand his field of investigation to include social sciences related to accounting and *Economia Aziendale*, according to an interdisciplinary approach.

We may observe that the information summarized above clearly indicates that Giannessi had a wide range of interests, being an all-round business economist, an accounting historian and a scholar capable of projecting himself onto the international stage, prone to interdisciplinary dialogue.

From an institutional perspective, Giannessi should also be remembered as a founder of the *Istituto di Ricerche Aziendali* (Institute for Research on the *Azienda*) of the University of Pisa in the academic year 1957–1958. Under his direction, the Institute progressively grew until it became a first-rate research centre in Italy and internationally, and established significant relationships with other Italian and foreign universities.

3 The theory of functional value and valuation

As we pointed out earlier, the subject of financial valuation is one of the preferred fields of investigation of the Tuscan School of *Economia Aziendale*. Ceccherelli and Giannessi are the members of this School who spent the most significant amount of energy in developing a well-grounded theory on the subject at issue. The theory of functional valuation, conceived by the former scholar and improved by the latter, is undoubtedly a peculiar theme of the Tuscan School that contributes to differentiate its system of thought from that of other Italian and foreign schools. The contributions of the two aforesaid scholars are examined in detail in the next sections.

3.1 The contribution of Alberto Ceccherelli

The themes of financial statements and, more specifically, financial valuation are common in Alberto Ceccherelli's research work. Since the end of the 1920s, the researcher took an interest in financial statements, with a specific focus on the financial statements of banks, and published on this theme first an article (1918) and then a monograph (1923). Subsequently, in 1928, he published a first essay focused on financial valuation and, after a book on extraordinary financial statements in 1933, he would resume the subject of financial valuation with two publications, one in 1939 and the other in 1949. Most importantly, in 1939 he would publish a consistent treatise entitled *Il linguaggio dei bilanci – Formazione e interpretazione dei bilanci commerciali* [*The language of financial statements. Preparation and interpretation of the business financial statements*], one of his most prominent and important works (Riparbelli 1960: p. 17), which was also translated into Spanish (Ceccherelli 1951). It is in this book that Ceccherelli definitively developed his own theory of financial valuation, resuming some considerations he had already presented in previous works.

To grasp the ultimate meaning of the theory developed by Ceccherelli on financial valuation, it seems appropriate to start by defining the function of the financial statement in the scholar's view. In fact, he intended it "as a technical-accounting procedure of determination and representation of the results for the period, which depend on enterprise's activity" (Ceccherelli 1939a: p. 3). In the logical framework proposed by Ceccherelli, financial statements "may have a control and a reporting function" (Ceccherelli 1939a: p. 9): while the first function is a form of "control of trends and efficiency", the second occurs "when directors, acting as agents, have to show with the financial statement the results of their activities and report to shareholders" (Ceccherelli 1939a: p. 9). In the Tuscan author's thought, it is clear that if control functions are always present,[4] reporting functions are only possible.[5] This is particularly true in a one-person enterprise, where although "the financial statements are inspired to the same notions and obeys the same rules … of the financial statements of limited companies, … nobody would ever think that such a financial statement should be considered as a report" (Ceccherelli 1939a: p. 11). We would like to add that this line of reasoning is also applicable for those enterprises that are managed by the shareholders themselves, like family-run firms, as common in Italy at that time as they are today.

After these introductory considerations, the two main aspects of the theory of financial valuation conceived by Ceccherelli can be identified, in our opinion, in the notion of "functional qualities" of assets and in the consequent notion of "functional value" (Ceccherelli 1939a: p. 192). Both notions are developed by referring to a limited area of capital, i.e. non-financial assets.[6]

In truth, the scholar's thought is essentially grounded on an axiom, i.e. that assets have a specific and indispensable function in each enterprise, that for which they have been originally purchased. In this regard, Ceccherelli wrote:

> assets … do not occupy an autonomous position in the capital of the firm: they have a useful existence, since they contribute, with others, to make a certain type of economic transformations possible, given that they make up a complex bound to the management of the firm and depending thereon.
>
> (Ceccherelli 1939a: p. 189)

As one can easily infer, the researcher is fully aware that assets are complementary elements, and not autonomous entities. This reveals a holistic vision of the financial position. The problem, according to Ceccherelli, should be adequately considered when conducting financial valuations. He clarified this point when he observed, referring to assets:

> In the valuation process, these assets lose, even when they take on a concrete form, their nature of economic goods, which, for their own intrinsic qualities, can be estimated at any time. In order to be estimated with this method, they should be detached from the complex by disaggregation of it.
>
> (Ceccherelli 1939a: pp. 189–190)

In Ceccherelli's vision, the purpose of financial valuation is "to translate into value the functional qualities of the firm assets that are considered as investment of funds for profit" (Ceccherelli 1939a: p. 196); the said qualities "summarise the attitudes and productive potential of the [aforesaid] assets" (Ceccherelli 1939a: p. 196).[7] Therefore, the attribution of values at year-end ultimately assumes the study of the operating capacities of the different balance sheet items, seen as parts of a unitary whole. This led to the consolidation of a first systemic vision of financial valuation, which marked the birth of a typical approach of the Tuscan School of *Economia Aziendale*, the so-called "valuation holism" (Gonnella 2008: p. 37). How, therefore, should valuation be conducted?

The aforesaid functional characteristics, when an asset is purchased, necessarily "find a quantitative expression – as Ceccherelli maintained – in their original cost" (1939a: pp. 196–197). This can be justified by recalling that "at that time, cost is … a measure of the functionality of the investment made, that is a measure of the assumed possibility that an adequate revenue is obtained from it" (Ceccherelli 1939a: pp. 197). Subsequently, valuation implies that the evolution of "functional qualities" and of the "degree of functionality" of assets are examined (Ceccherelli 1939a: p. 195). So we may have several different hypotheses: if the functionality level has remained unchanged, then the valuation shall always be based on the cost incurred at purchase (Ceccherelli 1939a: p. 195); if, instead, the degree of functionality changes, then we should apply the value "that, at the time considered, expresses the new degree of functionality of the assets, corresponding to the changed internal and external conditions of the firm" (Ceccherelli 1939a: p. 195). Should such functionality be decreased, the value will be reduced in accordance with the decreased functionality of the asset (Ceccherelli 1939a: p. 196), while, in the event of any "increase in functionality", the original cost will be taken as balance sheet value, as in the case of an unchanged degree of functionality, because the greater value – according to Ceccherelli – cannot "become part of an income that has been already realised" (Ceccherelli 1939a: p. 196). Clearly, in this last case, a typically prudential approach – in accordance with the conservatism principle – has been chosen to prevent the recognition of unrealized profits (Ceccherelli 1939a: p. 201; see also p. 196). Furthermore, we should not forget that, according to the then-applicable Code of Commerce, financial statements had to "demonstrate with evidence and truth the actually realized profits and the suffered losses" (art. 176, paragraph 2). All in all, we can say that Ceccherelli, believing deeply in the need to develop theories in strict adherence to the facts, acknowledges the provisions of law and respects them punctually. However, to a certain extent, he went well beyond that. He did not waive the opportunity to expose the asset to its functional value. Indeed, he proposed a technical–accounting solution suitable to book in the balance sheet the higher value of the assets even in case of an increase in their degree of functionality, however without affecting the determination of income. This is done by suggesting that the increase in value be booked both in the asset account, as a cost increase, and in the corresponding contra asset account called *fondo oscillazione valori* (Ceccherelli 1939a: p. 201).

The valuation process, therefore, consists in changing the original cost based on the changed production capacities of assets examined (Giannessi 1941: p. 649), because their contribution to income depends on such capacities (Ceccherelli 1939a: p. 195). Ceccherelli was rather clear on this point:

> all valuation procedures, … from the depreciation … to the future sale price of goods to be sold, … actually consider [the original cost] as a monetary

capital capable of producing a certain income, and, by translating it into balance sheet value, they change the measure according to the changes in the assumed degree of functionality of the associated investments.

(Ceccherelli 1939a: pp. 203–204)

This statement can be better understood by recalling how Ceccherelli defined "financial valuation":

valuating capital … does not mean … to assign values to the different assets that compose it, but rather to assign a value to the original and subsequent costs incurred for firm's operation that remain.

(Ceccherelli 1939a: p. 190)

The approach at issue, in the end, does not value assets as such, but estimates the residual value of the costs that have been incurred in the past to procure them.

However, there is a further element we deem essential to deeply grasp the thought of our scholar: original costs can be reviewed only by developing forecasts on future business trends (Ceccherelli 1939a: p. 198).[8] This is an aspect on which Ceccherelli insisted with a particular vigour:

Financial valuation … must … find its basis in a forecast of the future possibilities of the enterprise, inferred from the exploration of internal and external conditions, and be resolved in appropriate corrections of original costs.

(Ceccherelli 1939a: p. 201)

Therefore, values are based on forecasts, and precisely for this reason they are affected by the actual occurrence of said forecasts (Ceccherelli 1949: p. 4). The need to investigate the future makes financial statement valuation difficult and uncertain – as our author stressed (Ceccherelli 1939a: p. 197). How should we, therefore, face financial valuation? Even on this point Ceccherelli provided us with an unequivocal answer:

Uncertainty … should not mean to give up the solution of the problem, but being aware of the difficulties and orientation of the investigation not so much towards valuation rules and formulas, but rather towards the study of the interdependencies that bind values … to the firm's operations.

(Ceccherelli 1939a: p. 198)

In the excerpt above, we can detect a strong idea of the valuation theory conceived by Ceccherelli. According to him, in fact, no financial valuation can be performed by mechanically applying predefined valuation criteria and rules, as it actually requires a veritable reasoning based on an accurate analysis of the enterprise's activity. In fact, Ceccherelli introduces a radical change in the approach to the study of financial valuation in the Italian doctrine. Unlike other authors of the same period, he does not propose a mere list of valuation criteria with a description of their pros and cons (Giannessi 1960: p. 814), but rather a logical path to be followed to express valuation judgements. As he says:

> It is not the norms and rules, which uselessly tend to immutability, that can resolve the problem of valuation and the truth of the financial statements, but it is the correct interpretation ... [of] the economic phenomena of the *azienda* that helps clarifying the process of determination and valuation of values and allows for the best possible solutions.
>
> (Ceccherelli 1949: p. 12)[9]

This is also confirmed by the fact that, even when he describes the cost criterion, Ceccherelli immediately clarifies its strictly indicative nature. In this regard, he says:

> Financial valuation is oriented towards ... the cost criterion. That does not mean that assets must be valued at cost, but only that for their valuation ... one must take cost as a point of reference.
>
> (Ceccherelli 1939a: p. 191)

> The cost criterion ... cannot become a valuation rule.
>
> (Ceccherelli 1939a: p. 197)

Clearly enough, the scholar dislikes rigid valuation criteria and their – as we may say – mechanical application. This aspect clearly appears even when Ceccherelli, after dealing with the theoretical general principles of financial valuation, illustrates some application examples of the estimate of the various categories of assets. Two examples are worthwhile mentioning on this: the valuation of depreciable assets and the valuation of goods.

The valuation of depreciable assets, as is well known, is obtained indirectly by using the depreciation process. Ceccherelli develops his personal thesis on depreciation as well. After criticizing the doctrine of his time, which, in his opinion, was "more inclined towards research and a criticism of the formulae to be used to resolve the arithmetic calculation of rates, rather than towards the study of the fundamental elements of the problem" (Ceccherelli 1939a: p. 358), he deeply analyses exactly those elements. By so doing, he eventually put forward the proposal to adopt a mixed depreciation criterion, in which the depreciation rate is formed by a minimum constant part and by an additional part that varies proportionally to the profit of the period (Ceccherelli 1939a: p. 372).[10] So, higher depreciation rates will be applied in periods of prosperity, expecting future periods of depression that will negatively impact on the degree of functionality of the fixed asset. Conversely, lower depreciation rates will be used in periods of depression in view of the higher degree of functionality that will characterize future periods of prosperity. All in all, Ceccherelli's idea is to refer to a "depreciation rate that already includes the value of a provision for risks, that is to say the corrective elements of its uncertain measure, and consequently closer to the real world" (Ceccherelli 1939a: p. 372). This is, therefore, a flexible solution.[11]

The problem of the valuation of goods also reveals an elastic approach. Here the researcher starts by specifying that the issue of valuing goods cannot be tackled by using various kinds of valuation rules, "but should be identified in the criterion of the future contribution of inventories in generating future profits", which "implies an investigation of the market conditions and expected business and price trend" (Ceccherelli 1939a: p. 339). Specifically, the principle proposed by Ceccherelli is valuation "at a cost adjusted based on estimated future revenues" (Ceccherelli 1939a: p. 340). This essentially requires to reduce the cost on a precautionary basis in the case of "forecasts ... of decrease in prices based on ongoing trends" (Ceccherelli 1939a: p. 340) and to leave it unaltered in the opposite case of "expected future price increases, even if based on ongoing trends" (Ceccherelli 1939a: pp. 340–341): in this second instance, "increases [should], however, be recorded in the financial statements in a special indicative contra asset account" (Ceccherelli, 1939a: p. 341). The "criterion of the realisable value", as clarified by the author, differs from the simple rule of cost or current price, if lower (Ceccherelli 1939a: p. 341). The former, unlike the latter, "leaves its part to forecast and receives its deductions" (Ceccherelli 1939a: p. 341).

The criterion proposed by Ceccherelli leaves a larger freedom of action to directors, but if we look at the issue more in-depth, this is precisely the element that pushes the researcher to appreciate it, because "the greater flexibility ... allows for a better distribution, between the different annual financial statements, of profits and losses depending on the changing economic environment and on the related price changes" (Ceccherelli 1939a: p. 342).

The solutions proposed by Ceccherelli for the depreciation and valuation of goods, as described above, undoubtedly tend to favour a stabilization of income over time. However, in the researcher's logical framework, this is not a limitation, but a veritable strength. The flexibility of valuation, unlike one might think, is precisely required by the need to have more reliable financial statements. In his vision, the reliability of financial statements can only be obtained by assuming, for the determination of income, a multi-year perspective, by referring to

> time periods much longer than one year, that is to say periods corresponding to the length of an economic cycle, ... [i.e.] a time period long enough to allow for the manifestation, balancing and stabilization of the various market trends and price changes.
>
> (Ceccherelli 1939a: p. 207)

By so doing, he moved "the practical problem of financial valuation towards a logical solution" (Ceccherelli 1939a: p. 207).

At this point, a spontaneous question arises as to whether such an approach, considering its flexibility, is appropriate for the two functions of the financial statement: the control function and the reporting function. Ceccherelli answered rather explicitly:

> The greater freedom resulting from the sole obligation to comply, in preparing financial statements, with theoretical and technical principles regarding the subject matter without a specific indication of rules, would not reduce the warranties offered by the law to the stakeholders. Indeed, we could maintain that it would reinforce its scope because, on one hand, it would allow to apply the most appropriate criteria, on a case-by-case basis, ... on the other hand, would not permit to overcome the limits imposed by those principles, thus making directors even more responsible.
>
> (Ceccherelli 1949: p. 20)

At this point, it seems appropriate to observe that, if the problem of year-end valuation requires to examine firm economic phenomena and interpret them as correctly as possible, it is necessary to have a framework useful for this purpose. In this regard, it seems to us that in Ceccherelli's perspective, the said framework consists in the principles developed by *Economia Aziendale*, more specifically in the theory of the *azienda*, so dear to the author. It is precisely within the framework of the theory of the *azienda* that notions like functional qualities, degree of functionality and complementarity of assets find their natural placement. It is totally logical, therefore, that these notions are recalled precisely by Ceccherelli, who has studied the *azienda* as a phenomenon in depth and had developed a personal theory of the subject.

We may conclude that, in the scholar's view, valuation stems from the study of the production capacities of the factor in the system to which it belongs, after considering the internal and external conditions of the enterprise in a future perspective. Therefore, Ceccherelli does not suggest specific and pre-established rules, but teaches a logical line of reasoning by presenting general principles based on solid economic bases, by which the preparer of the financial statement could usefully be inspired when expressing their valuations. So the value is the result of a critical, cognitive, and interpretive process regarding the life of the enterprise and the environment where it lives and operates. This is the innovative contribution of Ceccherelli. In the notions of functional qualities and degree of functionality, as well as in the consequent notion of functional value, we can see the core of Ceccherelli's thought.

The theory expounded, albeit abstract, appears to be totally in line with the two functions of the financial statement recognized by Ceccherelli, that of control of trends and efficiency, and that of reporting to shareholders.

With his research on the subject of financial valuation, the scholar develops an original and rather complex personal theory that could be defined as a theory of functional value and contributes to elevating the subject of valuation from a technical–regulatory level to the doctrinal level.[12]

3.2 The contribution of Egidio Giannessi

More than 20 years after the first edition of the book on financial statements published by Master Ceccherelli, the disciple Giannessi also deals with the problem of financial valuation. He does it in a special chapter of his main work, *Le aziende di produzione originaria* (1960), a monograph in which, from a perspective midway between *Economia Aziendale* and accounting, he analyses farms, albeit it contains broader considerations pertaining to enterprises in general. We should note that this is the same book where the scholar develops for the first time his own general theory of the *azienda* (pp. 39–107); this book will be followed later by more works on the same subject (see: 1961 and 1969). We will start our reasoning precisely from a short reference to his ideas on the *azienda* as a phenomenon.

In Giannessi's theory, *azienda* is defined as a *"systematic, dynamic* and *probabilistic* phenomenon" (Giannessi 1956: p. 103). More specifically, it is seen as a "system of operations stemming from the combination of specific [production] factors and from the composition of internal and external forces" (1960: p. 51), having "as purpose the achievement of a given economic equilibrium, durable in time" (1960: p. 63). This is, in fact, in his vision of the *azienda*, the "end assigned" by men to the said entity (Giannessi 1969: p. 587). According to Giannessi, the economic equilibrium of the *azienda* exists when economic results ensure the adequate remuneration of production factors and a remunerative compensation to ownership, for a satisfactory period (Giannessi 1960: p. 75). Clearly, as extensively described by the scholar, different economic situations of equilibrium or disequilibrium may occur during the life of the entity, with a tendency that may be, in both cases, of an evolutive nature (improvement of the economic situation) or of an involutive nature (worsening of the economic situation) (Giannessi 1960: pp. 92–102). This having been stated, it will be easier to explain the peculiar notion of financial statement developed by the scholar.

In Giannessi's theoretical approach, "the financial statement is [conceived as] a tool for the conversion of dynamics into figures and for the reconversion of figures into economic trends" (Giannessi 1960: p. 801; see also p. 815), that is to say a tool – just like other ones used in the firm – to reflect and interpret entity dynamics. On the other hand, we should not forget that when Giannessi further develops Ceccherelli's theses, he conceives accounting as the doctrine that studies how to "reflect firm dynamics", by processing figures, and to "reconstruct said dynamics on logical bases", starting from the same figures (Giannessi 1960: p. 515). In particular, he specifies that:

> The financial statement is a tool through which a given dynamic position in the life of the entity is reflected.
>
> (Giannessi 1960: p. 799)

This vision, which stems from the acknowledgement of the continuous flow of enterprise life, leads to the recognition of the dual nature of the accounting document:

The financial statement has a historical and simultaneously probabilistic nature: it is historical because it contains data regarding the past of which it can offer an effective synthesis, and it is probabilistic because it contains data on the valuation of equipment, inventories and risks by which it somehow anticipates future operations.

(Giannessi 1969: p. 799)

Therefore, we could say that the financial statement is the linking ring between two dynamics: the activity conducted in the past and the activity foreseen for the future. This is the reason why Giannessi maintains that:

The financial statement ... does not give irrefutable results, but only *probabilistic results*, whose meaning is closely dependent on the assumptions made and on the higher or lower probability these have to be converted into real events.

(Giannessi 1960: p. 802)

Coming to the purpose of the financial statements in Giannessi's theory – a very interesting aspect for our research, indeed – Giannessi writes:

Financial statement information is formed to determine a "profit for the period", to be used in the reconstruction of the equilibrium positions of the *azienda* and in the identification of the characteristics of the motion by which this is animated.

(Giannessi 1960: p. 824; see also pp. 804, 806 and 824)

The purpose of financial statements and financial accounting is, therefore, to provide a basis for a judgement; first of all, of the income for the period, which is useful to make the point about the economic equilibrium of the *azienda*, which lies at the basis of its life.[13] In our opinion, this is the strong, and perhaps most interesting, idea in the theory of financial statements developed by the scholar. So, we might state that the financial statements, intended as such, should be essentially defined as a tool for the control and planning of the firm's activity, useful for directors to govern their enterprise in full awareness and in a rational manner. It is based on the financial statements, conceived and prepared as described, and particularly based on the profit recognized therein, that even the most important business decisions are made.[14] These, in a nutshell, are the main features of the theory of financial statements proposed by Giannessi in the work quoted above (1960). To complete the picture on this subject, it is useful to point out that in a subsequent work he would call the financial statements, intended as such, an "'actual' financial statement" (Giannessi 1969: p. 532), to be distinguished from the "financial statement to be published", that is the one with which "its preparers, in addition to determining a result that could be useful to manage the activity, pursue additional aims, such as the policy of dividends, the policy related to the tax office, the banks and third parties in general" (Giannessi 1969: p. 535). Among other things, Giannessi also says:

Companies, particularly when they are listed, try to *"... stabilize their results for the period* by using those that are most favourable – by using ... hidden reserves – to face negative results. In this way, and for this reason, the 'published' result never corresponds to the 'actual' result."

(Giannessi 1969: p. 535)

So:

an "actual" result, either positive or negative, may correspond to a "standard income", whose meaning is purely formal or, in other words, *political-operating* in nature.

(Giannessi 1969: p. 536)

We can see how Giannessi clearly distinguished between an "actual financial statement" and a "financial statement to be published". The "actual financial statement", to be submitted to the internal stakeholders of the enterprise, first of all its directors, who prepare it, must ensure a true view of firm dynamics, and for this reason will neither be regulated by accounting standards, nor admit earning management practices. The "financial statement to be published", which is prepared to provide information to the various external stakeholders, shows values that necessarily depend on the applicable law rules and accounting standards, not rarely aimed at stabilizing income, because it is the subject of income smoothing practices. Based on these considerations, in order not to misunderstand Giannessi's thought, we must point out that the perspective of the "actual financial statement" is the one that is observed preferentially, if not exclusively, by the scholar and to which he systematically refers developing his own "theory of functional valuation" (Giannessi 1960: p. 29).

But let us now come to the theory of financial valuation. First of all, we should remember that Giannessi, when he deals with the valuation issue, tackles the subject from a broader perspective, and examined the different types of valuations that can be found in the business domain: financial statement valuation, liquidation valuation, and valuation in buying or selling a business. However, one may not deny that the theme Giannessi develops more broadly is that of financial statement valuations, and particularly the notion of functional valuation. And he does this for a very precise reason, as, in his opinion, functional valuation is "the most significant expression of the valuation process" (Giannessi 1960: p. 598). This is explained by its peculiar recurrence and its specific function. Giannessi states, in this regard:

While ... [business valuations and liquidation valuations] occur once and only serve to determine the ways in which firm investment can be realized after a certain time, functional valuation is required at least once every period and is used to determine the basic positions of enterprise's equilibrium.

(Giannessi 1960: p. 598)

At this point, it is correct to say that, in Giannessi's vision, "the [functional] valuation process implies the definition of the notion of functionality", in the awareness that, with such a concept, one "identifies the position of each factor within the economic combination of the firm" (Giannessi 1960: p. 67). This explains why functional values summarize – in his view – the function of production factors in a specific enterprise (Giannessi 1960: pp. 738–739). Read the following excerpt:

> Production factors are *generators of services*, and they must be considered as such. The circumstance that an asset exists in the market in the free state or that it belongs to a production combination is determinant for the purpose of valuation.... In the latter case, the asset is no longer a free element, but a production factor: it is part of a system in which it has a specific destination. A production factor is purchased to carry out a given function and it remains indissolubly tied to that function until a change in its destination arrives.... Considering the production factor as a free market asset is like denying the existence of the firm as a system and of the links that characterise its structure and motion.... The valuation of production factors must take into account the function they are expected to perform in the firm as a system.
>
> (Giannessi 1960: pp. 697–698)[15]

To valuate means to grasp the economic attitude of the different production factors within the operating structure of which they are part. This is a crucial point in the work of the scholar, one that seems to find its logical premises in the investigations – initiated by Ceccherelli and later resumed and further developed by Giannessi himself – on how to combine production factors. For Giannessi, indeed, production factors, considered individually, have no usefulness for the *azienda*.[16] They become useful only if adequately combined with each other.[17] In other words, he believes that valuation could not neglect an important feature of the productive structure of the firm, that is to say the complementarity of the production factors. These ones must not be valued individually, as if they were autonomous entities, by observing them only in their intrinsic features, but rather as parts of a whole. In fact, the valuation of each asset is affected by how it is combined with the others (n–1) and by the relationships created among them.

Passing from facts to their representation, or – we may say – from the economy of the *azienda* to accounting, he transposes those conclusions on the level of the determination of financial statement values and highlights that:

> Two factors having an identical nature may have different values depending on the firm to which they belong and, within this firm, depending on the specific time when the valuation is done.
>
> (Giannessi 1960: p. 591)

> The essence of functional valuation lies in this: as long as assets remain in the firm, they have a given value; as soon as they removed from it, they will have another.
>
> (Giannessi 1960: p. 592)

The functional value varies, in fact, when the asset becomes part of a system other than the original. We speak, therefore, of functional valuation, because, to express a judgement, one must take into account the *function* of each asset in the productive combination. Giannessi writes:

> The valuation of production factors must take into account the function they are expected to perform in the firm. Any other criterion is absurd.
>
> (Giannessi 1960: p. 698)

And again:

> [The] differences, sometimes significant, observed between going-concern values and liquidation values … are nothing else, in summary, than the most significant expression of the diversity that exists between the free life of market goods and the combinatory and systematic life of the production factors of the firm.
>
> (Giannessi 1960: p. 699)

At this point, it is appropriate to remember that, apart from the excerpts quoted above, all Giannessi's work is imbued with the notion of functional capacity, a concept that, as he says: "allows for the application of the "functional value" to the assets of financial statements" (Giannessi 1960: p. 67). Hence, the need to grasp the course of the valuation process conceived by Giannessi.

The scholar identified three stages of the valuation process, along which the functional value is reached by successive approximations. Initially, "one should identify the [intrinsic] nature of assets" (Giannessi 1960: p. 591), so that a first attribution of value can be obtained. Then "assets must be referred to the firm as a system of which they are part", because "the firm value is not based on the sole nature of the assets, but also on the function they perform in the productive combination as factors"; this "suffices to cause changes in the original attributions of value" (Giannessi 1960: p. 591). Finally, "once the firm value has been determined … that value must be referred to the equilibrium positions and characteristics of the motion of the *azienda*" (Giannessi 1960: p. 591). Values will change again at this last stage because the possibility of utilizing production factors changes as a function of the type of equilibrium that is foreseen. So functional values, which are the final result of this valuation process, will be higher in case of equilibrium and an evolutionary motion of firm, and lower in the opposite case of disequilibrium and regressive motion (Giannessi 1960: pp. 591–592). It seems we may conclude that the functional value of assets, in Giannessi's theoretical system, is affected by three factors: 1) the intrinsic characteristics of the asset considered; 2) how that asset relates to the remaining ones, forming, all together, a productive combination; and 3) the conditions of economic–financial equilibrium that characterize the dynamics of the *azienda*. At this point, it is useful to point out that the valuation activity, intended as described above, takes the form of a very complex analytical process that requires, on the one hand, an in-depth study of different firm variables – i.e. the characteristics of production factors, their combination patterns, the state and tendency of firm's equilibrium – and, on the other hand, presupposes an equally extensive know-how not only in the field of accounting, but also in that of *Economia Aziendale*.

Clearly, the valuation process described above requires forecasting the future enterprise trends, particularly with the purpose of evaluating the protection of the economic–financial equilibrium over time. Our scholar proves to be fully aware of this when he maintains:

> The valuation process, although based on the observation of facts that taken together may be defined as "historical", is also the synthesis of probable events which the firm may face in the future.
>
> (Giannessi 1982b: p. 1)

and

> financial statement valuation depends on the development of plans and their implementation.
>
> (Giannessi 1981: p. 68; see also p. 70)[18]

A particularly interesting aspect is the relationship that is established, in this peculiar conception of the valuation process, between profit and economic equilibrium of the *azienda*. This is, in fact, a circular relationship. Giannessi highlights this problem when he writes:

> Equilibrium positions cannot be identified if the remuneration of production factors and the return to ownership are not previously determined; the remuneration of factors and the return to ownership cannot be determined if the survival of the equilibrium positions over time has not previously been guaranteed.
>
> (Giannessi 1960: p. 591; see also: Giannessi 1961: p. 27)

We may add that the valuation process conceived by Giannessi needs to be developed by successive approximations, according to an iterative approach that requires preparers of financial statements to carefully examine the effects that are produced, from time to time, during successive steps, on two fronts: that of the profit for the period and that of the economic equilibrium, until a satisfying solution is reached.

Up to this point, the investigation focused on the most general aspects of Giannessi's notions on the theme of financial statement valuation. However, we should remark that Giannessi tackled the problem of functional valuation not only on an abstract level, by developing a general theory, but also by dwelling on the specific valuation methods of the different types of assets, that is to say by reasoning on specific applications. Rather innovative insights are found even in this part. The aspect that deserves attention more than others is the approach adopted by Giannessi to develop this subject. Unlike other authors of his time (e.g. Onida 1940 and Riparbelli 1943) and also unlike Ceccherelli, he did not propose a critical review of valuation criteria to be used for the different classes of assets, but rather described the main causal factors of their functional value, which, at an operating level, are characterized as the main pieces of information to be examined in order to form a valuation judgement. A few examples may be useful.

According to Giannessi, for example, in order to determine the functional value of equipment and machinery, one should primarily obtain accounting data like the "historical cost", "extraordinary maintenance and repair costs" and the "reproduction cost" (Giannessi 1960: pp. 678–679). However, these data are not sufficient. Let us see what he writes in this regard:

> The historical cost, extraordinary maintenance and repair costs and the reproduction cost are all useful elements to be used for judgement, but do not consist in the judgement itself. In order to express the latter and formulate the functional valuation of the machine, one must adjust the data so obtained to the specific situation of the firm and the market to which the calculation refers.
>
> (Giannessi 1960: p. 681)

Clearly enough, then, in Giannessi's theoretical system the valuation of equipment and machinery requires the formulation of a veritable judgement, which must rest on adequate pieces of information. Then he accurately indicates a set of informative elements to be examined for valuation:

> Among the circumstances that may affect the functional value of a machine we may mention the positions of equilibrium of firm, the direction of pertinent motion, production and sales volumes, the technical economic and financial situation and any other element capable of distinguishing a given productive combination from another; market circumstances may include the general and particular conditions of the economy, price fluctuations and the erosion of the currency.
>
> (Giannessi 1960: p. 679; see also pp. 820–821)

The functional values stemming from such a valuation process may be lower or higher than the purchase cost of the asset. As Giannessi clarified, the former case is the norm, the second the exception (Giannessi 1960: pp. 686–689). From a bookkeeping perspective, in the first case, you will have to depreciate, while in the second, when you have increases in functional value due to the improvement of the degree of functionality of assets, such increases "must always be neutralised by contra asset accounts of the same amount" (Giannessi 1960: p. 764). In substance, the author aligns his position with that of Ceccherelli and proposes, for the cases in which "the recognition of an increase in value is useful for the determination of the equilibrium positions of the firm" (Giannessi 1960:

pp. 764–765), the adoption of an appropriate technical–accounting solution to present the higher value both in asset accounts and in contra asset accounts of the balance sheet, without affecting – for reasons of prudence – the determination of the year's income.

The approach that consists in examining the various elements for judgement to be considered in financial statement valuation is also found in the functional valuation of products. When he discusses the products of farms, Giannessi identifies three first elements for judgement: the destination of products (reuse in production or sale in the market), the state of negotiations (presence or absence of sales agreements of various kinds or commitments to sign agreements), the degree of preservability of products (products that can be preserved or that can be preserved only by using refrigeration processes, products that can be preserved with simpler means) (Giannessi 1960: pp. 711–714). The value of products must take into account the various possible situations that concern said parameters. But that is not all. Giannessi recalls, more generally, the need to take into due consideration "all the technical, economic and financial conditions that identify product batches" (Giannessi 1960: p. 714). In this regard, Giannessi specifies:

> Technical conditions are important for the relationship existing between products to be reused in production and products to be directly sold in the market; the economic conditions for the relationship existing between historical pricing and the probabilistic determination of prices; the financial conditions for the interest the firm may have to sell immediately, or wait for the most appropriate time.
>
> (Giannessi 1960: p. 714; see also pp. 821–822)

A first conclusion we may draw from the excerpts above is that, for Giannessi, valuation is a logical operation that transcends any rigid and mechanical application of valuation criteria.[19] Rather, valuation consists in formulating a veritable subjective judgement based on the analysis of an adequate information basis. In other words, it is a matter of forming a judgement starting from an adequate system of quantitative and qualitative information elements, concerning essential aspects of the firm and its surrounding environment.[20] These elements for judgement must be identified on a case-by-case basis, in connection with the asset to be estimated; this is the reason why they change between assets. The judgement so formed is a summary of the different pieces of information available, although it differs from each one of them. In this regard Giannessi says: "The functional criterion uses all the data available, both historical and related to the market, but does not coincide with any of them" (Giannessi 1960: p. 709). This having been said, it makes sense to wonder: what is the role played by valuation criteria in the theory of valuation at issue. We may answer that they lose their *status* of valuation rules and take on the role of elements for judgement, together with other kinds of information to be used for valuation. This is a *leitmotiv* of Giannessi's thought.

In other words, Giannessi developed a valuation logic to be followed as a guidance to perform financial statement valuation. Consistently, in the examination of the theme, he did not propose specific rules "ready for use" to be applied as they are, but offered useful indications concerning the elements to be used for the formulation of valuation.

This is a valuation logic not so easy to apply and strongly subjective, indeed. It is not easy to apply it because it requires a significant investigation process for each asset, aimed at identifying the different elements for judgement, collecting – to the extent possible and convenient – specific information on each element, examining said information and eventually forming the valuation; it is strongly subjective because the valuations and the resulting income "depend on the notion each one may have of the functionality and the way in which the concept is interpreted and referred to the circumstances of time and space in which the valuation has to be formulated" (Giannessi 1960: p. 68).

As one can easily infer, such an approach to valuation leaves broad margins for creativity to the preparers of financial statements, but perhaps this is precisely the strength of the approach considered, because it gives a more rational and reliable view of the equilibrium positions of the firm. This does not mean that such a logic does not require objectivity from the appraiser. On the contrary, Giannessi explicitly maintains that "the functional valuation process ... must be carried out in full objectivity" (Giannessi 1960: p. 607). It is also true that, since said process concerns the internal financial statements – which "directors prepare for their own use and reference" (Giannessi 1969: p. 532), with the function of providing useful information for the control and planning of firm activities – one does not understand why directors should not be really objective: what would be the point in lying to themselves by adopting earning management policies?

Undoubtedly, the theory of functional valuation proposed by Giannessi rests on solid economic bases. It was developed in close compliance with the notion of *azienda* proposed by the scholar. The features of the *azienda* – systematic, dynamic and probabilistic – and the end that characterizes it – the economic equilibrium durable in time – are all elements that recur also in functional valuation. In the scholar's perspective, the framework of the theory of functional valuation is precisely that of the principles of *Economia Aziendale*, and primarily of the general theory of the *azienda*, a subject on which Giannessi made huge efforts to create his personal view.[21]

We think we may say, as a conclusion, that with Giannessi the theory of functional value is investigated in depth and enriched with contents essentially for two reasons: the extension to all the assets and the reference to the economic equilibrium of the firm. In fact, the functional value in Giannessi's version, on the one hand, is a notion that can be no longer referred to the sole non-financial assets, but – thanks to a process of generalization – also to the financial assets; on the other hand, it also takes into account the situation and motion of the economic equilibrium that characterizes the enterprise considered.

4 Concluding remarks

Our research highlighted that, over half a century ago, two scholars, first Cec-cherelli and then Giannessi, developed a theory of financial valuation that focused on the notion of functionality, that is to say on the capacity of the asset to contribute to the production processes of a give firm. Even more, we should point out that the notion of functionality, in that theory of functional value, becomes the actual key point and distinctive element of the theory itself. The two Italian scholars thought that the valuation issue could not be tackled with simple valuation rules, so they looked for a general principle that could be used as a helpful pattern of behaviour in the formulation of value judgements. Their proposal is that valuation, being a process that transcends a simple mechanistic application of predefined valuation criteria, requires a rather complex logical reasoning starting from the observation of the specific characteristics of the asset, of the specific firm and of its external context.

Functional value, as conceived by Ceccherelli and Giannessi, has a peculiar feature: unlike other types of values (e.g. historical cost, current cash equivalent, etc.) it does not immediately refer to a real or assumed economic transaction, but stems from a firm-specific valuation. More specifically, it is a value in use, estimated in function of the usefulness of the production factor for the enterprise that uses it. This does not mean that data like the historical cost, the replacement cost, the net realization value or other values derived from the market are not contemplated in the valuation process, but that, together with others, they are no longer taken as such but take on – especially in Giannessi's theory – the simplest role of elements for judgement. This means that the close and direct connection between value and economic transaction, typical of other valuation theories (see Lee 1998: p. 26), is lost, precisely because the functional value is peculiar for each *azienda*. Indeed, in our opinion, the actual essence of the functional value lies in its uniqueness for the specific reference entity.

At this point, for a more in-depth insight in the intrinsic nature of functional value, we may say that it has a systematic, dynamic and probabilistic nature.

Its systematic nature stems from the fact that the functional value of an asset can be expressed only by considering its actual production capacities within a given productive combination. In other words, with functional valuation, the complementary nature of production factors is more effectively expressed in the financial statements.[22] We should add that, while other Italian scholars had already mentioned the connection of production factors in their texts,[23] in func-tional valuation the link between the complementarity of production factors and financial statement values took on the nature of a veritable qualifying item. It is for this reason that some would say that functional value has an intrinsically relational nature.[24] Ceccherelli and Giannessi advocated a holistic view of the valuation problem, according to which the different assets should be valued as parts of a whole, by duly considering the complementarity connections existing between them. So, the financial statement, from being a mere aggregate of values, becomes a veritable "system of values" (Onida, 1940: 74). It is not perhaps wrong to maintain that functional valuation is the most evident expression of the holistic approach to the valuation problem that is typical of the Italian tradition.

On the other hand, the dynamic nature of the functional value can be grasped by reflecting on the fact that valuation, according to the theory examined, is based on elements of judgement that are historical, contemporary and future with respect to the balance sheet date. Therefore, valuation is performed according to an approach that we may define as diachronic. This is, in fact, an attempt at reflecting the dynamic nature of the enterprise in terms of financial valuation.

Finally, functional valuation also has a probabilistic nature, a feature deriving from its state of being significantly affected by the future perspectives and trends of the firm and the surrounding economic environment. Clearly, then, financial results are significantly affected by the reliability of the directors' forecasts during the valuation.

As we have already pointed out multiple times, the functional valuation of any asset is based on the personal judgement of preparers of financial statement. Said judgement is strongly subjective and uncertain. The discretional nature of all sorts of valuations is even reinforced, in this case, because the valuation is no longer bound to some kind of criterion, but is guided by a principle. The values obtained by applying the various valuation criteria, such as the historical cost or the replacement cost, are no longer exclusive references, but only some among the "n" quantitative and qualitative elements on which the judgement is based. This means there is a greater degree of freedom. On the other hand, since this kind of valuation will have a higher number of valuation parameters on which said judgement should be based, it is clear that this fact in itself inevitably increases the subjectivity and uncertainty of the same. In addition to that, we should say that being the valuation based on a guiding principle rather than on a rigid binding valuation criterion, the resulting values are more difficult to audit. Furthermore, functional values can be more easily manipulated because they are strongly affected by the "personal equation" of the preparer of financial statements. For this reason, a financial statement prepared with functional values will seem to be scarcely effective for the purpose of controlling the action of directors, because their responsibility would be evaluated based on strongly subjective values, that can be more easily altered by themselves, rather than referring, for instance, to more impartial market values. Then we should point out that, since each director, even after expressing the most objective judgement, may give a personally interpretation of the functional value, financial statements with functional values are poorly indicated for comparative analyses aimed at assessing the performance of different enterprises. Finally, we should add that the provision of a wide information base containing qualitative and quantitative data, their careful examination and the formulation of a judgement based on said information are all activities that make the functional valuation process a rather difficult one to implement or, in any case, a very demanding one in terms of time and energy. Problems might then be worsened by the circular relationship existing between income for the period and condition of perspective economic equilibrium, as we pointed out earlier. On the other hand, it is difficult to think that one could concretely implement such a process without preparing an *ad-hoc* information system, whose use also involves increased costs. We have undoubtedly listed the weaknesses of functional valuation. However, functional valuation also presents equally significant strengths.

The first aspect we should mention is that the approach based on the functional value tries to translate into values certain natural characteristics of the enterprise, such as its systemic and dynamic nature, as well as the conditions that lie at the basis of its survival, such as reaching and maintaining a condition of economic equilibrium. Then, functional values are perhaps those that, more than others, summarize the above-mentioned firm characteristics. But that is not all. Since they stem from an entity-specific valuation, they also reflect the expectations, the assumptions, and the intentions of directors. Clearly, therefore, the information we can infer from the financial statements prepared with functional values is particularly useful, as we said earlier, to help managers make decisions, also regarding strategic problems. This is the reason why said values are consistent with the notion of the financial statements as a tool for the control of the economic trends of enterprise. However, we cannot exclude that income and financial position data obtained by applying functional values may also be useful for minority shareholders and for creditors, if it is true that – unlike, for example, with values expressed by the market – they are derived from facts and information sometimes confidential and only available to the management. We should not forget that it is precisely for this reason that functional values – when not distorted by opportunistic behaviour – might be more effective for the control of the managers' actions, since these would be evaluated on financial statement data based on their forecasts and plans.

At this point, it is appropriate to observe that the theory of functional value, as we have already pointed out, is defined as a system of ideas resting on:

- solid economic bases, particularly on specific and strong theories of the *azienda*;
- a peculiar conception of *Economia Aziendale*, of accounting, and on the existence of a specific relationship between them; and
- a specific theory of financial statements.

Ceccherelli and Giannessi are scholars characterized by large scientific views, especially by interests that simultaneously spanned from accounting to *Economia Aziendale*. In their works, the arguments of both disciplines are so interconnected with each other that it is really difficult, or even impossible, to establish where each of them starts or ends. More specifically, we have seen that for both the Tuscan scholars *Economia Aziendale* consists of general principles regarding the operation of the enterprise (the "theory of the *azienda*"), while accounting is the science that studies and explains the figures representing the dynamics of a firm in order to be able to grasp its economic trends.[25] In the views of both scholars, the two disciplines benefit from one another. While accounting, by collecting and processing data regarding the operation of the *azienda*, offers *Economia Aziendale* the natural "raw material" on which to build its processes for the interpretation of the investigated phenomenon, *Economia Aziendale*, by studying the methods of operation of the enterprise, is characterized as a preparatory science to accounting and is its natural framework. Ceccherelli and Giannessi then share a notion of the financial statements mainly as a private tool for the internal control of firm trends, which is the perspective they both adopted in their analyses also to develop the theory of valuation. On the other hand, this is the same perspective adopted by other Italian scholars of that period, which finds its justification in some characteristics of the Italian economic system of those years, which was characterized by a prevalence of small-size firms and, only in rare cases, of large-size firms albeit family-run or public-owned. In substance, that was an economic system characterized by a strong concentration of ownership, overlap between ownership and control, and a scarce development of the stock market. It would be only years later, since the beginning of the Seventies, that Italian accounting started to ask itself questions on the financial statements intended as a report to stakeholders, which is required to satisfy public interest purposes (Poli 1971: pp. 113ff.).

The aspects described above seem to be sufficient to explain the origin of the theory of functional value that, leaving aside the significant differences in the conceptions of the two authors,[26] refers, in a nutshell, to the nature and operating principles of the enterprise, and has been conceived in the perspective of financial statements aimed at meeting primarily the need for information of directors and fulfilling the function of a tool for the economic control of operations.

While approaching the conclusion of this chapter, we should develop some considerations on the legacy left by the theory of functional value from a scientific point of view.

Ceccherelli and Giannessi are scholars who significantly contributed in Italy to the growth of accounting and *Economia Aziendale*. Some of the most interesting contributions are certainly the investigations they carried out on financial valuation, which resulted in the theory of functional value. This theory presents innovative elements at least from two reasons: the approach adopted for the investigation and the propositions formulated.

As to the first point, that is to say the approach adopted for the investigation, we had the opportunity to observe an original aspect: Ceccherelli and Giannessi, unlike other contemporary authors, tackled the study of financial valuation not by merely describing the different valuation criteria to highlight the pros and cons of each one, but rather tried to devise a veritable valuation logic of a wider scope. By so doing, they raised the level of the analysis from the discussion of technical rules to the development of an authentic universal guiding principle, that of functional valuation. This chapter also demonstrates that the two authors conceived their theses starting from the study of the causal factors of the value of assets, thus conceiving a theory of value in a Schumpeterian sense,[27] with a specific reference to the phenomenon of the *azienda*. This has been their great innovation, and not only at the Italian level.

As to the second point recalled above, the propositions formulated by the two authors, the innovation here lies in the fact that the functional value is seen as a value in use. It is not easy to find a valuation approach of this kind in Italy and in other countries.[28] In this sense, they offer a perspective on financial valuation that differs from those that recall values directly or indirectly associated with market transactions.

The formulation of a general principle, of a guiding idea, aimed at addressing the process of valuation, allows Italian accounting to accomplish a significant progress in the investigation field at issue and, considering the role of this matter, in the accounting itself. By so doing, Ceccherelli and Giannessi succeeded in achieving, at least in part, their already described aspiration to develop in particular the doctrinal side of accounting, although this contribution did not impact accounting regulation and practice (see Alexander and Servalli 2011).[29]

Today, after so many years from the development of the theories examined, the functional value still arouses interest (see, among others: Iannone 1993; Marasca 1999: pp. 58–63; Musaio 2005: p. 13; Tozzi *et al.* 2012: p. 110; Adamo 2013: p. 591; Corsi 2013: pp. 6–7; Paolini 2013: p. 51). This proves that it is a rather well-rooted theory in the Italian doctrine, which does not seem to be outdated yet.

Notes

1 The quotations of Italian writings were translated into English by the author of the chapter.

2 The three students, according to Bertini, in giving "their own personal contribution to the development of the Tuscan School", showed that they were "all perfectly aligned with the positions of Alberto Ceccherelli" (2010: p. 681).

3 It was Giannessi who realized that the notion of "order" could be referred to the *azienda* as a phenomenon. In fact, he maintained that the life of an organization depends on the existence of a threefold order within it: between the factors that globally make up the manufacturing combination (combinatory order), between the operations that cannot be isolated but must make up a system (systematic order), between the firm forces and the environmental forces that must be composed in harmony (composition order) (Giannessi 1960: pp. 51–56; 1961: pp. 21 and 58–64).

4 When Quagli describes "the function of the financial statement as a *tool for the ex ante and the ex post control of firm operations* to the benefit of internal decision-makers", he precisely referred to Ceccherelli (Quagli 2015: p. 6).

5   The financial statements may play the role of a report, so, while the phrase "financial statements" (*bilancio*) may, in some cases, absorb and include the meaning of report, the function of the report cannot be identified or used to describe the technical-accounting procedure that is specifically referred to when using the phrase "financial statements".

(Ceccherelli 1939a: p. 11)

6 It could be interesting to recall how the scholar maintained that "the economic and financial assets occupy a different position vis-à-vis the valuation issue" (Ceccherelli 1939a: pp. 183 and 198–203).

7 Inspired by the studies of the Austrian economist Carl Menger (1925), and particularly by the notion of complementarity of assets examined by him, Ceccherelli concluded that

the criterion of the complementarity of assets easily leads to the deduction that the most notable feature of assets, in the economic aspect, is the one that derives from how they participate in the production process, as a consequence of which each of them acquire special functional qualities.

(Ceccherelli 1931: p. 198)

8 "Financial valuations are essentially based on forecasts" (Ceccherelli 1939a: p. 198).

9 "Theory and technique may offer healthy general principles, but they cannot generalize solutions, they can offer interpretive criteria, but they cannot build the mechanics of financial statements" (Ceccherelli 1949: p. 8).

10 Ceccherelli stated: "The variability of the economic environment and market conditions produces a parallel variability of income for the company, which often justifies a variable cost allocation to different financial years" (Ceccherelli 1939a: p. 370).

11 "The subject [of depreciation] is particularly complex and cannot find a rule that can be summarised in invariable schemes and formulae" (Ceccherelli 1939a: p. 371).

12 Concerning the distinction between accounting intended as a doctrine, a technique and an art, see, *inter alia*, Giannessi (1960: pp. 465 and 743).

13 It is a fundamental basis for judgement, but certainly not the only one. As Giannessi himself said: "The income is not suitable to reflect the equilibrium status of the entity; it could be one of the elements for judgement, but not the only and absolute elements for judgement" (Giannessi 1960: p. 74).

14 Giannessi, in this regard, remarked that based on the final result

the protagonists of the life of the enterprise may decide to extend or restrict production, venture in far-away markets or reduce the operating range of the entity, to implement or not implement programs for the renewal of plants, of financing, particularly those with a medium and long term, distribution of products, advertising campaigns, and so on ... As we can see, the results of financial statements, in spite of their extreme uncertainty, are an important element for judgement and can have a remarkable influence on the further developments of operations.

(Giannessi 1969: pp. 532–533)

15 The functional value of production factors is affected by all the circumstances that direct the motion of a firm by pushing it towards the points of maximum profitability or towards those of maximum non-profitability and of failure. (Giannessi 1960: pp. 698–699).

16 A factor provided with a degree "x" of usefulness may not find its full utilization in the firm if the other factors do not own "y", "z", etc. usefulness capable of combining with it in the most profitable manner.

(Giannessi 1969: p. 513)

17 "A firm combination is not such if the factors that perform a function in production are not proportional with each other" (Giannessi 1969: p. 513).

18 "The valuation of assets is ... linked to the results of probabilistic calculation" (Giannessi 1960: p. 781). "If the probabilistic calculation is excessively coarse or wrong, the results will lose their essential meaning" (Giannessi 1981: p. 66).

19 "The problem of valuations – as Giannessi maintains – cannot be resolved with the choice of any criterion from those existing, the application of a "simple rule" dictated by a law or found in any of the many accounting manuals" (Giannessi 1981: p. 66).

20 "*Valuation is not an exclusively quantitative problem* ... Figures substantiate the judgement that expresses the quantitative-qualitative position of an asset at a given time compared to the environmental complex that makes up its orbit" (Giannessi 1960: p. 589).

21 It is not by chance that Bertini identified precisely in the notion of "functional valuation ... the connection that links indissolubly *Economia Aziendale* to Giannessi's Accounting" (Bertini 1994: p. 99).

22 A few years later, Ferrero would point out that "complementarity relationships should be taken into account ..., since not taking said relationships and their 'weight' into account means to determine a shareholders' equity and an associated year's income based on a gross *conceptual error*" (Ferrero 1995: p. 105).
23 We can already find various levels of reference to the complementarity capital components and the consequent implications on the level of financial valuation in, *inter alias*: Pantaleoni 1904: pp. 219–221; Besta 1909: II, p. 14; Zappa 1910: pp. 112–113; Alfieri 1923: p. 268; De Gobbis 1925: pp. 122–123. Zappa, particularly, viewed the financial position as a "fund of coexistent values", that is "a whole that ... determines the quantity of parts" (Zappa 1920–1929: pp. 3 and 15).
24 "Each individual value ..., although referred to given elements, does grasp *relational* aspects together with peculiar aspects" (Corticelli 1981: p. 95).
25 For more insights on the development of Italian *Ragioneria* in close connection with *Economia Aziendale*, see, *inter alia*, Zan (1994), Zambon (1996), Viganò (1998, 2013), Zambon and Zan (2000, 2013), Canziani (2013).
26 The visions of the two authors, as already pointed out, differ mainly as regards the possibility to implement or not income smoothing policies, to which Ceccherelli was favourable, while Giannessi was contrary.
27 Schumpeter, a well-known economist with a great historical–doctrinal culture, conceived the theory of value as a "causal explanation of the phenomenon of value" (Schumpeter 2006: p. 309).
28 For an accurate overview of the different valuation theories proposed by Anglo-Saxon scholars, see: Lee 1998 and 2009; Belkaoui 2004: pp. 533–552.
29 It is certainly not a sporadic case, if Lee is right when he observes that: "The financial accounting theory contributions of writers such as Hatfield, Paton, Chambers, and Sterling can be argued to have had marginal impact on the general state of practice and education" (Lee 2009: p. 157).

References

Adamo, S. (2013), *Le rivelazioni di esercizio delle imprese. Scritture complesse e sintesi periodiche*, Bari: Cacucci.
Alexander, D., and Servalli, S. (2011), "Economia aziendale and financial valuations in Italy: Some contradictions and insights", *Accounting History* 16, 291–312.
Alfieri, V. (1923), "Le rilevazioni amministrative", *Rivista Italiana di Ragioneria* 23, 265–275.
Antonelli, V. (2014), *La storia della ragioneria nel pensiero di Alberto Ceccherelli*, Roma: Rirea.
Antonelli, V. and Sargiacomo, M. (2015), "Alberto Ceccherelli (1885–1958): Pioneer in the History of Accounting Practice and Leader in International Dissemination", *Accounting History Review* 25, 121–144.
Antoni, T. (1979), "Ricordo di Gino Zappa e di Alberto Ceccherelli", *Rivista Italiana di Ragioneria e di Economia Aziendale* 79, 78–83.
Bandettini, A., Catturi, G., Franceschi Ferraris, R., and Pezzoli, S. (1996), *La scuola toscana di Economia Aziendale: Alberto Ceccherelli ed i suoi primi allievi*, Padova: Cedam.
Belkaoui, A.R. (2004), *Accounting Theory*, Andover: Cengage Learning EMEA.
Bertini, U. (1994), *Giannessi, l'economia aziendale e la ragioneria, in Atti della giornata di studi giannessiani*, Pisa, 30 ottobre 1992, Milano: Giuffrè.
Bertini, U. (2010), "La scuola toscana di ragioneria e di economia aziendale", *Rivista Italiana di Ragioneria e di Economia Aziendale* 110, 675–693.

Besta, F. (1909), *La Ragioneria, Parte prima, Ragioneria generale*, Vol. II, Milano: Vallardi.

Canziani, A. (2013), Accounting and "Economia Aziendale" in Italy, 1911 Afterward, in Y. Biondi and S. Zambon (eds), *Accounting and Business Economics. Insights from National Traditions*, London: Routledge.

Ceccherelli, A. (1910), *Le scritture commerciali nelle antiche aziende fiorentine*, Firenze: Lastrucci.

Ceccherelli, A. (1913a), *I libri di mercatura della Banca Medici e l'applicazione della partita doppia a Firenze nel secolo decimoquarto*, Firenze: Bemporad.

Ceccherelli, A. (1913b), "Un libro di conti tenuto da B. Cellini al Duca Cosimo Medici", *Rivista Emiliana di Ragioneria* 5, 21–30.

Ceccherelli, A. (1914a), "Le funzioni contabili e giuridiche del bilancio delle società medievali", *Rivista Italiana di Ragioneria* 14, 371–378.

Ceccherelli, A. (1914b), "Le funzioni contabili e giuridiche del bilancio delle società medievali (Continuazione)", *Rivista Italiana di Ragioneria* 14, 391–395.

Ceccherelli, A. (1914c), "Le funzioni contabili e giuridiche del bilancio delle società medievali (Continuazione e fine)", *Rivista Italiana di Ragioneria* 14, 436–445.

Ceccherelli, A. (1915), *La logismologia*, Milano: Vallardi.

Ceccherelli, A. (1918), "Caratteristiche del Bilancio Bancario", *Rivista Italiana di Ragioneria* 18, 20–35.

Ceccherelli, A. (1921), *La tecnica del bilancio con speciale riguardo alle aziende bancarie*, Milano: Vallardi.

Ceccherelli, A. (1922), *L'indirizzo teorico negli studi di ragioneria: prime linee di una introduzione allo studio della ragioneria generale*, Firenze: Ariani.

Ceccherelli, A. (1923), *Introduzione allo studio della ragioneria generale. Gli organismi aziendali*, Firenze: Le Monnier.

Ceccherelli, A. (1928), *Note sulle valutazioni contabili e sulla formazione dei bilanci commerciali*, Firenze: Tipografia dei Sordomuti.

Ceccherelli, A. (1930), *Istituzioni di ragioneria*, Firenze: Le Monnier.

Ceccherelli, A. (1931), *Le prospettive economiche e finanziarie nelle aziende commerciali. Vol. I. Gli elementi statistico contabili dell'indagine prospettiva*, Firenze: Le Monnier.

Ceccherelli, A. (1933), *Formazione e interpretazione dei bilanci straordinari in alcuni casi previsti dal Codice di Commercio*, Milano: Giuffrè.

Ceccherelli, A. (1934), *La ragioneria nel sistema delle discipline economiche e commerciali. Discorso inaugurale dell'anno accademico 1933–1934 presso il Regio Istituto Superiore di Scienze Economiche e Commerciali di Firenze*, Firenze: Ricci.

Ceccherelli, A. (1936a), *Il problema dei costi nelle prospettive economiche e finanziarie delle imprese*, Firenze: Seeber.

Ceccherelli, A. (1936b), *Le rilevazione dei costi in relazione al fenomeno dei cicli economici*, Firenze: Carlo Cya.

Ceccherelli, A. (1939a), *Il linguaggio dei bilanci. Formazione e interpretazione dei bilanci commerciali*, Firenze: Le Monnier.

Ceccherelli, A. (1939b), "Valutazioni di bilancio", *Rivista Italiana di Scienze Commerciali* 3, 36–45.

Ceccherelli, A. (1948), *Economia Aziendale e amministrazione delle imprese*, Firenze: Barbera.

Ceccherelli, A. (1949), *Valutazioni di bilancio e disposizioni di legge*, Roma: Castaldi.

Ceccherelli, A. (1951), *El lenguaje del balance. Traducción de la cuarta edición italiana*, Madrid: Instituto de Censores Jurados de Cuentas de España.

122   *E. Gonnella*

Ceccherelli, A. (1952), *Le funzioni professionali del commercialista. Ragioneria, tecnica, procedura*, Milano: Vallardi.

Ceccherelli, A. (1959), "La posizione attuale della ragioneria negli studi e nell'insegnamento", *Rivista Italiana di Ragioneria* 59, 1–8.

Ceccherelli, A. (1964), *Problemi di Economia Aziendale*, Pisa: Cursi.

Corsi, K. (2013), *La comunicazione dell'impairment test dell'avviamento. Tra riflessioni teoriche ed evidenze empiriche*, Torino: Giappichelli.

Corticelli, R. (1981), Carattere specifico della valutazione di bilancio e accoglimento generale di principi contabili: considerazioni, in *Bilancio di esercizio e amministrazione delle imprese. Studi in onore di Pietro Onida*, Milano: Giuffrè.

Corticelli, R. (1982), "Egidio Giannessi: il suo generoso impegno per l'Università", *Rivista Italiana di Ragioneria e di Economia Aziendale* 83, 488–493.

De Gobbis, F. (1925), *Il bilancio delle società anonime*, Milano: Società Editrice Dante Alighieri.

Ferrero, G. (1995), *La valutazione del capitale di bilancio, edizione aggiornata a cura di U. Bocchino*, Milano: Giuffrè.

Ferraris Franceschi, R. (1992), Prefazione, in Egidio Giannessi, *Considerazioni introduttive sul metodo storico*, Milano: Giuffrè.

Ferraris Franceschi, R. (2013), "Egidio Giannessi: un precursore dell'internazionalizzazione", *Contabilità e Cultura Aziendale* 13, 153–165.

Giannessi, E. (1935), *I costi di produzione nelle imprese tessili cotoniere*, Firenze: Seeber.

Giannessi, E. (1941), "Rassegna di economia aziendale", *Studi Corporativi* 12, 644–658.

Giannessi, E. (1943), *Costi e prezzi-tipo nelle aziende industriali*, Milano: Giuffrè.

Giannessi, E. (1954a), *Attuali tendenze delle dottrine economico-tecniche italiane*, Pisa: Cursi.

Giannessi, E. (1954b), *Die Finanzbedarfsgleichung im Produktionsbetrieb und die Möglichkeit ihrer Darstellung*, Köln und Opladen: Westdeutscher.

Giannessi, E. (1955), *L'equazione del fabbisogno di finanziamento nelle aziende di produzione e le possibili vie della sua soluzione*, Pisa: Colombo Cursi.

Giannessi, E. (1956), *Il piano finanziario nel sistema dei piani d'azienda*, Pisa: Libreria Goliardica.

Giannessi, E. (1958a), "Der Kreislauf zwischen Kosten und Preisen als bestimmender Faktor der Gleichgewichtsbedingungen im System der Unternehmung", *Zeitschrift für handelswissenschaftliche Forschung* 10, 613–649.

Giannessi, E. (1958b), *Il Kreislauf tra costi e prezzi come elemento determinante delle condizioni di equilibrio del sistema d'azienda: prolusione tenuta nell'Aula magna storica della Università degli studi di Pisa l'11 dicembre 1957*, Pisa: Cursi.

Giannessi, E. (1960), *Le aziende di produzione originaria, Vol. I, Le aziende agricole*, Pisa: Cursi.

Giannessi, E. (1961), *Interpretazione del concetto di azienda pubblica*, Milano: Giuffrè.

Giannessi, E. (1962), *A Equação do Financiamento nas Empresas (Possível Vias da Sua Solução)*, Lisboa: Portugália Editora.

Giannessi, E. (1966), *Harrington Emerson*, Pisa: Pellegrini.

Giannessi, E. (1969), Considerazioni critiche intorno al concetto di azienda, in *Scritti in onore di Giordano dell'Amore. Saggi di discipline aziendali, Vol. 1*, Milano: Giuffrè.

Giannessi, E. (1970), *Frederich Winslow Taylor*, Pisa: Pellegrini.

Giannessi, E. (1971), *Ricordo di Alberto Riparbelli*, Pisa: Cursi.

Giannessi, E. (1974), Human and Electronic Brain in Business Life, in Accademia nazionale di ragioneria (eds), *Papers on Business Administration, Vol. 1*, Milano: Giuffrè.

Giannessi, E. (1979), *Appunti di Economia Aziendale con particolare riferimento alle aziende agricole*, Pisa: Pacini.

Giannessi, E. (1980), *I precursori in Economia Aziendale*, Milano: Giuffrè.

Giannessi, E. (1981), *Possibilità e limiti della programmazione*, Pisa.

Giannessi, E. (1982a), *Il Kreislauf tra costi e prezzi come elemento determinante delle condizioni di equilibrio del sistema d'azienda*, Milano: Giuffrè.

Giannessi, E. (1982b), *L'equazione del fabbisogno di finanziamento nelle aziende di produzione e le possibili vie della sua soluzione*, Milano: Giuffrè.

Giannessi, E. (1992), *Considerazioni introduttive sul metodo storico*, Milano: Giuffrè.

Gonnella, E. (2008), *Osservazioni sul problema delle valutazioni di bilancio nella dottrina italiana: dal "valore di scambio" al "valore funzionale"*, Roma: Rirea.

Iannone, G. (1993), La valutazione funzionale: applicabilità nel contesto civilistico attuale, *Rivista Italiana di Ragioneria e di Economia Aziendale* 93.

Kaplan, A. (2014), "European management and European business schools: Insights from the history of business schools", *European Management Journal* 32, 529–534.

Lee, T.A. (1998), *Income and Value Measurement. Theory and Practice*, London: Chapman & Hall.

Lee, T.A. (2009), Financial Accounting Theory, in J.R. Edwards and S.P. Walker (eds), *The Routledge Companion to Accounting History*, London: Routledge.

Marasca, S. (1999), *Le valutazioni nel bilancio d'esercizio*, Torino: Giappichelli.

Mariani, M. (1968), L'indirizzo teorico negli studi di ragioneria, in A. Riparbelli (eds), *Atti del seminario sulle opere del Prof. Alberto Ceccherelli tenuto nell'anno accademico 1967–68*, Firenze: Coppini.

Mattessich, R. (2003), "Accounting research and researchers of the nineteenth century and the beginning of the twentieth century: an international survey of authors, ideas and publications", *Accounting, Business and Financial History* 13, 171–205.

Menger, C. (1925), Principi fondamentali di Economia, Bari: Laterza.

Miolo Vitali, P. and Gonnella, E. (2006), "Egidio Giannessi: la figura del Maestro e il suo fondo bibliotecario", *Rivista Italiana di Ragioneria e di Economia Aziendale* 106, 576–589.

Musaio, A. (2005), *La riforma del diritto societario. Profili economico-aziendali*, Milano: FrancoAngeli.

Negru, I. (2013), "Revisiting the concept of schools of thought in economics: The example of the Austrian School", *American Journal of Economics and Sociology* 72, 983–1008.

Onida P. (1940), *Il bilancio d'esercizio nelle imprese. Significato economico del bilancio: problemi di valutazione*, Milano: Giuffrè.

Pantaleoni M. (1904), "Alcune osservazioni sulle attribuzioni di valori in assenza di formazione di prezzi di mercato", *Giornale degli Economisti* 28, 203–231.

Paolini, A. (2013), L'oggetto della rilevazione periodica: il reddito di esercizio ed il capitale di funzionamento, in L. Marchi (eds), *Introduzione alla contabilità d'impresa*, Torino: Giappichelli.

Pezzoli, S. (1996), Profilo di Alberto Ceccherelli: un Maestro della Ragioneria e dell'Economia Aziendale, in A. Bandettini, G. Catturi, R. Franceschi Ferraris and S. Pezzoli (eds), *La scuola toscana di Economia Aziendale: Alberto Ceccherelli ed i suoi primi allievi*, Padova: Cedam.

Poli, R. (1971), *Il bilancio d'esercizio: evoluzioni e prospettive nell'economia dei paesi industrialmente progrediti*, Milano: Giuffrè.

Quagli, A. (2015), *Bilancio di esercizio e principi contabili*, Torino: Giappichelli.

Riparbelli, A. (1943), *Aspetti tecnico-contabili delle disposizioni del nuovo codice civile in materia di bilanci di società per azioni*, Firenze: Coppini.

Riparbelli, A. (1960), *La vita e l'opera di Alberto Ceccherelli*, Firenze: Le Monnier.

Riparbelli, A. (1968), Ricordando Alberto Ceccherelli nel decennio della sua scomparsa, in A. Riparbelli (eds), *Atti del seminario sulle opere del Prof. Alberto Ceccherelli tenuto nell'anno accademico 1967–68*, Firenze: Coppini.

Schumpeter, J.A. (2006), *History of Economic Analysis*, London: Routledge.

Tozzi, I., Aprile, R., Russo, M., Baldarelli, M.G., Semprini, L. and Gigli, S. (2012), L'impatto dell'adozione degli IAS/IFRS sui bilanci delle aziende di servizi, in L. Marchi and L. Potito (eds), *L'impatto dell'adozione degli IAS/IFRS sui bilanci delle imprese italiane quotate*, Milano: FrancoAngeli.

Viganò, E. (1998), "Accounting and business economics traditions in Italy", *European Accounting Review* 7, 381–403.

Viganò, E. (2013), Accounting and Business Economics Traditions in Italy, in Y. Biondi and S. Zambon (eds), *Accounting and Business Economics. Insights from National Traditions*, London: Routledge.

Zambon, S. (1996), "Accounting and business economics traditions: A missing European connection?", *European Accounting Review* 5, 401–411.

Zambon, S. and Zan, L. (2000), "Accounting relativism: The unstable relationship between income measurement and theories of the firm", *Accounting, Organizations and Society* 25, 799–822.

Zambon, S. and Zan, L. (2013), Accounting Relativism: The Unstable Relationship Between Income Measurement and Theories of Firm, in Y. Biondi and S. Zambon (eds), *Accounting and Business Economics. Insights from National Traditions*, London: Routledge.

Zan, L. (1994), "Toward a history of accounting histories", *European Accounting Review* 3, 255–307.

Zappa, G. (1910), Le valutazioni di bilancio con particolare riguardo ai bilanci delle società per azioni, Milano: Società Editrice Libraria.

Zappa, G. (1920–1929), *La determinazione del reddito nelle imprese commerciali. I valori di conto in relazione alla formazione dei bilanci*, Roma: Anonima Libraria Italiana.

6 The financial statements in Aldo Amaduzzi's thought

Antonio Costa and Alessandra Tafuro*

1 Aldo Amaduzzi: an academic profile

Aldo Amaduzzi (1904–1991) belongs to the generation of the Masters who gave birth and impetus to Economia Aziendale through the development of logic models and general theories.

Amaduzzi graduated in 1925 in Venice and began teaching, at first as a substitute, Business Mathematics and Accounting at the Royal Technical Institute of Camerino and then, as the winner of the public competition, in Fiume. There, in addition to teaching, he carried out his professional career as a chartered accountant.

In November 1930 he won the competition for the role of Accounting Assistant in the Royal National Institute of Economic Sciences of Venice where he worked with Pietro D'Alvise until October 1932.

In 1934 he obtained the qualification for teaching Business Mathematics and General Accounting, and in 1936 he won the university chair and started to teach at the University of Catania (where he was also Dean). From 1939 to 1947 he taught in Bari and was also the Dean and Rector; in 1940 he became full professor. During the period 1947–1965 he taught his courses at the University of Genoa and then moved to Rome where he finished his university career in 1980 with the appointment of Professor Emeritus.

His scientific production is very copious and includes, approximately, 40 monographs and 100 articles in addition to many conference papers.

His first publication took place in 1926, when he published his thesis on "The merger of the companies" defended in 1925 with his Master Gino Zappa. Later he composed several essays that were the result of what he learned from both his theoretical experience and professional practice.

In the 1930s, he printed the first edition of his course of *Ragioneria applicata alle società commerciali associazioni in partecipazione, commissioni e rappresentanze, aziende divise* (1932) and then he wrote the volume *Aziende di erogazione. Primi problemi di organizzazione, gestione, rilevazione* (1936).

Probably the time spent in Genoa was the most fertile. In fact, he published some of his greatest works: *Il sistema produttivo dell'impresa nelle condizioni del suo equilibrio e nel suo andamento* (1948); *Conflitto ed equilibrio di interessi nel bilancio dell'impresa* (1949); *L'azienda nel suo sistema e nell'ordine delle rilevazioni* (1957); *La contabilità dei costi* (1959), *Le gestioni comuni* (1961); *Manuale di contabilità aziendale* (1968).

In parallel to the major works, he continued to write numerous essays. Among the last, in chronological order, we recall: "Situazioni e prospettive degli studi aziendali" (1977); "Profili dell'impresa" (1988), "Funzione auto-rigeneratrice dell'impresa ed evoluzione dei principi" (1989); "Economia aziendale e ragioneria nella concezione dell'azienda come sistema" (1991b).

When remembering some of his major works, it should be specified that the scientific production of Amaduzzi, despite having been conditioned by the teachings of his Master, is characterized by the originality with which he questions, expands and completes the definitions and the theories proposed by the scholars of the time (especially Besta and Zappa).

The major differences inherent in the definition of *azienda* proposed by the three Masters are reflected in the concepts of income and capital and therefore on the accounting system that each one proposed, and considered to be the most appropriate and effective to quantify these variables.

With regard to the definition of the *azienda* developed by Besta, Amaduzzi, without denying the central role of capital, highlights the key role of the human in the economic life. In addition, for Besta, the *azienda* does not have the coordination, variability and probabilistic features that are typical of real economic phenomena.

Amaduzzi broadly endorses the Zappa idea, but conceives the object of the *azienda* as a going concern only as trendy concept, representing the liquidation and termination phases as some possible phases of the *azienda*'s life.

In summary, the contribution of Amaduzzi to the progress of the *azienda* concept is particularly evident in the affirmation of the *azienda* as an open and dynamic system, which is in constant exchange with the environment and ever-changing in its components due to the variability of internal constraints and of environmental conditions.

With regard to the concepts of capital and income, the Author believes that they are phenomena which, though distinct, are united.

In defining capital, Amaduzzi specifies that the economic nature of the assets constituting gross capital is based, as well as on other characteristics, on their ability to produce income. Capital, therefore, through the instrumentality of its economic components, gives rise to income. As a result, it is unquestionable that the latter, if not distributed, increases the value of capital.

These conceptual issues are immediately reflected in the accounting system developed by Amaduzzi (System of capital and income) which, although having a lot in common with the income system of Zappa, differs from this in the following ways:

- for the object of the accounting recognition represented, as the name itself highlights, no longer only by income, but by capital and its result;
- for the possible use of the new system both in the for-profit oriented enterprises and in non-profit enterprises.

With regard to accounting, it is clarified that for Amaduzzi (1963: p. 34) the concept of economic administration is given by the management of the company itself, aiming to achieve corporate purposes.

Economic matters, then, are accomplished by carrying out three processes: organization, management and accounting. That division, undoubtedly inherited from Zappa, has different contents that – at the same time – are interconnected due to the substantially unitary character of the economic administration.

In fact, for Amaduzzi (1963: p. 36), Economia Aziendale is the science that studies the unified economic administration of companies, while the organization and accounting are simply complementary branches of a unified knowledge.

For Amaduzzi (1963: p. 41), accounting is understood as the doctrine that studies the processes of early accounting recognition, concurrent and subsequent to the administration of the economic phenomena of the company, adhering to the management and the organization processes in the company system, through their accounting recognition. Here, the harmony with the classification proposed by Besta regarding the economic control functions depending on when they are carried out (before, concurrent and subsequent control) is evident.

However, the evolution, compared to the traditional theory in the field of accountancy, lies mainly in the fact that the object's detection dynamics are investigated and interpreted according to the Economia Aziendale principles. The purposes of accounting, in fact, do not end in the mere reporting of company affairs to comply with an administrative obligation, but extend to encompass the qualitative and quantitative determinations of economic administration events (Amaduzzi 1963: p. 41).

However, we note that Amaduzzi acknowledged the possible confusion that could be made between the contents of the unitary discipline (Economia Aziendale) and those of the partial discipline (Accounting), and, as pointed out by the doctrine (Costa 2001: p. 249), Amaduzzi often focused on the differences and connections between the two disciplines coming to the conclusion for which Economia Aziendale investigates and explains the laws that govern the existence of the companies, while accounting verifies its compliance.

Economia Aziendale, in fact, is the science that defines the principles that guide the preparation and interpretation of data from accounting, and it is defined by the author as a fundamentally theoretical science. He would call this "pure Economia Aziendale"; its purity is intended to indicate that it must be cultivated to reach a universal validity of propositions (Amaduzzi 1990: p. 10).

The Master, therefore, states that the principles of unitary doctrine differ from that of the partial doctrine (Amaduzzi 1990: pp. 10–16). While the former adhere to an abstract universe, and are set and verified with the aid of logic, the latter refer to individual entities and companies and are set and verified using mathematical tools.

2 Introduction

The purpose of this chapter is to provide an interpretive key of the theoretical model of financial statements proposed by Aldo Amaduzzi (1904–1991). From a methodological point of view, using a deductive approach, we analysed his key scientific contributions that largely retrace the conceptual development of his Master Gino Zappa.

Amaduzzi has been recognized by Italian doctrine as a lively disciple of Zappa, at least in the initial phase of his training. Nevertheless, he developed his own thinking, resulting from the synthesis of the experiences lived in the different contexts in which he carried out his scientific activity. Amaduzzi shared the systemic vision of the *azienda* proposed by Zappa (1963: p. 20) but he clarified the concept by proposing the following definition:

> Azienda is a system of economic forces which develops, in the environment of which it is a complementary part, a process of production or consumption, or production and consumption together to the benefit of the economic subject and also of the individuals who cooperate with it.[1]

Amaduzzi made an original contribution to the study of Economia Aziendale: he meticulously investigated aspects of financial and economic nature related to management compared to which capital and income are merely derived aspects. A more direct vision of administrative aspects, thus, allowed the Author to develop a broader *theory of equilibrium* considering it in terms of finance, economics and equity.

In the wake of Zappa's thought, Amaduzzi expressed the relationship between income and capital as follows: "capital, therefore, has a structure of goods that can be considered in terms of the bond that it has in the production cycle, and from which it receives economic benefit, namely value" (Amaduzzi 1963: p. 157).[2]

The originality of Aldo Amaduzzi's contribution lies exactly in his detailed study of the observations proposed by Zappa on "sistema del reddito" (income-based accounting system).

Zappa, to this, observed,

> some discordant notes, indexes without a doubt of great complexity, even in concrete accounting records. Among other non-conformities, at least one has to be considered: not rarely, certain accounts are entrusted to detect, at the same time, both numeraire variations and income components. Income and expenses, and currency trading; a rise and an extinction of the assimilated ready cash values, and trading of credit and debt are often determined in an indistinct series of the same accounts.
>
> (Zappa 1937: pp. 423–424)[3]

Based on these considerations, and placing himself in an evolutionary logic compared to the original formulation of Zappa, Amaduzzi reaffirms the centrality of cash dynamic for the creation of wealth in the company, but he transforms the cash aspect into a financial aspect because he is convinced that "the enterprise system, which is an economic system, is carried out through monetary and financial manifestations".

He feels the need, therefore, to include the *non-cash* variations related to financing debt and credits in the *financial aspect* of management, recognizing a greater appropriateness of this form of detection of transactions in representing the facts of management, given their participation in the production process.

It follows that the accounts, and therefore the values that are expressed in financial statements, are affected by this "transposition" of credit and debts in the financial aspect of the management: a conclusion at which Amaduzzi admits he arrived through a *gradual construction*.

Also, he tends to specify that such choice, made with extreme caution, allows us to highlight the results coming from financial operations, distinguishing them from economic ones, without submerging Zappa's basic concept that considers the *numerarie* variations as original variations, which is the idea at the basis of the theory.

A further touch of originality in Amaduzzi's studies is found in the interests that gravitate inside and outside of the company and are such that they affect not only the conditions of the general equilibrium of the same company, but also the preparation and interpretation of financial statements.

In fact, he defines the same document as the *seat of balance and conflict of interest* such that one can't speak of an *objective or true financial statement*, but of a *subjectively interpretable financial statement*, that is the result of conjectures and estimations of future trends made by dominant stakeholders and thus, are based on criteria which, by nature, are not objective.

3 Amaduzzi's thoughts on company equilibrium

An essential element, at the centre of the studies of Aldo Amaduzzi, is the concept of equilibrium and its implications in business. In fact, feeling the need to go beyond the studies already proposed by pure economists, such as Pareto and Mayer, he focuses on developing his own "economic theory of business equilibrium". This theory was presented in the monograph *L'impresa nelle condizioni prospettiche del suo equilibrio* published in 1948, in which he offers some thoughts that will shape much of his later and copious bibliography (Amaduzzi 1991b: pp. 323–336).

Maintaining the general conditions of equilibrium is, for Amaduzzi, the prerequisite for the continuity and for the pursuit of any goal that the shareholders have prefixed. In this sense, for the Master the principle of perspective company equilibrium, that lasts over time, can be considered a *purposive objective* (Amaduzzi 1990: p. 11). For him, in fact, "equilibrium conditions do not express a calm situation, but the alleged conditions for a future trend" (Amaduzzi 1963: p. 200).

For the Author it is fundamental to set up, within the company, a planning process to determine the equilibrium that he himself defines "prospective, since it refers to future conditions, and dynamic, in that it refers to a deployed trend over time" (Amaduzzi 1968: p. 49). The Master insists on this concept specifying that "the company's mission is to generate and self-generate production processes and achieve equilibrium conditions permanently" (Amaduzzi 1989: p. 8). Unlike the other scholars of his time, Amaduzzi often resorts to mathematical logic to address business issues and to better understand the principles of operation of the business system (Paolini 2014: p. 16).

The analysis of the nature of the management operations is part of a larger pattern in which the business system is divided, in fact there are four *particular* subsystems, namely: economic, financial, monetary and patrimonial.

The benefit of this mathematical approach is perceived in its ability to better express and model the conditions of general equilibrium through the formulation of equations that express the same in the long and in the short term. Amaduzzi, with the help of mathematical calculations, quantifies the results achieved through management, highlighting the degree of economic efficiency (*economicità*) achieved – also an effect of the character of complementarity existing among the individual subsystems – designed to meet the conditions of a general equilibrium related to the whole business system.

In his *Manuale di contabilità aziendale* (1968) he specifies that "saying a company is a system is like saying that the facts of the company are related to each other by the laws of nature, as in every other field of creation".

The management of a company, therefore, is characterized by a series of transactions that, regardless of when they occur (past, present, future), are mutually conditioning.

> It means, therefore, that the management of a company is given by a chain of operations, each of which affects all the others that are performed at the same time and which will be performed in the future, as is conditioned by those that were performed in the past, are performed at the same time, and that will be performed in the future.
>
> (Amaduzzi 1968: p. 16)[4]

In particular, in the work *L'azienda nel suo sistema e nell'ordine delle sue rilevazioni*[5] (Amaduzzi 1963: p. 202), the Master points out that "the balance of the whole is function of the balance of the parts" and he continues reiterating that "equilibrium conditions are connected by relations that arise from a systematic and dynamic conception of the entity" (Amaduzzi 1963: p. 220).

It follows that such a systemic view of the company allows for the investigation of economic facts according to the principles of unity and continuity, taking into account both the temporal horizon and the spatial one (Amaduzzi 1949: p. 16).

Nonetheless, he specifies that "when speaking of the company as a system, we establish the so-called mechanistic analogy, we compare it, that is, to a mechanical system, but this does not negate the system nor deny the subjective acting forces" (Amaduzzi 1963: pp. 20–21).

He clarifies, then, that the use of the analogy of mechanical systems is a question of method that can help determine the quantitative requirements of balance, without excluding, however, the indeterminacy of the system itself or the presence and action of subjective forces.

The study of the particular equilibrium conditions, in a systemic logic, lets us affirm that the factors that most influence the value of the income produced are:

- the level of economic efficiency achieved through management;
- the proper relation established between the investment and funding structures in relation to the patrimonial, financial and monetary aspects, which, among others, are also conditioned by the broader economic environment to which the company belongs.

The *azienda*, in fact, being by definition an open and dynamic system, is in constant interaction with the environment and tends to change constantly as a result of various internal constraints and external environmental conditions: in this respect, the Master believes that "the variability of the economic process manifests itself through macro-micro-economic interrelations" (Amaduzzi 1981: pp. 684–685).

4 Conflict and balance of interests in financial statements according to Aldo Amaduzzi

The topic of the different interests that converge in a company is further examined by Amaduzzi in his works relating to financial statements. Among these, the essay *Conflitto ed equilibrio di interessi nel bilancio dell'impresa*[6] (1949) is particularly important.

In this work, the Author identifies financial statements as the "site of a conflict of interest, as a place where diverse interests, which themselves require different considered values, find rational or irrational composition, rational or irrational fissure" (Amaduzzi 1949: p. 10).[7]

For Amaduzzi, interests are divided into objective and subjective. The former are those dictated by phenomenology inherent to the business system, and the environment around it and, therefore, derive from the need to maintain appropriate conditions of corporate equilibrium; the latter, however, are those dictated by the aspirations of internal parties (shareholders, directors, employees, etc.) or external stakeholders (lenders, suppliers, the State, the Treasury, competitors etc.).

Amaduzzi, consequently, claims the need for a careful analysis on all the interests in order to identify those that are "compliant" with or "opposed" to the maintenance of the equilibrium conditions over time which, as he pointed out, is the actual objective interest of the company. In his view, therefore, those who have the task of drawing up the financial statements also have the responsibility to reconcile and settle the needs of all stakeholders, in accordance with the conditions necessary for the pursuit of a lasting equilibrium of the company.

Amaduzzi argues that the simultaneous presence of both objective and subjective interests that may contrast the general interest of the company can make the significance of the result achieved by the company *relative*. Indeed, he notes that

> the profit or loss that appears in financial statements is relative, and it may not respect the conditions of corporate equilibrium, may not balance the possible harmony between objective interests and prudential operations made by persons responsible for the company.
>
> (Amaduzzi 1949: pp. 96–97)[8]

The accounting result, in fact, may be an expression of interests conflicting with the conditions of good governance and might reveal values that, even though they show a semblance of formal correctness, may not result from a *wise combination of values* to which, instead, the person appointed to prepare financial statements should aspire.

The Master, therefore, in his dissertation, finds that: "the financial statements are a document inspired by a particular interest, or by a given group of reconcilable interests, and therein lies the key which gives meaning to the document, and gives to the document itself its demonstrative task" (Amaduzzi 1949: p. 144).[9]

At this point, it is worth remembering that the categories of accounting document users increased following the doctrinal and legal evolution on the topic of financial statements that also affected the importance of the information function assigned to them (Adamo 2005: pp. 36–43). The document in question, in fact, is no longer drawn up solely for internal uses (measurement of the wealth produced), but also to satisfy the disclosure requirements of the economic subject and all those who are interested in the business system.

Consequently, the recognition and measurement of accounting entries have to be the object of particular attention. This forces the manager to question the adequacy of the criteria for the definition, recognition and measurement of the same accounting entries, such that we can achieve a proper synthesis capable of expressing a measure of wealth and, at the same time, protect those who have an interest that the company persists.

Amaduzzi shares the view of the financial statements as a *system of symbols* proposed by Pantaleoni (1904) that, however, also recognized the need to have a correct key with which to interpret the document contents.

Drawing on this original interpretation, Amaduzzi can be considered – along with Fabio Besta (1893: p. 12), Napoleone Rossi and Pietro Onida (1951: p. 4) – a precursor of the theory of the differentiations of financial statements and of the relativity of evaluation policies according to the purposes assigned to the document itself. This formulation, only recently, has become the subject of attention for international scholars of Accounting.

For Amaduzzi, if on one hand, the interests of those who are interested in the business activities influence the evaluations of those who prepare the financial statements, on the other, the external information produced affects the choices of the various stakeholders. Therefore, the evaluations are not the result of a "rational" rule of evaluation, nor are they the consequences "of the ability to predict, or of the will to achieve certain results of a type". Consequently, they are understood as "the result of a game of interests, of which only one part finds reconciliation in the financial statements" (Amaduzzi 1949: p. 13).

The financial statements, which should be the main tool with which to communicate the company's performance to the outside, according to Amaduzzi "says what its compiler, in correspondence to the simple or combined interests, wants it to say" (Amaduzzi 1949: p. 144).

Considering the characteristics of Italian companies, for the Author, the assessments are aimed at protecting the dominant interests of the group of majority shareholders. In this regard, taking into account the differences between US and Italian companies concerning who takes on the role of dominant stakeholder, Amaduzzi can be considered a precursor of the *positive accounting theory* (Melis 2007).

The main difference between the considerations developed by the overseas scholars and Amaduzzi is found in the object of their analysis. The Master, in fact, based his analysis on the reality of the typical company of his country in the first decade of the twentieth century, a period during which the accounting regulations were very limited and financial statements were drawn up without the use of generally accepted accounting principles. US scholars, however, came to similar conclusions by observing a context in which the reference company type was the great American public listed company, required to prepare financial statements according to specific accounting rules and accounting principles.

5 The financial statements as a "system of values" deriving from the application of principles and criteria of evaluation

Amaduzzi argues that,

> Of the goals to be entrusted to the financial statements, there is one, among those examined so far, from which it is not possible to derogate, and that effectively represents the core of the "indicative combination" in the document. It is that of indicating the economic result (profit or loss) that we should attribute (and possibly take all or any partially out) to the year, compatibly with the maintenance of all other conditions of company equilibrium.
>
> (Amaduzzi 1949: p. 48)[10]

Financial statements, essentially, seek to examine the ways in which the company performs the function of the creation of wealth: the preparation of the document, therefore, must take into account the reasonable prospects of ensuring the on-going of the business.

The document in question examines the managerial events from an economic and financial point of view, presenting a very broad content, because, the results of the management of a specific accounting period are succinctly expressed in it. It summarizes the management of the company as a whole, as a whole unit, and not as a sum of individual transactions or management events that are independently investigated.

The Author, to clarify his thoughts, proposes the concept of "economic–financial circuit" of business management. Capital, though in general terms can be seen as a set of economic goods, in practice is the coordination of a number of factors that are complementary within the technical–economic and income process. Operating capital, as a result of the above economic–financial circuit, takes on a composite structure characterized by both generic factors (the nature of which is monetary) and specific factors (the nature of which is economic). It, therefore, is an expression of the continuous exchanges that occur as a result of the economic–financial circuit, in which money is invested in the acquisition of production factors which, combined, are placed on the market, generating a cash return (Angeloni 2013: pp. 369–370).

Capital, therefore, for Amaduzzi, takes on value and meaning depending on the role that it plays in the economic–financial circuit: consequently, its elements need to be assessed in view of their ability to be a part of future production cycles of the company. Specifically for dependence of income on the aforementioned circuit, it is also explained by the Author as,

> the positive financial result (profit) or negative (loss) determined on the basis of a comparison between the values attributed directly or indirectly to inputs used in operations and values attributed directly or indirectly to operating revenue achieved in relation to the uses of those factors.
>
> (Amaduzzi 1963: p. 167)[11]

The Master further reiterates the importance of the reflection of the business continuity concern basis in the financial statements noting "The values of the components of financial statements are to be understood as parts of a value system, and influenced by the forecasts and prospects of the opportunities for the use and application of economic resources in later times" (Amaduzzi and Paolone 1986: p. 121).

Amaduzzi says that,

> the substantial correlation between the financial aspect and the economic aspect of business operations, considered in the drawing up of financial statements in which the balance sheet and the profit and loss account should include yearly values of equity and accrual income, cannot be obtained within a single set of financial statements.
>
> (Amaduzzi 1970: pp. 20–21)[12]

This demonstrates how the principle of accrual income with reference to the values of capital and income implies that during the drawing up of the financial statements the compiler should take into account physical usage time longer than the period of the financial statements.

The company financial statements, therefore, can be defined as a document that not only derives from the application of accounting methods, but also derives mainly from decisions of management behaviour, proposed by the management at various levels, up to the supreme administrative bodies, general meetings or those who have to decide on its approval.

Amaduzzi notes that it is the task of accounting, not only to provide data regarding the administration of the company, but also to point out the informative ability, the degree of reliability or uncertainty that they contain, the attitude they have towards reporting the verification or not of conditions of corporate equilibrium (Amaduzzi 1963: p. 454).

The Master states that "the financial statement is not the mere result of numerical rules which, on the basis of the technique of double entry, allows for the formation of numerical tables containing equalities and verification of formal accuracy" (Amaduzzi 1970: p. 11).[13] Indeed, for the Author the preparation of financial statements requires a more complex process comprising a set of findings and non-accounting assessments aimed at the evaluation of the determined arithmetic balance.

The estimated values, on which the construction of capital and income are based, must be unique and must come from a unique economic reasoning given the economic situation in which the company operates: for Amaduzzi income and capital, during operation of the company "express two parts of the same dynamic, not only does the capital express a stasis of forces, but forces acting toward the future" (Amaduzzi 1939: p. 22).

The problem of evaluation for the determination of income assignable to the year is based primarily on presumptive calculations, on forecasts that aim at allocating the results of economic events over time, generally attributable to more years. The creation of reserves of various types is also aimed at this purpose.

The evaluation process – following a principle of prudence, within the limits imposed by the criterion not to defer expected losses to the future – should help to normalize the economic results of the various years, to equitably allocate the income to the individual accounting period without damaging the allocation of income to future years, that is, without compromising the future operability of the enterprise, neither from an economic standpoint, nor from a financial standpoint.

On the ties that should exist between evaluations of the financial statements and the financial prospective circumstances of the life of the business, Amaduzzi makes reference to the work of Taggart – *Profit and financial statement adjustments* (1934) – in which the Author examines the adjustments of book values arising from the need to ensure normalcy to the future financial management. He points out that the future financial normality is one of the prerequisites of economic normality.

However, Amaduzzi does not share the thought of Taggart regarding the "too intimate relations he places between circulating capital and profits", whereas, the latter can be determined only following an increase in operating capital.

The number of times the capital invested is renewed in the production of the various businesses and the presumed economic cycles of renewal are elements to consider to achieve this goal as part of the financial and economic outlook of the enterprise, framed in future market trends, and more generally in future environmental situations.

The most important factor – in the value system of the financial statements – which affects the allocation of yearly operating income – is the evaluation of non-monetary active and passive resources.

Amaduzzi argues that we must be "very cautious in affirming evaluation criteria that they are capable of expressing the uniformity of a performance of the enterprise, subject to, with the markets in which the company operates, the most unpredictable changes" (Amaduzzi 1939: p. 34).[14] Therefore, he prefers to talk about deductions by specifying that:

1   The values of investment and inventories to be deferred to subsequent years have their foundation in the future lucrative processes of the business and in the future fulfillment of processes already initiated that can lead to a more appropriate overall orientation of the evaluation of the various types of inventories.
2   The orientation can only be general, because it is only in the specific case of individual enterprises and/or in a given situation concerning given perspectives, that one can reach the determination of specific criterion of evaluation.
3   The awareness of the complexity and variability of the phenomena to be assessed also advises not to give general informative criteria of assessments by indicating – albeit as a general criterion – certain types of values. This awareness leads to "a more logical indication of general criteria, on the basis of given types of threshold values, outside of which the feedback would no longer respond to a sincere economic administration".[15]

The availability destined to sales can be evaluated within the maximum limit given by the *presunto valore di realizzo* "net realizable value", minus the costs that, directly or indirectly, are likely to be incurred in the future. He also tends to point out that, in this case, the value of interest is the maximum limit, considering that if you wanted to indicate a minimum limit this could be found in the lowest among the many possible configurations of cost.

What he proposes is not an evaluation rule, but a guideline based on the economic essence of the phenomenon that the value must express and that must necessarily be known. The upper limit, stated in *net realizable value*, meanwhile lets us not defer expected losses to the future. The search for the most suitable value, when the *net realizable value* exceeds the calculated cost configurations, allows you to assign yearly operational income in compliance with the future functionality of the enterprise.

Amaduzzi points out that the application of this general rule should be contextualized in the entire system of values of financial statements that allows for, in the face of uncertain inevitable forecasts, the establishment of "special reserve funds" for the guarantee of third parties.

Therefore, with respect to fixed assets and other values subject to reduction, Amaduzzi argues that these factors may be gradually amortized taking into account that in different years they are listed in financial statements at a value that must not exceed a certain limit. This limit is given by the value that, during the planned period of utilization of plants, will be covered, along with other costs, by the alleged yearly operating revenues and the possible revenue achieved by the sale of the good.

As a result, the Master is convinced that, in relation to the uncertain evaluation of fixed assets and in the light of the existing economic and accounting connection between the various attributions of value, you can set up risk reserves and reserve funds. Other appropriate guidelines for the evaluation of other kinds of investments may derive from what he calls "general informative criterion" (criterio generale informatore). Therefore, the value of fixed assets, cannot normally exceed, in the regular yearly financial statements, that determined according to the alleged utility deriving from investment in future lucrative processes.

By analogy, therefore, the value of passive liabilities must be included in the revenues and the minimum limit given by their *costi futuri presunti* (presumed future costs). Thus, they do not defer to the future expected losses allowing, if it were necessary, a fair distribution of profits over the years spanning the course of the profitable process.

Amaduzzi states that he prefers to indicate "the guiding criteria of the evaluation in financial statements of the various classes of passive liabilities", based on the existing mutual relations between the parties and the whole: the various investments, in fact, must be examined in their role as complementary to the unitary production process, over the course of development within the company.

For the Author, the same reason for the economic–administrative complementarity among the financial statement values probably justifies "the simplistic procedures often followed in practice when the single yearly values irrationally implemented as such, are generally adjusted for the unitary consideration of the business situation by a policy of reserves or by adjustments to certain values".[16]

However, the Master concludes by saying that, in any case, such a procedure must also be considered *irrational*. The unitary determination of the State enterprise, though necessary, can't overlook the rationality of the individual attribution of values to the various differential investments made during business.

6 Concluding remarks

Studies conducted by Aldo Amaduzzi detect a close interdependence between the cognitive purposes attributed to the financial statements and the accounting policies used in the preparation of the same.

In particular, at the basis of the evaluation processes, the systemic nature of the assets to be estimated is underlined, considering both the economic utility of the individual business means and its relative characteristics of instrumentality and complementarity that distinguish them during the course of production processes.

Another aspect considered with particular attention during the preparation of the financial statements is the principle of *going concern* the interpretation of which is not always easy, especially when it is necessary to define the appropriate criteria for assessing the operations still in progress at the end of an administrative period.

This principle, as is known, goes back to the concept of creating value over time: it refers, therefore, to a company that intends to extend its activities over the years. Consequently, it is also considered appropriate to apply in a consistent manner the evaluation criteria, not only in order to determine the yearly results referable to multiple administrative periods more correctly, but also to make possible a comparison of the same over time, thus enhancing the disclosure function of financial statements. The evaluation criteria proposed by Italian Masters provide the opportunity to consider, not only the historical values of investments or financing, but also the corresponding values of prospective realization and extinction, establishing the most appropriate correlations between them according to the probabilistic nature of business activities and the true purpose of each company. It is precisely in this aspect that Italians scholars identify one of the main problems associated with the adoption of the model of financial statements prepared according to international standards (International Accouting Standards (IAS)/International Financial Reporting Standards (IFRS)). Several scholars, for example, show that the assumptions, on which the evaluation using fair value is based, are difficult to reconcile with the principle of continuity of management, often creating conditions to go in derogation from the principle of prudence (Pizzo 2000: p. 89; Costa 2004: p. 161).

The evaluation of the assets according to the criterion of fair value, in fact, is based on the assumption that the identification of the exchange values in relation to a possible external scenario could lead to identify a situation essentially static, more consistent with a process of liquidation activities than with the continuation of the same.

In the IAS/IFRS model financial statements, this evaluation approach applied to the individual accounting entries shows an atomistic approach that does not highlight the systemic relations among the assets that make up working capital. This approach, of course, ignores the concept of *azienda* as formulated by Italian Masters.

We should add to this that while the model of the Italian financial statements has the task of guaranteeing the integrity of the share capital to protect creditors, the Anglo-Saxon model is designed to support the decisions of both current and future investors of a company (Azzali 2002; Tafuro 2011). In the Anglo-Saxon view, in fact, the information provided in the financial statements tends to influence the decisions of investors – to increase, maintain or liquidate their company shares – evaluating both the current and prospective performance of the company and while also considering alternative investments.

Internationally, it is customary to use the term "business" in a financial sense. This is not only a problem in terminology, but also a substantive one. In fact, the Italian doctrine defines the *azienda* as a living organism capable of persisting over time and it is, therefore, essential that its activities and its results are interpreted considering the long-term perspective. In contrast, in the Anglo-American view, the "economic" concept of *azienda* is completely absent. Indeed, it is conceived as a capital investment that, according to a speculative approach, might also be re-sold on the same day.

Amaduzzi, in 1962, pointed out that, in general, abroad there has not been a development of *Economia Aziendale* as a prerequisite for the advancement of accounting theories that, on the contrary, have been considered singularly. The Master, therefore, did not share "the opinion of those who believe that we Italians are not aiming at the development of the accounting theories, and we can be overcome by recent formal foreign generalizations in accounting that we are, instead, closely following" (Amaduzzi 1962: p. 332).[17]

The approach proposed by the international standards seems to guide financial statement evaluations towards a prospective logic of a financial nature, while studies in Italian literature (Lionzo 2005, pp. 38–39) for some time now have shown that financial statements themselves can't express the company's ability to generate cash in the future.

At most the financial statements may provide useful elements about its ability, especially when it is included in a broader informative system. In this regard Amaduzzi observed that "It is known that the limitation comes from the uncertainty of the course of investments and financing, and from the reflection of this uncertainty on the values historically acquired" (Amaduzzi 1989: p. 2).[18] For this reason, he argued it would be necessary "to update some crucial chapters on the annual financial statements".

Actually Amaduzzi (1989: pp. 2–3) already highlighted the vital role of the company consisting of the *"capacity for monetary self-regeneration of investments"*: this means that the production of cash flows, then, can be understood as an expression of a point of reference to which all stakeholders can refer to consider their own decisions carefully.

Notes

* This Chapter was jointly written by the authors. However, it is possible to allocate Sections 1, 3, 6 to Antonio Costa, and Sections 2, 4, 5 to Alessandra Tafuro.

1   L'azienda è un sistema di forze economiche che sviluppa, nell'ambiente di cui è parte complementare, un processo di produzione, o di consumo, o di produzione e di consumo insieme a favore del soggetto economico ed altresì degli individui che vi cooperano.

2   "Il capitale ha dunque una struttura di beni che può essere considerata in funzione del vincolo che ha nel circuito produttivo e che da tale legame riceve utilità economica e cioè valore."

3   … alcune note discordanti, indici non dubbi di notevole complessità anche nelle rilevazioni concrete. Tra le altre disarmonie una ancora almeno deve essere qui pure considerata: non raramente dati conti sono deputati ad un tempo alla rilevazione di variazioni numerarie e di componenti di reddito. Entrate e uscite numerarie e negoziazione di monete; sorgere ed estinguersi di valori numerari assimilati e

negoziazioni di crediti e di debiti sono determinati spesso in serie indistinte negli stessi conti.

4   Vuol dire perciò che la gestione di un'azienda è data da una catena di operazioni, ognuna delle quali condiziona tutte le altre che sono compiute nello stesso tempo e che saranno compiute in avvenire, così come è condizionata da quelle che furono compiute in passato, che sono compiute nello stesso tempo, e che saranno compiute in futuro.

5   The business system and the order of its recordings.

6   Conflict and equilibrium of interest in corporate financial statements.

7   "Sede di un conflitto d'interessi, come un luogo ove interessi disparati, che esigono, di per sé considerati valori diversi, trovano razionale o irrazionale componimento, razionale o irrazionale scissura."

8   "La cifra dell'utile o della perdita che appare in bilancio è relativa, può non rispettare le condizioni di equilibrio aziendale, può non contemperare la possibile concordia tra interessi obiettivi e fra operazioni prudenziali di persone responsabili dell'azienda."

9   "il bilancio è un documento ispirato da un dato interesse o da un dato gruppo di interessi conciliabili, ed in ciò sta la chiave che dà significato al documento e dà al documento stesso il suo compito dimostrativo."

10   Fra gli scopi da affidare al bilancio ce n'è uno, di quelli finora esaminati, da cui non si può derogare, e che rappresenta effettivamente il fulcro della "combinazione" segnaletica del documento, ed è quello di indicare il risultato economico (utile o perdita) che si conviene attribuire (e prelevare in tutto od in parte eventualmente) all'esercizio, compatibilmente con il mantenimento di tutte le altre condizioni dell'equilibrio aziendale.

11   Il risultato economico positivo (utile) o negativo (perdita) determinato in base al confronto fra valori attribuiti direttamente o indirettamente a fattori produttivi utilizzati nell'esercizio, e valori attribuiti direttamente o indirettamente a proventi di esercizio conseguiti in relazione alle avvenute utilizzazioni di quei fattori.

12   La correlazione sostanziale tra l'aspetto finanziario e l'aspetto economico delle operazioni aziendali, curata per formare bilanci di esercizio che nello stato patrimoniale e nel conto perdite e profitti accolgano valori di capitale netto e di reddito di competenza economica dell'esercizio, non può essere ottenuta nell'ambito di un solo bilancio.

13   "Il bilancio non è la mera risultante di regole numeriche che, sulla base della tecnica della partita doppia, consentono la formazione di prospetti numerici presentanti uguaglianza e verifiche di esattezza formale."

14   "Occorre essere molto cauti nell'affermare criteri di valutazione che siano atti ad esprimere l'uniformità di un andamento dell'impresa, soggetto, con i mercati nei quali l'impresa vive, alle più imprevedibili variazioni."

15   "Tale consapevolezza porta ad indicare più logicamente i criteri generali, sulla base di date specie di valori limiti, al di fuori dei quali le valutazioni non risponderebbero più ad una sincera direttiva di amministrazione economica."

16   "I procedimenti semplicistici spesso seguiti nella pratica quando le valutazioni singole di esercizio irrazionalmente attuate come tali, siano globalmente rettificate, per la considerazione unitaria della situazione d'impresa mediante la politica delle riserve o mediante rettifiche di alcuni valori."

17   "Omississ ... l'opinione di chi crede che noi Italiani non miriamo allo sviluppo anche delle teorie contabili, e che possiamo essere superati da recenti formali generalizzazioni straniere di contabilità che pur stiamo attentamente seguendo."

18   "Si sa che la limitatezza deriva dall'incertezza del decorso degli investimenti e dei finanziamenti in essere, e dal riflesso che di tale incertezza sui valori storicamente acquisiti."

References

Adamo, S. (2005), *Dalla conoscenza alla comunicazione: il ruolo dell'informazione periodica di bilancio*, in Atti dell'VIII Convegno Nazionale Società italiana di storia della ragioneria, Atri-Silvi, 22–23 settembre 2005, Roma: RIREA.

Amaduzzi, A. (1932), *Appunti di ragioneria applicata: società commerciali, commissioni e rappresentanze, partecipazioni in merci*, Padova: Cedam.

Amaduzzi, A. (1936), *Aziende di erogazione: primi problemi di organizzazione, gestione e rilevazione*, Milano: Principato Editore.

Amaduzzi, A. (1939), *Aspetti di problemi di valutazione nelle imprese commerciali*, Padova: Cedam.

Amaduzzi, A. (1949), *Conflitto ed equilibrio di interessi nel bilancio dell'impresa*, Bari: Cacucci Editore.

Amaduzzi, A. (1957), *L'azienda nel suo sistema e nell'ordine delle rilevazioni*, Torino: Utet.

Amaduzzi, A. (1959), *La contabilità dei costi*, Genova: M. Bozzi Editore.

Amaduzzi, A. (1961), *Le gestioni comuni: gestioni societarie, associazioni in partecipazioni, aziende divise, gestioni speciali*, Torino: Utet.

Amaduzzi, A. (1962), "Sviluppi delle nostre teorie contabili e confronto con recenti generalizzazioni", *Rivista Dottori Commercialisti* 4, 331–351.

Amaduzzi, A. (1963), *L'azienda nel suo sistema e nell'ordine delle sue rilevazioni*, Torino: UTET.

Amaduzzi, A. (1968), *Manuale di contabilità aziendale*, Torino: UTET.

Amaduzzi, A. (1970), *Tematica sui bilanci delle società azionarie*, Roma: Kappa.

Amaduzzi, A. (1972), "Il sistema aziendale e i suoi sottosistemi", *Rivista Italiana di Ragioneria e di Economia Aziendale*, 1, 3–7.

Amaduzzi, A. (1977), "Situazioni e prospettive degli studi aziendali", *Rivista Italiana di Ragioneria e di Economia Aziendale*, 1, 3–6.

Amaduzzi, A. (1981), L'equilibrio delle imprese nella teoria e nella realtà contemporanea con riguardo al rapporto tra investimenti – finanziamenti, in AA.VV., *Studi in onore di Pietro Onida*, Milano: Giuffrè Editore.

Amaduzzi, A. (1988), "Profili dell'impresa", *Rivista Italiana di Ragioneria e di Economia Aziendale*, 1/2, 2–9.

Amaduzzi, A. (1989), "Funzione auto-rigeneratrice dell'impresa ed evoluzione dei principi", *Rivista Italiana di Ragioneria e di Economia Aziendale*, 1–2, 8.

Amaduzzi, A. (1990), "Il sistema degli studi aziendali sulla base di principi", *Rivista Italiana di Ragioneria e di Economia Aziendale*, 1–2, 6–18.

Amaduzzi, A. (1991a), "Economia aziendale e ragioneria nella concezione dell'azienda come 'sistema'", *Rivista di Ragioneria, Tecnica Commerciale*, Diritto, Economia, 2, 9-14.

Amaduzzi, A. (1991b), "Ricordo di Aldo Amaduzzi", *Rivista Italiana di Ragioneria e di Economia Aziendale*, luglio-agosto, 323–336.

Amaduzzi, A. (1992), *L'azienda nel suo sistema e nei suoi principi*, Torino: UTET.

Amaduzzi, A. and Paolone, G. (1986), *I bilanci di esercizio delle imprese*, Torino: UTET.

Angeloni, S. (2013), "Aldo Amaduzzi: one of the best Italian Scholars in business disciplines", *Review of International Comparative Management*, 14, 3, 367–376.

Azzali, S. (2002), *Il bilancio consolidato secondo i principi contabili internazionali*, Milano: Il Sole 24 Ore.

Besta, F. (1893), *La ragioneria*, Milano: Vallardi.

142   *A. Costa and A. Tafuro*

Costa, A. (2004), *L'azienda, l'economia globale e i principi contabili internazionali*, Bari: Cacucci Editore.
Costa, M. (2001), *Le concezioni della ragioneria nella dottrina italiana. Profili storici e storiografici nella sistematica delle discipline aziendali*, Torino: Giappichelli Editore
Lionzo, A. (2005), *Il sistema dei valori di bilancio nella prospettiva dei principi contabili internazionali*, Milano: Franco Angeli.
Melis, A. (2007), "Financial Statements and Positive Accounting Theory: The Early Contribution of Aldo Amaduzzi", *Accounting, Business & Financial History*, 17, 1, 53–62
Onida, P. (1951), *Il bilancio d'esercizio nelle imprese: significato economico del bilancio, problemi di valutazione*, 4th Ed., Milano: Giuffrè Editore.
Pantaleoni, M. (1904), "Alcune osservazioni sulle attribuzioni di valori in assenza di formazioni di prezzi di mercato", *Giornale degli economisti*, 28, 203–221.
Paolini, A. (2014), L'azienda, in Marchi L., (ed.), *Introduzione all'economia aziendale: Il sistema delle operazioni e le condizioni di equilibrio aziendale*, 4th edn, Torino: Giappichelli Editore.
Pizzo, M. (2000), *Il fair value nel bilancio d'esercizio*, Padova: Cedam.
Serra, L. (1999), *Storia della ragioneria italiana*, Milano: Giuffrè Editore.
Tafuro, A. (2011), *The fair value accounting for the usefulness of financial information*, Roma: RIREA.
Taggart, P. (1934), *Profit and financial statement adjustments*, London: Sir Isaac Pitman and Sons.
Zappa, G. (1937), *Il reddito d'impresa*, Milano: Giuffrè Editore.

7 The contribution of Lino Azzini to Financial Accounting and Group Accounting in Italy

Stefano Azzali and Luca Fornaciari*

1 Introduction

The main aim of the chapter is to outline Lino Azzini's contribution to the development of Accounting Studies in Italy (Galassi 1987), taking into account that basic principles of "Economia Aziendale" consider Accounting to be closely linked to Management and Organization. Azzini's academic career started at the University of Venice (Italy), where he worked for several years under Gino Zappa, the founder of the discipline of "Economia Aziendale". As Full Professor at the University of Parma, Azzini taught and researched mainly Accounting and "Economia Aziendale", making several significant contributions to the literature.

This chapter first provides biographical details of Azzini, and three subsequent sections focus on the main areas of his academic activity: (1) "Economia Aziendale"; (2) Financial Accounting; (3) Group Accounting. The main characteristic of Azzini's research is his unified approach to management, organization and information systems of a firm. In his view, the financial statement is an instrument that managers use to meet stakeholder needs through earnings management within the Generally Accepted Accounting Principles, and to ensure a long-term life-cycle for the firm, with satisfactory remuneration for all institutional interests. In Azzini's studies on Financial Accounting, capital maintenance methodologies are an aspect of the determination of income, the main information in the financial statements. Azzini was thus a precursor in social and environmental accounting and Fair Value accounting, two fields that were to develop significantly in subsequent years. Finally, Azzini made a significant contribution to Group Accounting, suggesting a Theory of Groups based on the Entity Theory, which also characterizes consolidation methodologies.

2 Short biography

Lino Azzini was born in Borgo Val di Taro (Parma, Italy) on 12 December 1908 and graduated with honours in Accounting from Ca' Foscari University, Venice, in 1930. After a period teaching in high schools, he became Assistant Researcher at the Laboratory of Accounting in the Department of Economics of Ca' Foscari University. He worked in Venice for nearly 25 years as Assistant and Collaborator of Gino Zappa, the founder of "Economia Aziendale". This collaboration continued to the death of Gino Zappa in 1960, and resulted in several publications, written jointly with Gino Zappa and Giuseppe Cudini. Azzini's academic research, closely based on the work of Gino Zappa, followed three main strands: the improvement of "Economia Aziendale"; Financial Accounting Studies with an accounting approach based on the mathematical approach in all kinds of firms and methods of capital maintenance; Group Accounting based on the Entity Theory. Publications in these fields brought Azzini a Chair in Accounting at the beginning of the 1960s. After a short period at the University of Urbino (Italy), he moved to the University of Parma, where he remained up to his retirement in 1984. His time there can be divided into two periods: the first period, up to 1964, when he cooperated as an External or Visiting Professor and the longer intensely productive period 1965–1984 when he was a key figure in the founding and growth of the Economics Faculty, and particularly the section named after "Gino Zappa".

Azzini taught accounting and auditing courses, and introduced new courses such as Group Accounting and "Economia Aziendale" as obligatory subjects for students taking a degree in Business and Economics.

He was Director of the "Gino Zappa" Section for several years up to his retirement. Under his leadership, research and teaching flourished in amount and quality. Lino Azzini died in Milan, on 2 May 1986.

3 "Economia Aziendale"

Lino Azzini was lucky enough to be a student and then research assistant of Gino Zappa at the University of Ca' Foscari in Venice from the 1930s to the 1950s. The two collaborated on many publications, Azzini being in full agreement with the principles of research in "Economia Aziendale". From the 1960s to the 1980s, his contributions to the literature can be classified into three main areas: (1) "Economia Aziendale"; (2) Financial Accounting (financial reporting represented with equations, capital maintenance methodologies); (3) Group Accounting. This classification is subject to limitations, but roughly corresponds to Azzini's academic interests over time. In the 1930s and 1940s, his work was mainly on Financial Accounting, although it looked towards several concepts in "Economia Aziendale". In the 1950s, his research focused on "Economia Aziendale", although he also worked on capital maintenance methodologies and Group Accounting, making a significant contribution to Accounting.

Below, we summarize the main issues that Azzini researched in the process of development of "Economia Aziendale". In the 1950s and 1960s, his publications focused on profit organizations (Azzini 1954, 1956b, 1957, 1961, 1962a, 1962b, 1963, 1964a).

Most of these studies were published before Azzini became Full Professor. They investigate profit firms, mainly in manufacturing industry, with regard to investment, productivity, financial situation and risks related to long-term price dynamics. They developed important concepts of "Economia Aziendale" and disseminated the discipline in the Italian academic community. They are based on the work of Aldo Amaduzzi, Alberto Ceccherelli, Egidio Giannessi, Pietro Onida and Pasquale Saraceno as well as Gino Zappa.

Azzini's academic focus next moved to the institutions of "Economia Aziendale", although his contributions were applicable to other kinds of organizations (Azzini 1969a, 1969b, 1978, 1987a, 1987b).

Azzini published *Istituzioni di economia d'azienda* in 1978, and updated it in 1982, at the end of his academic career. This is probably one of his key works as it improved the development of the basic assumptions of "Economia Aziendale". The book has three parts described below. Part One covers the notion of "Azienda", or firm, and its essential factors (employee, manager, Board of Directors, capital), different types of firm (profit, non-profit, public administration, households, listed, non-listed), aspects of administration (management, organization and information systems), context (i.e. the prevailing legal system, market economy, industry specialization, financial system, corporate governance), and provides a systemic approach to the analysis of organizations. Part One is the most consistent with the work of Gino Zappa and systematically presents an overview of the key concepts of "Economia Aziendale". In Part Two, Azzini described how performance can be measured using an accounting approach for three types of firm (profit, family and non-profit/public administration), underlining the specific aspects of each type (net income in profit firms and net savings in households, non-profit and public administration firms). Part Three covers planning, specifying the instruments of planning and implementation strategies.

4 Financial Accounting

Azzini's main Financial Accounting publications are Azzini 1949, Azzini 1951a, Azzini 1951b, Azzini 1952, Azzini 1956a, Azzini 1966, Azzini 1976.

The textbooks written with Gino Zappa and Giuseppe Cudini introduced double-entry bookkeeping methods and were widely adopted in high schools. Many publications presented concepts of the new discipline of "Economia Aziendale" which were subsequently further developed by other scholars. Azzini focused on Accounting Studies, but in the context of other functions of the firm like organization and management, and various kinds of organizations like non-profit organizations, public administration and households. The accounting system was developed with a mathematical approach: double-entry bookkeeping and financial reporting were studied as equations (Masini 1995, 1957; Galassi and Cilloni 2006, 2010, 2012) where all values deriving from operations could be recognized and summarized. This approach, common to other authors (Masini 1970), was suggested for all kinds of organizations including profit and non-profit firms, public administrations and households. The financial statements are a summary of accounting data showing values deriving from company operations and processes. Like his mentor Gino Zappa, Azzini interpreted these values as being closely connected with management and organization, and with different kinds of organizations. His particular contribution was to develop a classification based on important criteria: (a) a separation between values that represent financial and economic aspects of operations; (b) a distinction between revenues and expenses directly connected with cash flow and accruals (discretionally and non-discretionally). The first classification is connected with the double-entry bookkeeping methods and is consistent with the "theory of income system" introduced by Gino Zappa and developed in Italy by several scholars. The second classification underlines the relative objectivity of revenues and expenses directly connected with cash flow and the high level of discretion characterizing most accruals. In fact, as laid down by the Generally Accepted Accounting Principles, discretionary accruals need to be adequately disclosed and controlled to prevent fraud and unwarranted management earning, which exacerbate the agency conflict between investors and manager. Azzini linked the financial reporting with "the company economic dimension that represents how managers realize the objectives of the enterprise" (Azzini 1982: p. 198): he noted however that information disclosed in financial reporting does not give a complete picture of firm performance, and wrote that it was "necessary to supplement knowledge of the economic and financial dimension with other information". Azzini thus identified very early on the need for research into social and environmental accounting.

In the matching principle, Azzini heavily criticized the association between independent assessment of individual components of the financial statements. He believed that it is not correct to evaluate assets, liabilities, revenues, expenses, gains and losses taking into account only the direct relations with operations and economic processes. He was in favour of interpreting the matching principle on the basis of a dynamic and systematic view of the company, and believed that it was important to evaluate the elements of the financial report considering forward data and company prospects, not only historical information.

In Financial Accounting studies, Azzini made a special contribution to the topic of capital maintenance methodologies.

This work was mainly carried out at the end of Azzini's distinguished academic career, and together with his contributions on Groups and on financial reporting, is some of the most important contributions to literature. He saw capital maintenance as an important aspect of the determination of income because a "necessary condition to have a positive income is the maintenance of the initial capital every year" (Azzini 1982: p. 284). Capital maintenance is an essential condition for the long-term development of the firm. He developed the concept in three different models for different aspects of the firm:

1   Stability of money and firm.
2   Changes in the purchase power of money.
3   Growth or crisis in the firm.

In the first model, the determination of income is simplified because it is not necessary to take into account changes of purchase power of money or the changes in the size or complexity of the firm and its environment. Capital maintenance without changes in purchase power and under the hypothesis of firm stability, i.e. the expected revenues and gains cover the expected costs, expenses and losses in a process which satisfies stakeholders, is called "Real and monetary capital maintenance". In conditions of firm and money stability, management can plan and forecast production with a high level of objectivity, and all the components of financial statements benefit from this. The determination of a positive income assures the real monetary capital maintenance. The problem, of course, is that such conditions prevail only in theory; the dynamics of the financial and economic systems in the real world are not coherent with a stability condition.

In the second model, the volatility of the purchasing power of money is combined with a relative stability of the firm in production conditions. Prices vary for monetary or economic reasons. The purchasing power of money is the mean of prices over the entire market, or industry market, weighted with amounts traded. Changes in purchasing power affect the accounting system, the determination of income and capital maintenance. Specifically, a reduction in purchasing power of money reduces the value of cash, cash equivalent, receivables and debts. A financial statement following the capital maintenance principle needs to take into account past and forward variations in the purchasing power of money. Methodologies of this type are based on indexes, which are determined by national institutions to measure the periodical variations. Items on the income statement and balance sheet are updated using these indexes, so that income and capital maintenance can be determined according to the purchase power of money existing at the beginning of the year. Azzini put forward criticisms of the model mainly relating to the use of unreliable indexes for measuring the variation in purchase power.

The third model is based on a dynamic firm that is growing or surviving. Growth entails an increase in production volumes, size, structure, processes, and transformation of management, information and organizational systems. Survival of the firm entails a going concern even during financial or economic crisis. Azzini developed this model mainly from an internal firm perspective, where the financial statement and related determination of income was an instrument to manage the firm consistently with the capital maintenance objectives. In both growth and survival phases, capital maintenance is realized with reserves of income deriving from evaluation criteria of assets, liabilities, revenues and expenses that take into account the expected development or survival of the firm. Measurement criteria are based on past costs and other evaluation criteria that ensure the development or the restructuring of the firm. Azzini believed that the best capital to maintain is the "economic capital" defined as the effective capital determined with the actualization of future income of the firm (Onida 1951; Provasoli 1974; Andrei 2004, 2008; Andrei and Quagli 2010). Azzini's use of evaluation criteria other than past costs for fair and market values was a precursor of Fair Value accounting used today in International Accounting Standards (IAS)/International Financial Reporting Standards (IFRS) financial reporting.

The difference is that today's Fair Value accounting mainly meets investor need for disclosure of unrealized income represented in comprehensive income. Azzini's model, on the other hand, met management's need to ensure balanced growth, consistent with economic capital maintenance and satisfactory stakeholder remuneration.

5 Group Accounting

One of Azzini's key contributions to literature was his work on Group Accounting (Azzini, 1964b, 1968, 1974, 1975a, 1975b).

After Azzini's apprenticeship under Gino Zappa in Venice, the 1960s and 1970s were decades of academic maturity. Within "Economia Aziendale", Azzini developed a Theory of Groups based on the Entity Theory (Moonitz 1951). He started from the concept of Group as a single Entity that includes branches characterized by formal and legal autonomy. From this he developed the notion of income and capital related to Groups and the procedure for aggregating and consolidating the information system of individual branches in a single consolidated financial report. This notion and procedure are described in more detail below.

5.1 The concept of Group

Azzini's book *I gruppi aziendali* researched Group economics and how it was defined. He defined the Group as an Entity whose units have the following two basic characteristics:

- formal and legal autonomy;
- substantial (economic and financial) dependence on the Group.

A Group is a firm whose units are formally and legally independent. Within the Group, however, each unit loses its autonomy and becomes a complementary and interdependent component. Unity and autonomy of the Group and formal independence of the units are the fundamental characteristics of the Group (Azzini 1968: pp. 26–27).

The structure of the Group was based on legally independent units, each of which has legal rights and duties. Both unlimited and limited companies can form a Group, but it is more frequent for limited companies as financial risk can be limited, which is among the main reasons for setting up a Group. The approach introduced a clear distinction between Groups and other business combinations. For Azzini, the Group is an Entity made up of legally independent firms defined as units. Other business combinations are more or less intense forms of cooperation between entities that are both legally and economically independent.

But with a full Group structure, the units are economically and financially dependent on the Group, which aims to achieve stakeholder objectives. Azzini stated that in any unit there exist specific interests, such as the interests of minority shareholders, creditors and employees, which represent conditions that the Group must meet in order to achieve its overall goals.

The influence of Gino Zappa was decisive; Azzini developed his theory by applying Zappa's Theory of the Firm to Groups. Each Group is an autonomous Entity: without autonomy there is no Entity (Azzini 1968: p. 36). Applying this criterion to the units of the Group, Azzini established boundaries between the Group (where units are not autonomous) and other forms of business combinations (where units are autonomous).

This definition marked significant progress in studies on business combinations and is still useful today. Azzini analysed in a unified manner the Group's economy, and considered all issues as issues relating to the whole. Considering the Group as an Entity rather than as a collection of individual firms, Azzini underlined the importance of taking the Entity as a starting point (Andrei 1994; Azzini 1968; Rinaldi 1990; Zambon 1996; D'Amico 1999; Azzali 2002) in analysing the Group's economy.

Azzini's definition conflicted with the definition based on Property Theory, where affiliates are considered as an economic extension of the parent company. In Property Theory, subsidiaries are considered as investments of the parent company: both the analysis of the economy of the Group and the preparation of financial statements are performed from the parent company point of view.

Azzini went on to analyse the main benefits associated with Groups. The main purpose of the Group is to share and mitigate risks. The presence of legally independent units allows splitting and limiting the risks among the units, through the equity, asset, liability, revenues, expenses and operational activity managed in the affiliates. A further purpose of a Group is to make the production system flexible. The typical structure of the Group makes it possible to enter or leave a business sector or industry simply through the purchase, setting up or sale of legally independent companies. It also means that the Group can choose the most efficient size. The Group structure also provides significant financial advantages: it makes it possible to multiply financial resources, because each unit, on the basis of its reputation as part of the Group, can attract equity and debt resources. Next, the Group structure makes it possible to minimize risks on financial resources invested by the parent company or shareholders. Azzini examined these aspects in detail, and his work described the multiplication "power" of equity investments that tie the units to the Group.

Further benefits of a Group are found in development processes. The classification proposed by Azzini was based on observation of the economic environment of the 1960s and 1970s, but is still applicable today. External development, or the acquisition of other companies, is the main way Groups are formed. Autonomous companies become units dependent on the Group. This process is often the result of the evolution of relationships between units, which agree to strengthen their cooperation through the establishment of a Group. The units exchange economic autonomy for the expected benefits of being in a Group. Azzini outlined two other formation processes, both characterized by internal development of the Entity. In the first, the Group is formed by the spinoff of one or more units, and it meets a need to reorganize management. In the second, the new units are set up to operate in new lines of business or in new geographical areas.

Azzini next focused his attention on the structure of the Group, particularly equity relationships. He described the Group as a set of investments that directly and/or indirectly link the units to the parent company. He used diagrams to illustrate Group structures, describing the flow characteristics in terms of the intensity of the control, Group management and the role of the parent company in the holding.

Holdings are essentially companies that manage investments, although Azzini distinguished pure from mixed holdings (Azzini 1968: p. 85). Pure holding companies guide, coordinate and supervise the management of the Group without participating in the economic and technical management of the business. They are responsible for Group management strategies, planning, organization of units, and maintaining coherence between performance and objectives. Mixed holdings, in addition to these activities, are also actively involved in operative management of the single units of the Group and their coordination.

Azzini's diagrams also show equity relationships that describe the strength of the holding control over subsidiary (Azzini 1968: p. 88). He showed two equity relationships, which differ according to the presence or absence of indirect control.

The first indicator, "Direct Investment Percentage – DIP", is the share (unitary or percentage) of the equity owned by the holding company to exercise control over the subsidiaries. The second indicator, "Indirect Investment Percentage – IIP" is the share (unitary or percentage) of the equity of the subsidiary indirectly acquired by the holding company, with their own resources. The two indicators are the same in the presence of only direct relationship, but differ if there are indirect ones. To illustrate this, here is an example from *I gruppi aziendali* (Azzini 1968: p. 93), in which A is the holding of the Group that participates directly in B and indirectly in C and D.

The IIP is determined by multiplying the percentage expressing the direct and indirect holdings. For example, A indirectly controls D through B and C. However, to control D, A has invested resources amounting to 33.6 per cent ($0.8 \times 0.7 \times 0.6$) of equity of D. IIP is useful to show the benefit for the parent company, which with relatively low financial resources controls the majority of the share of affiliates and the real percentage of investment.

The last important aspect of Group economics researched by Azzini was the distinction between economic and financial Groups. In economic Groups, the

Figure 7.1 Direct and indirect control.

Table 7.1 Benefit from indirect investment

Units	"Direct investment percentage"		"Indirect investment percentage"	
	Holding	Minority interests	Holding	Minority interests
A	1		1	
B	0.8	0.2	0.8	0.2
C	0.7	0.3	0.56	0.44
D	0.6	0.4	0.336	0.664

units are linked by relationships of cooperation and technical complementarity, while in financial Groups there are only financial and economic relationships (Azzini 1968: p. 113). Azzini notes however that the distinction is not always clear, as it is very common for Groups to show both characteristics. The issue is however central to his work on Group economics, especially with reference to his ideas on determination and presentation of Group performance.

5.2 Group financial reporting and the consolidation process

Another important topic analysed by Azzini is the determination and representation of Group performances. The Group financial report is the document necessary to study the economic and financial performances of the Group, to understand operating policies and make forecasts. This however is not possible using a financial report from only a single unit, because the unit is strongly influenced by the Group's strategies. Azzini distinguishes internal from external financial reporting. Internal reporting provides useful information to the Board of Directors for the management of the Group, whereas external reporting is an instrument of communication towards Group stakeholders, and has to comply with legal and professional standards.

Azzini emphasizes the need to draw up financial reports at Group level to determine the performance of the Group, the net income, the net equity, changes in cash flows together with their analytical components (revenues, expenses, assets, liabilities, cash flow from operating activities, from investment and from financial activities). Group income, consistent with his definition of a Group, is the result of systematic management of the units (Azzini 1968: p. 197) and shows its economic performance (Azzini 1968: p. 195). Considering the Group as an Entity with a particular structure, the best indicator of performance is its combined income. But Group income is not the sum of the results of the individual units, (Azzini 1968: p. 196) because the aggregated income needs to be cleaned from values related to intra-groups transactions.

Group equity represents the wealth available to the Group at any given time (Azzini 1968: p. 223) and, like Group income, it does not come from the simple aggregation of equities of the holding and its subsidiaries.

To determine the Group performance, Azzini proposed two methods (Azzini 1968: p. 202) which were subsequently defined as (Andrei 1994, 2002): a) direct method; b) indirect method. Following the definition of a Group as an Entity, the direct method determines Group performance by directly observing and recording its operations and processes (Azzini 1968: p. 202). The direct method first determines Group income, equity and all the other components of financial reporting related to the Entity "Group". Only in the second phase it is divided among units, according to Group strategy and the needs of stakeholders converging in the parent company and affiliates.

Azzini's second method differs from the direct method and determines Group performance with a consolidation procedure of the financial reports of the units in the consolidation area. First, each unit drafts a financial statement that includes values from intragroup transactions. In the second phase, the parent company uses the financial statement of units to draw up a consolidated financial statement.

The first method is not feasible for legal requirements, because the law requires consolidated financial reporting to show complete financial reporting of subsidiaries in the separate financial reporting of the parent company. But beyond legal obligations in both drafting and analysing consolidated information, it is important to remember the unitary management of the Group and that the direct method of determination of Group performances is useful for audit purposes.

Azzini distinguished Group financial reporting from consolidated financial reporting, considering consolidated financial reporting to be a type of Group financial reporting. Consolidated financial statements effectively show income and equity in economic Groups, thanks to the homogeneity that characterizes units in a consolidation area, but they may not be suitable for financial Groups, where units are involved in different industries or different segments of manufacturing or services industry. In financial Groups, separate financial reporting by the parent company, showing investments in associated companies evaluated using the equity method, is probably the best solution for the determination of the income and equity.

In other words, Azzini found that consolidated financial reporting was not necessarily appropriate simply because it has higher informative power only for Groups made up of units which are homogenous and complementary from the

Table 7.2 Method of performance measurement in different groups

Group financial statement		
Economic Group	Financial Group	Group with both economic and financial characteristics
Analytical Method	Concise Method	Mixed Method
Consolidated Financial Statement covering all homogenous units	Parent Company (Separate) Financial Statement, with investment in affiliates evaluated with equity method	Consolidated Financial Statement (only for homogenous activities) and evaluation of investment in affiliates with equity method

technical point of view. He believed it was necessary to investigate the economic characteristics of the Group, in terms of integration and complementarity of the activities of the units, before selecting the method of measuring Group performance. He proposed three methods of determining income and equity of a Group: (1) Analytical Method for economic Groups; (2) Concise Method for financial Groups; (3) Mixed Method for Groups having both economic and financial aspects.

The Analytical Method entails the consolidation of the partial value systems of units into each of the elementary components (assets, liabilities, costs and revenues). The result is consolidated financial reporting with the integral consolidation method in which the net equity of the Group must be broken down into parent company investments, with separate disclosure of Group net equity attributable to minority shareholders in subsidiaries. The Analytical Method is particularly suitable for economic Groups, where units have strong interdependency and technical as well as economic complementarity. Azzini emphasizes that in these Groups, consolidated financial reporting is useful to appreciate the Group's economic and financial situation, because the consolidation of homogeneous financial reporting of the units is functional to the determination of significant and reliable Group performance.

The Concise Method, on the other hand, determines the income and capital of the Group by evaluating investment in affiliates in the financial reporting of the parent company using the equity method. This method is suitable for financial Groups, where companies carry out non-integrated and non-complementary activities.

The Mixed Method entails the simultaneous use of the above two methods: the financial reporting values of the complementary and interdependent units are consolidated and the equity method is adopted as evaluation criterion for non-homogeneous investment.

Azzini also analysed the consolidation process, in particular intragroup operations. He described consolidation as a process of adjustment of aggregated values using the sum of the financial statements of single units, line by line. It takes into account: (a) the elimination of investment with the corresponding equity value, and the related treatment of positive or negative consolidation differences; (b) the elimination of value deriving from two main types of intragroup transactions: (1) reciprocal values; (2) unrealized intragroup income. Reciprocal values are credits, debts, revenues and expenses arising from intragroup transactions, and Azzini underlines the need to eliminate them because they originate from internal transactions, and in order to prevent duplication of assets, liabilities, revenues and expenses: these eliminations do not change the net equity and net income due to the same value but opposite sign of assets and liabilities or revenues and expenses. The values of unrealized intragroup income derive from intragroup price policies, and are particularly significant because eliminating them alters the net income and net equity of Group.

Following Entity Theory, Azzini's work looked forward to today's IAS/IFRS standards on consolidated financial statement, perceiving the usefulness of Entity

Theory in the consolidation procedure and similar treatment of minority interests and control shareholders.

6 Conclusion

Thanks to his collaboration with the eminent Gino Zappa at the University of Venice in the 1930s, 1940s and 1950s, Lino Azzini played a leading role in the birth of "Economia Aziendale" as a discipline and its spread and development in Italy. As Chair of "Economia Aziendale" at the University of Parma, where he was for nearly 20 years director of the section named after his mentor, Azzini worked on developing the essentials of "Economia Aziendale" and made a significant contribution to Accounting literature and to the organization of university courses.

His main areas of research were the basics of "Economia Aziendale" and Financial Accounting, and he also made a significant contribution to methodology of capital maintenance and to the theory of Group Accounting based on the Entity Concept.

In the last years of his illustrious career, Azzini published a book dedicated to Gino Zappa (*Institutions of Economia Aziendale* (1st edition 1978, 2nd edition 1982)). It clarified basic concepts of "Economia Aziendale", like the notion of the firm, the classification of firms, the subdivision of administration into management, organization and information systems, and the context including market and sector. It described the systematic approach to the study of companies, the activities of companies and methods of selecting and collecting data for financial reporting, and company planning. One of the innovative aspects of Azzini's work is that it covered not only profit firms but also public administration, non-profit organizations and households. He for example suggested a specific approach to accounting and financial reporting based on equations with information adapted into three main versions; for profit organizations where the result is the income, for public administration and for households where the result is savings. These concepts contributed to the development of "Economia Aziendale" in Italy. Azzini was aware that financial reporting was not sufficient to represent all aspects of company life and suggested it should be supplemented by other information, thus looking forward to the field of social and environmental accounting.

Azzini also made an important contribution on methodologies of capital maintenance. He presented it as an aspect of the determination of income in three main contexts: (1) Stability of money and firm; (2) Changes in the purchase power of money; and (3) Growth or crisis in the firm. He found that management needs to take into account the goal of capital maintenance with an effective use of evaluation criteria of assets, liabilities, revenue and expenses. When money changes its purchasing power or when companies are growing or restructuring, the financial report needs to update the historical values with indexes of inflation using evaluation criteria fitting the changing circumstances. It is possible to interpret this contribution as Azzini being an early proponent of Fair Value accounting as an instrument to assure economic capital maintenance.

Finally, Azzini's most important contribution to literature concerned Group Accounting and consolidated financial reporting. He applied the basic assumptions of "Economia Aziendale" to the Group, as a single autonomous Entity that includes units independent from the legal point of view. This definition, based on substantial domination by the holding company of the affiliates, is helpful to differentiate the Group from the other various forms of Business Combinations. As a consequence of this definition, Group Accounting requires its own specifications. Azzini suggested an original and direct method of organization of Group Accounting based on the Entity Theory. He believed data should be consolidated only for economic Groups, in order to ensure homogeneity of the data. In fact, IAS/IFRS establish the consolidation of data independently of the nature of the Group, but they suggest segment reporting in the notes, with homogenous values grouped for geographical or business units. However, the IAS/IFRS consolidated financial statement showing heterogeneous values from units operating in different industries could be less useful.

Azzini bequeathed a significant body of research, and today researchers at the University of Parma and other Italian universities are continuing to develop his work in the income approach to accounting, capital maintenance methodologies and Group Accounting.

Note

* This study is the result of cooperation between Stefano Azzali and Luca Fornaciari who wrote Sections 1, 2, 3, 4 and 6 and 5, 5.1 and 5.2 respectively.

References

AA.VV. (1987), *Saggi di Economia aziendale per Lino Azzini*, Milano: Giuffrè.

Andrei, P. (1994), *Il bilancio consolidato nei gruppi internazionali*, Milano: Giuffré.

Andrei, P. (2004), *Valori storici e valori correnti nel bilancio di esercizio*, Milano: Giuffrè.

Andrei, P. (2008), "Fair value, significatività e attendibilità dell'informativa di bilancio", *Rivista Italiana di Ragioneria e di Economia Aziendale* 9–10.

Andrei, P. and Quagli, A. (2010), "Il fair value nel bilancio di esercizio: potenzialità e limiti nella prospettiva della dottrina economico-aziendale italiana", in Airoldi G, Brunetti G, Corbetta G. and Invernizzi G. (eds), *Economia Aziendale & Management. Scritti in onore di Vittorio Coda*, Milan: Egea.

Azzali, S. (2002), *Il reddito e il capitale di gruppo. Valore e sua determinazione nei gruppi aziendali*, Milano: Giuffrè.

Azzini, L. (1949), *Ragioneria generale* (with Gino Zappa and Giuseppe Cudini), Milano: Giuffrè.

Azzini, L. (1951a), *Computisteria* (with Gino Zappa and Giuseppe Cudini), Milano: Giuffrè.

Azzini, L. (1951b), *Ragioneria applicata alle aziende private* (with Gino Zappa and Giuseppe Cudini), Milano: Giuffrè.

Azzini, L. (1952), *Complementi di ragioneria applicata alle aziende private. Le associazioni in partecipazione. Le imprese divise* (with Gino Zappa and Giuseppe Cudini), Milan: Giuffrè.

Azzini, L. (1954), *Investimenti e produttività nelle imprese industriali*, Milano: Giuffrè.

Azzini, L. (1956a), *Esercitazioni di ragioneria generale da svolgere* (with Gino Zappa and Giuseppe Cudini), Milan: Giuffrè.

Azzini, L. (1956b), "Alcuni aspetti della banca in economia di azienda", *in Il risparmio*, Milan, Year V, File 8.

Azzini, L. (1957*), Le situazioni d'impresa investigate nella dinamica economia delle produzioni*, Milano: Giuffrè.

Azzini, L. (1961), "L'elasticità della gestione", in AA.VV., *Saggi di economia aziendale e sociale in memoria di Gino Zappa*, Vol. 1, Milano: Giuffrè.

Azzini, L. (1962a), *Le situazioni finanziarie investigate nella dinamica economia delle aziende*, Milano: Giuffrè.

Azzini, L. (1962b), "Le situazioni finanziarie investigate nella dinamica economia delle aziende", *Rivista dei dottori commercialisti* 6.

Azzini, L. (1963), *Le negoziazioni con prezzo a riferimento nei processi produttivi*, Milano: Giuffrè.

Azzini, L. (1964a), *I processi produttivi e i rischi di andamento dei prezzi nel tempo*, Milan: Giuffrè.

Azzini, L. (1964b), *Autonomia e collaborazione tra le aziende*, Milano: Giuffrè.

Azzini, L. (1966), "L'organizzazione delle rilevazioni, svolte secondo le tecniche più recenti", in AA.VV., *Studi di tecnica economica, organizzazione e ragioneria in memoria del Prof. Gaetano Corsani*, Vol. I, Pisa: Cursi.

Azzini, L. (1968), *I gruppi aziendali*, Milano: Giuffrè.

Azzini, L. (1969a), "Del significato delle decisioni d'azienda", *Journal UEC. Europaische Zeitschrift fur prufung und Beratung* 4.

Azzini, L. (1969b), "Alcune osservazioni sul significato delle decisioni d'azienda", in AA.VV., *Studi e ricerche della Facoltà di Economia e Commercio dell'Università degli Studi di Parma*, VI, Parma.

Azzini, L. (1974), "The multinational company, the large-scale enterprise of the future", *Accademia nazionale di ragioneria*, Paper on business administration: Milano.

Azzini, L. (1975a), "L'impresa multinazionale, grande impresa del futuro", in AA.VV., *Studi di ragioneria, organizzazione e tecnica economica in memoria di Alberto Riparbelli*, Pisa: Cursi.

Azzini, L. (1975b), 'Considerazioni sul reddito d'impresa e conservazione del capitale', in AA.VV., *Scritti in onore di Ugo Caparra*, Milano: Etaslibri.

Azzini, L. (1976), *Flussi di valori, reddito e conservazione del capitale nelle imprese*, Milano: Giuffrè.

Azzini L. (1978), *Istituzioni di economia d'azienda*, Milano: Giuffré.

Azzini, L. (1982), *Istituzioni di economia d'azienda*, Milan: Giuffrè.

Azzini, L. (1987a), "L'inflazione nelle aziende", in AA.VV., *Scritti di Economia Aziendale per Egidio Giannessi*, Pisa: Pacini.

Azzini, L. (1987b), "Le tipiche funzioni delle aziende di consumo e delle aziende di produzione nel sistema economico. Le conseguenti relazioni tra di esse", in AA.VV., *Scritti in onore del Prof. Domenico Amodeo*, Padova: Cedam.

D'Amico, E. (1999), *Teorie di gruppo e tecniche contabili di formazione dei bilanci consolidati*, Cedam: Padova.

Galassi, G. (1987), "Prefazione", in AA.VV., *Saggi di Economia aziendale per Lino Azzini*, Giuffrè.

Galassi, G. and Cilloni, A. (2006), "Momento del reddito e logica ricorsiva in contabilità e in economia d'azienda. Le equazioni di Lino Azzini e di Carlo Masini: sviluppi metodologici", *Rivista Italiana di Ragioneria e di Economia Aziendale* 7–8.

Galassi, G. and Cilloni, A. (2010), "Sintesi, determinazioni quantitative ex-post, ex-ante, e variabili stocastiche in Economia Aziendale. Le equazioni di Lino Azzini e di Carlo Masini. Ulteriori sviluppi metodologici", *Rivista Italiana di Ragioneria e di Economia Aziendale* 5–6.

Galassi, G. and Cilloni, A. (2012), "Determinazioni analitiche e di sintesi, quantità fisiche e monetarie, nella logica di ottimizzazione economico-aziendale. I software applicativi. Le equazioni di Lino Azzini e di Carlo Masini: nuovi sviluppi metodologici", *Rivista Italiana di Ragioneria e di Economia Aziendale* 3–4.

Masini, C. (1955), *La dinamica economica nei sistemi dei valori d'azienda: valutazioni e rivalutazioni*, Milano: Giuffrè.

Masini, C. (1957), *I bilanci d'impresa. Principi e concetti*, Milan: Giuffrè.

Masini, C. (1970), *Lavoro e risparmio*, Torino: Utet.

Moonitz, M. (1951), *The entity theory of consolidated statements*, New York: The Foundation Press.

Onida, P. (1951), *Il bilancio d'esercizio nelle imprese. Significato economico del bilancio. Problemi di valutazione*, Milano: Giuffrè.

Provasoli, A. (1974), *Il bilancio d'esercizio destinato a pubblicazione*, Milan: Giuffrè.

Rinaldi, L. (1990), *Il bilancio consolidato. Teorie di gruppo e assestamento delle partecipazioni*, Milano: Giuffrè.

Viganò, A. (1979), *Le immobilizzazioni tecniche investigate nella dinamica economica d'impresa (principi e concetti)*, Milano: Giuffrè.

Zambon, S. (1996), *Entità e proprietà nei bilanci d'esercizio*, Padova: Cedam.

8   The contributions of Carlo Masini to accounting theories

Paolo Andrei and Silvano Corbella*

1 Introduction

This chapter aims to highlight the major contributions made by Carlo Masini in the field of financial accounting. In particular, the purpose of this study is to contextualize Masini's thinking against the scientific and cultural background of his life, in an attempt to underline how his way of thinking was firmly rooted in and consonant with his times, while also being marked by his unexcelled ability to look to the future and even be ahead of his time thanks to some of his felicitous insights.

Against this backdrop, the chapter is structured as follows: this Section provides a biographical sketch of Carlo Masini, surveys the author's main publications, and outlines the core features of Italy's dominant scientific thinking in the field of financial accounting at the time.[1] The following three Sections identify and discuss some of the main contributions that can be attributed to Carlo Masini, while emphasizing his sagacious foresight and the consonance of his thinking with the times. More specifically: (i) Section 2 is dedicated to the topic of "rivalutazioni fuori esercizio" (non-recurring revaluations) also in light of the accounting models based on historical costs and/or current values proposed by financial accounting studies; (ii) Section 3 is devoted to analysing goodwill and the so-called "esercizi economici particolari" (business unit) as interpreted by Carlo Masini; (iii) Section 4 discusses the "accounting equation" upon which the Masinian accounting logic is based and which creates conceptual connections between mathematical models and accounting methodologies. Finally, the chapter ends with some concluding remarks in Section 5.

1.1 Carlo Masini: a thumbnail biographical sketch

Carlo Masini was born in Milan on 6 November 1914. After graduating from Bocconi University in 1940, he builds upon the trail blazed by his mentor Gino Zappa and begins to teach and research primarily at Bocconi University, where he becomes full professor in 1963, and where he establishes the "Istituto di Economia Aziendale" before moving on to direct it in 1981. He also helps set up the activities run by the "Scuola di Direzione Aziendale" (School of Management). Meanwhile, he works at other prestigious Italian universities including Università Ca' Foscari in Venice, Parma State University and the Polytechnic University of Milan. He is also appointed President of the "Accademia Italiana di Ragioneria" (The Italian Academy of Accounting), later renamed "Accademia Italiana di Economia Aziendale". In addition to his university career, Masini fills prominent roles in civil society, always driven by an indomitable spirit to seek the "common good". Among these roles, he is elected President of "Ospedale Maggiore" in Milan and a member of the executive board of "Cassa di Risparmio delle Province Lombarde". Carlo Masini's research work leads to countless innovative publications in the field of "Economia Aziendale", accounting, management, organization and public administration. His contributions "are never insignificant or commonplace, but instead are aimed at provoking thought and at looking beyond the surface of things in a bid to uncover the truth beneath them, which … is the very duty of every researcher" (Coda 2015: p. 1). Spurred by this deep conviction, he succeeds in steering many of his students towards the academic profession, helping them develop their research skills with rigor and dedication. To this day, many of them are still working successfully within a number of Italian universities. After being appointed Professor Emeritus at Bocconi University, Carlo Masini dies in Milan on 20 September 1995.

1.2 The scientific production of Carlo Masini in its cultural and scientific context

1.2.1 The publications of Carlo Masini

The major publications by Carlo Masini, which deal with and elaborate on financial accounting issues, extend over a considerable span of time from 1946 to 1978 (Masini 1946, 1955, 1957, 1961, 1970, 1978), i.e. historically speaking, from the immediate post-war period heralding Italy's dizzying economic boom to the dark years following the youth protests of 1968, which give rise to out-and-out attacks on the rule of law by revolutionary political fringes.

However, this extensive time frame may be narrowed down to those works (Masini 1955, 1970), which, on either end of the spectrum, remain the mainstays of Masini's thinking. A more restricted scope, albeit still marked by tremendous upheaval and important social changes spanning 15 years from 1955 to 1970, is thus offered. During this time, a number of key cultural and scientific questions in the field of financial accounting come increasingly to the fore in Italy. These soon turn into "dominant" questions that seemingly flesh out the relatively stable and consolidated framework of those assumptions underlying the study of financial accounting. These assumptions will be dealt with in the following sub-Section with a special emphasis on financial statements.

1.2.2   The cultural and scientific background to the works of
Carlo Masini

The financial accounting theories dominating the 15-year period at hand are firmly tied to Gino Zappa's thinking (see Chapter 4 in this volume). A few rare exceptions notwithstanding (see Chapter 3 in this volume), Zappa's principles, which have driven the income-based accounting system and were developed within the newly opened-up field of "Economia Aziendale", seem widely accepted as a starting point for further scientific investigation. Still, without going into the details of those accounting theories which provide the backdrop to Masini's thinking, it is worth pointing out the "system of assumptions", which are significant in theoretical terms as well as in pragmatic and operational terms and which derive from the dominant cultural and scientific framework. The analysis of such a system of assumptions then allows us to understand where Carlo Masini stands in relation to the system itself and how he seems to act as a catalyst for further developments.

In brief, the well-established mainstays, which were consolidated in the 15-year period under scrutiny here and which substantiate the aforementioned system, may be summed up in the following points:

1   As an act of administration, financial statements are virtually aimed at gaining knowledge within the company. The internal financial statement is the only bearer of scientific dignity, whereas the published version of the financial statement is merely a corollary to the internal one (Canziani 1997: p. 189).

2   Financial statements are essentially a "behavioural tool" which are made available to the subjects managing the company.[2] Because the financial statements represents a source of information accessible (also) to external recipients, it equally affects their behaviours, thus influencing their decisions, actions – or lack thereof – following up on the content of the message transmitted by the preparers.

3   There may be more than one set of financial statements. Multiple financial statements may be differentiated according to their recipients (internal vs. external recipients, such as banks and tax authorities).

4   The notion of income defined as "distributable income" seems to take centre stage when preparing the financial statement. Such notion is characterized by the determination of a profit which, if distributed to the owner(s), will not harm any economic activities and, as such, is the result of smoothing provisions put in place to protect – including through the creation of hidden reserves – uncertain future incomes (see Chapter 12 in this volume).

Interestingly, the mainstays mentioned earlier have found fertile ground in Italy insofar as the accounting regulation, which is compulsory for "Società per Azioni" (S.p.A., i.e. public-limited companies) only, was rather generic and hardly effective. Stemming from the outdated *Codice Civile* of 1942, it merely contained a few highly open-ended articles allowing the managers ample room for discretion (Verona 2006: p. 14).

Thus, there is reason to wonder where Carlo Masini stands on the issue of financial statements in relation to the system of assumptions outlined so far. The short answer would be that, although Carlo Masini was "a man of his times", firmly aligned with the prevalent way of thinking of Zappa and his coevals (Coda 2015), he was still capable of illuminating insights that afforded him views of where accounting studies were headed. And while holding on to contemporary theories, his foresight enabled him to spearhead new "pathways" that have gradually been channelled into the dominant accounting paradigm.

To understand the meaning of this last statement, we must first and foremost understand, with the benefit of hindsight, what these pathways were and how they gelled into a "new system of assumptions" that progressively replaced the previous one. In this respect, the "breaking" point is often associated, by convention, with two specific events that took place in the early 1970s, when Carlo Masini published *Lavoro e Risparmio*, the last book containing some relevant chapters on Accounting.

Such established events can be traced back to: i) the decision of the Court of Milan of 23 December 1968 (the so-called "Standa case") which states, among other things, that the legislation governing financial statements is a compulsory provision aimed at protecting the company's stakeholders; ii) the so-called "accounting mini-reform" (Law n. 216 of 7 June 1974) to ensure greater transparency by regulating the content of the profit-and-loss statement, and by referring to the application of "fair accounting principles" ("corretti principi contabili") through Presidential Decree n. 136 of 1975.

These events, which have a strong legal significance, usher in a new accounting season that gradually undergoes an increasingly stricter statutory legislation culminating: (i) in the 1991 transposition rules relating to the fourth EU directive (Legislative Decree n. 127 of 1991) and subsequent amendments; (ii) in the 2005 adoption of the highly technical International Accounting Standards (IAS)/International Financial Reporting Standards (IFRS), which have been made enforceable by EU regulations. Against this progressively stricter set of regulations, the earlier "system of assumptions", forming the basis of financial statements, undergoes a radical change:

1 Financial statements become increasingly more relevant as a source of external knowledge. In the literature, eminent scholars delve into the field of published financial statements, which are thus given scientific dignity (i.e. Provasoli 1974).

2 Financial statements gradually feature the concept of "information tool" alongside the concept of "behavioural tool" in an effort to reach the various subjects directly and indirectly interested in the company's financial position;[3] such subjects, whose interests are considered worthy of protection, may rely on the (ever stricter) legal framework governing the content of the financial statements.

3   There is only "one" financial statement, showing the net income earned during the accounting period and the year-end owners' equity. This financial statement must be the one intended for publication, which must be prepared in accordance with the current accounting regulation (Cattaneo and Manzonetto 1992). Any "other" financial statement is meant for information only and for other "measurement purposes" so much so that it does not[4] qualify as a financial statement, but rather as a statement of liquidation, statement of merger, etc.

4   Financial statements prepared in accordance with the accounting regulation are designed to measure the so-called realized income,[5] which implies that an income is generated through revenues recorded only "upon providing the non-monetary transaction entitling the beneficiary to collect the negotiated selling price" (Campanini 1991: p. 239), net of expenses related with such revenues according to the matching principle. The concept of realized income: (i) on the one hand, is based on the cost principle; (ii) on the other hand, it removes any references to any income smoothing purposes meant to maintain a balance in future management developments. By contrast, in the IAS/IFRS accounting system, introduced nation-wide in 2005, the financial statements tend to measure an income that is the result of a system which is still partly tied to historical values and partly to the fair value (*amplius* Lionzo 2005).

Therefore, set against a background that has gradually emerged from the end of the 1960s to the present day, Carlo Masini stands out, as mentioned earlier, for his sharp and pioneering insights and for his great innovativeness in "conceptualizing" notions that had already been consolidated, partly because he resorted to the "exactness" of mathematical representation. Some examples of such ability feature a predominantly "technical" content and a focus "confined" to a specific theme. The following Sections are devoted to this. Here instead we point to the broader and farsighted "preview" of the role of financial statements.

As early as 1955 Masini began to see financial statements as an information tool geared towards calculating the income for the accounting period by observing the "economia di azienda" (business economics), whereas such income, "without any attributes", indicates a quantitative determination expressing an (income-related) aspect of firm performance (Masini 1955: pp. 590–597). Masini does not go so far as to deny the plurality of financial statements and to predict the importance of published financial statements. In fact, in Masini's view, the income is "typical of internal financial statements" resulting in "determinations for other such purposes as … 'government financial statements' which are subject, among other things, to the influence of accounting and tax regulations" (Masini 1955: p. 592) that affect the fair representation of the "economia di azienda". Nevertheless, Masini is able to look ahead and lay down a principle that will later be taken on board by unanimous consent and applied to Accounting studies: financial statements are aimed primarily at "making information available", it being the tool that circulates information on the company's performance.

2 System of values homogeneity: non-recurring revaluations

One of the most significant contributions made by Carlo Masini in the field of accounting theories – in which his farsighted acumen in interpreting corporate economic dynamics is evident and still current today – is doubtless his inquiry into the homogeneity of the system of accounting values and into any prospective solutions aimed at this complex question.

In Masini (1955) – a volume composed of 973 pages – the author addresses the issue of the changes occurring in the system of corporate accounting values as a result of the variability in corporate and environment dynamics. In this regard, thanks to a rigorously probing and logical reasoning, he offers a thorough methodology for determining and overcoming the problems arising from this variability.

After explaining the logic behind the use of the nominal value in corporate accounting systems, the treatise focuses on the currency trends in relation to various Italian business sectors, before going on to define a reference model based on the periodical cross-check of "recurring revaluations" and "non-recurring revaluations". In particular, in light of what the first parts of the volume have brought to the fore, the author, through subsequent approximations, suggests using a rigorous conceptual framework capable of defining the most evident issues that, in changing economic contexts, may affect the homogeneity of the system of accounting values, thus offering an interpreting tool of corporate dynamics as well as a relevant model for determining and overcoming any limitations inherent in the use of non-homogeneous values in financial statements.[6]

As is known, the accounting systems based on the application of the "historical cost" criterion – systems which were then generally adopted by companies and which are still implemented in several cases – do not take into account, as a first approximation, any change in value of assets and liabilities that may have arisen from changes in the environmental and corporate conditions.[7]

Masini observes how corporate phenomena, combined with environmental circumstances that may influence their future trends, could point to economic dynamics having a significant impact on the homogeneity of the financial statements according to the "historical cost" parameter, in particular as regards the diachronic creation of assets and liabilities values. Thus, especially in times of highly dynamic economic life, the evaluations based on the "historical cost" parameter seem unfit to fully capture the shifts in the system of accounting values since the conditions of homogeneity of the values making up the system are entirely neglected.[8] Under such circumstances, the performance indicators may lead to the creation of an unreliable net income due to various factors such as costs or portions of costs, whose original value is no longer indicative of the expected benefits associated with it.

To reestablish adequate homogeneity among the data of assets and liabilities and, above all, to appreciate the contribution towards the formation of the net income in a reliable manner, Masini also points out that it would be appropriate to go through a *general revaluation* of the system of accounting values, which should be carried out according to the rationale briefly outlined here.

- The revaluation process of assets and liabilities should be carried out whenever instances of value fluctuations occur at intervals long enough to enable the observation of the effects of the economic vitality on the corporate system.[9]
- The general revaluation should be carried out keeping in mind all the causes leading to the variations in value, including those relating to increasing inflationary processes ("monetary causes"), those derived from economic changes in market conditions (external "economic causes") as well as those linked to any changed corporate strategies (internal "economic causes") among which business combinations (mergers, acquisitions, divisions, transfers of assets, etc.) are worth remembering.
- The revaluation method is a quantitative determination process that is additional to the year-end valuation procedure in that the two combined processes can lead to the economic observation of the company's accounting values in its dynamic evolution.[10] It is also worth noting that the general revaluation of the assets and the liabilities is not, at least as a first approximation, a method to be implemented at the end of each accounting period.[11] Rather, it is an extraordinary valuation process[12] aimed at determining the value that shall be assigned to those assets in a bid to arrive at a more reliable estimate of the income attributable to subsequent periods.
- The economic significance meaning of the revaluations carried out through the abovementioned process takes on specific connotations within the context of quantitative determinations. We can define any appreciation or depreciation attributable to the general revaluation as an overall adjustment of equity derived from "non-recurring" processes. It follows that the revaluation balance resulting from adjusting assets and liabilities deriving from changes in the environment of the company does not affect the net income in the restatement period. Conversely, it enables an indirect adjustment of the income realized in previous periods, while also allowing for a more reliable quantitative estimate of any future performance.
- The process whereby the general revaluation of the net assets can be achieved must be understood as a single process, i.e. the reassessment of the individual assets and liabilities is significant only in a systemic perspective that may help interpret its contribution as a set of complementary parts constituting a whole.

The approach adopted by Masini in 1955 to tease out the problems affecting the homogeneity of the system of corporate accounting values and of any related financial statement computations would seem, on the surface, to foreshadow by a number of years the international debate on the adoption of the fair value when compiling financial statements.[13] It is nonetheless worth pointing out how the model proposed by the author is noticeably distant from the atomistic logic behind the current use of the fair value,[14] also in view of the fact that Masini's purpose-driven thinking is deeply rooted in the idea of the financial statement as a "behavioural tool" made available to the managers, whereas all the accounting principles (both domestic and international) have been developed by focusing on the financial statement as an external "information tool" (see Section 1.2.2., *supra*).

According to Masini's logic, while the consistency analysis of those single values that can be attributed to assets and liabilities may be a useful aid when going through the general reassessment process, the decision as to whether these may be accepted must be set against the wider context of a company's accounting values.

By way of illustration, if we observe the revaluation process of both tangible and intangible fixed assets, as contemplated by the IAS/IFRSs (*revaluation model* as per IAS 16 and 38), we can note how this is conveyed through methods that are different from the ones indicated above. In particular, two main differences are the following: (i) the first one refers to the "persistence" of the values taken into account to carry out the reassessment insofar as the IAS cited above do not state clearly that the values must reflect stable market conditions and management activities; (ii) the second one, on the other hand, refers to the lack of any references to a systemic logic which should underpin the entire revaluation process. In fact, the process suggested by Masini, whereby the adjustment of those values attributable to the company's assets and liabilities must be understood as a single process, i.e. the reassessment of the individual production factors acquires meaning only in a systemic perspective that may help interpret its contribution as a set of complementary parts constituting a whole. Indeed, the estimate of the fair values of single assets and liabilities could provide preliminary data aimed at the general revaluation process. However, they cannot be accepted as "new values" in the accounting system, as the revaluation method calls for a reassessment of the values through a valuation system that recognizes the complementarity and interdependence relationships between the various components of the company's accounting system.

With this in mind, it seems therefore plausible to claim that the methodological approaches relying on the use of the fair value-based valuation systems may come to our aid when going through the general revaluation process, although the decision as to whether these may be accepted must be set against the wider context of a company's accounting values. In fact, the fair value of individual assets can only offer some clues as to the company's environment and conditions, which must be analysed as a whole in order to appreciate their full extent and their chances of being recognized. In other words, it is necessary to ascertain whether the new estimate of the net assets value is a reliable sign of the expected benefits of the company's system which, taking into account the complementarity of its constituting factors,[15] may provide an adequate framework for estimating future incomes.

In conclusion, the general revaluation method suggested by Masini could be better suited – as far as the adoption of the fair value is concerned – to giving renewed homogeneity to the system of accounting values on the following grounds:

- First, an analysis performed at wide enough intervals allows us to observe more precisely the effects of the company's dynamics and environment on the net assets value, thus enabling us to understand long-term changes and not merely accidental ones.
- Second, whereas the accounting models based on the fair value have adopted an "atomistic" approach to evaluate assets and liabilities, the revaluation method, if applied correctly, is likely to capture system-wide any new relationships existing between the elements constituting the company's capital, based on a rationale that tends to recognize the expected benefits of specific production costs within the context of those correlations affecting their use in the specific corporate context of which they are a complementary part.

Furthermore, the assessment of the company's economic value is of particular importance in Carlo Masini's approach. In fact, the capital's economic value is a precious tool for interpreting the values allocatable to the various assets. The analytical value estimate provides an initial approximation in the general revaluation process and may gain full acceptance only if the updated values are deemed consistent with the assessment of the economic entity they are complementary to.

The revaluation method, viewed as a value alignment process aimed at a more reliable assessment of the net income, leads to the creation of "non-recurring" values. The revaluation balance is therefore considered a change in value that does not affect directly the income, in that it allows both to consistently appreciate the performance of the current accounting period and to suitably assess the ongoing processes at the reporting date in an attempt to obtain a reliable assessment of future income flows generated by the company.

3 "Operating segments" and goodwill in Carlo Masini's thinking

This Section is devoted to two further contributions that emerge from Carlo Masini's thinking in the field of financial accounting. Unlike the contribution discussed in the previous Section, these two contributions are less innovative and are concerned with narrower domains. However, it seems appropriate to briefly outline them here as they are emblematic of Carlo Masini's ability to tackle less innovative concepts (such as goodwill), while "looking ahead" and foreshadowing problems and solutions that were brought up many decades later in financial accounting studies.

The first area under scrutiny here is that of "operating segments". These "are set up when it is possible to see a 'relative economic unity' within the wider 'corporate economic unity'" (Masini 1961: p. 82), i.e. a significant business subunit comprising a mix of operations and production processes. "When one combines operations and processes in which correlated variations in economic values of opposite sign occur, the computation must necessarily include 'business segments'" (Masini 1961: p. 81), i.e. within the context of the wider scope of the reporting period comprising all corporate activities and processes.

Indeed, on several occasions, Carlo Masini devotes considerable time in his publications to the topic of "business units", thus foreshadowing the focus of this field of study which, decades later, will be incorporated by the IAS/IFRSs with the concept of Cash Generating Unit (CGU) and operating segment. In fact, it is well known that:

i   The concept of CGU is central to IAS 36 in order to implement the impairment test. A CGU is the smallest "identifiable group of assets" generating cash inflows that are largely independent of the cash inflows from other assets or groups of assets. The idea is to identify assets within a business unit, which, once aggregated, generate independent cash flows. To be sure, the different definition notwithstanding (which emphasizes assets as opposed to processes), a CGU establishes an "operating segment" to the extent in which it is a business subunit generating "correlated variations in economic values of opposite sign" (Masini 1961: p. 81).

ii The concept of operating segment is central to IFRS 8 for the purpose of presenting financial and descriptive information about the reportable segments of a company. Reportable segments are operating segments or aggregations of operating segments that meet specified criteria. Pursuant to IFRS 8, an operating segment is a component of an entity – that engages in business activities from which it may earn revenues and incur expenses – whose operating results are reviewed regularly by the entity's chief operating decision maker to make decisions about resources to be allocated to the segment and assess its performance – for which discrete financial information is available. Indeed, any comment meant to highlight the alignment between the concept of operating segment and "business units" is superfluous.

Nevertheless, the contribution made by Carlo Masini, which we wish to underscore here, is not confined to his ability to see, decades earlier, the importance of studying such corporate subsystems. His contribution does instead extend to insisting on the need not to use uncritically the "partitions" being discussed as if they were a "whole": the measurements and disclosure by subsystems, such as the CGUs and the operating segments, always imply abstractions that "split" the unity of the corresponding system – the whole company – thus introducing an "*of which*", which is only apparently disconnected from the whole and which is in fact indissolubly tied to it. Interestingly, Carlo Masini in his writings always warned against an uncritical use of these "business units", underlining the need for an increased awareness of the limitations denoting significance: as for "business units", whenever possible, only uncertain gross results may be assessed; if more business units are identified within a company, then many are the connections linking them in terms of the relationships between corporate events and market events.

As regards goodwill, the focus is even narrower. In rereading Carlo Masini's writings in preparation for this chapter, some passages stood out, in hindsight, for their consonance with the technical solutions provided by the IAS/IFRSs.

In particular, two excerpts are worth concentrating on.

With respect to the surcharge paid as goodwill in a business combination, Masini underlines:

> If recognized on the assets side …, the surcharge … will be amortized in the future. Should it not be amortized, it is assumed that even in the future, in an indefinite future, the capital will be negotiable to the extent it is being paid in the present.
>
> (Masini 1961: pp. 103–104)

Thus, the quoted passage left open, some 50 years ago, the possibility that goodwill could be left unamortized; a matter that has never been taken on board by national laws and accounting practice. Nonetheless, starting from 2005, the application of the IAS/IFRSs has introduced also in the Italian context the category of intangible assets with an indefinite useful life, which are exempted from the amortization process on account of the fact that there is no foreseeable limit to the period over which the asset is expected to generate net cash inflows for the entity. It is thus evident how Carlo Masini was a pioneer ahead of his times. Similarly, it is interesting to note how the author does not fall into the trap of speaking of "infinite" useful life when referring to intangible assets, but of "indefinite" life, as the IAS/IFRSs state today.

The second excerpt worth mentioning is concerned with price formation in a business combination. To this end, Carlo Masini points to (Masini 1961: p. 105): i) on the one hand, the need to express "the values of assets and liabilities … calculated as forecast … at the time of the sale" i.e. at current values; ii) on the other hand, the fact that goodwill must be included "as the difference between the total price paid and the net capital calculated according to the revaluation criteria" as suggested by the theory put forward in Section 2 of this chapter. Indeed, the same situation – as previously sketched out – seems to emerge in terms of goodwill amortization: Carlo Masini stands by a technical solution that, for years, has been deemed incorrect (as in the previous case) or has been neglected (as in the case at hand) by national regulations and practices and which has later been adopted by the IAS/IFRSs. In particular, with respect to the abovementioned excerpt, Carlo Masini foreshadows the rigorousness of those international principles that force us to avoid recognizing the so-called "false goodwill" (i.e. the overall goodwill comprising any surplus value on tangible assets arising from the fair value assessment and any intangible assets not yet recognized in the balance sheet), while recommending instead that only the so-called "core goodwill", i.e. the "real" goodwill be included, as it is attributable (only) to the expected capacity to generate earnings flows, thus avoiding any contamination caused by the inclusion of goodwill due to the aforementioned surplus values on assets already recognized and the fair value of intangible assets not recognized by the acquired company.

4 Symbolic and mathematical representation of the system of corporate accounting values

A particular contribution made by Carlo Masini following the conceptualization and consolidation of the corporate quantitative determination process is the elaboration of a mathematical formalization of the financial statements by means of "equations" (or rather, "mathematical identities"[16]): this is a symbolic re-expression of the different components of the system of accounting values aimed at fully appreciating the meaning of each kind of values interpreted according to a systemic logic and to its relationships with all other accounting values.

By means of subsequent approximations, Masini highlights the existing relationships between the various components of the system of accounting values, while outlining an overall interpretation of the corporate performance, both in terms of income and capital, which is represented, as far as manufacturing companies are concerned, by the following general formula:[17]

$$_{t_n}\underline{P}^{(S)}_{t_h} + (-\Pi_{t_{h-1}} - {_e}C_h - {_e}P^{(L)}_h - {_e}I_h - {_e}T_h + {_e}R_h - q_{t_h} + \Pi_{t_h} - g_{t_h} +$$

$$- {_e}P^{(L')}_h - {_e}P^{(S)}_h) = (N'_{t_{h-1}} + N_h - \underline{N_h} - N'_{t_h}) + N'_{t_h} + (-M^{(V)'}_{t_{h-1}} + \underline{M^{(V)}_h} - M^{(V)}_h +$$

$$+ M^{(V)'}_{t_h}) - M^{(V)'}_{t_h} + \Pi_{t_h} + Q_{t_h} - \underline{q_{t_h}} - P^{(G)}_{t_h}$$

where the various symbols stand for:

$_{t_n}\underline{P}^{(S)}_{t_h}$: equity at the time t_h. With the t_n symbol placed on the left, the time of the latest change in capital, which remains constant until time t_h, is highlighted.

$\Pi_{t_{h-1}}$: amount of inventories at the beginning of the h-th accounting period (final inventories of the $h-1$ accounting period).

Π_{t_h}: amount of inventories at the end of the h-th accounting period.

$_eC_h$: total amount of expenses incurred during the h-th accounting period.

$_eR_h$: total revenues earned during the h-th accounting period.

$_eP^{(L)}_h$: amount of employment compensation incurred during the h-th accounting period according to existing contractual clauses.

$_eP^{(L')}_h$: total amount of additional employment compensation incurred during the h-th accounting period.

$_eI_h$: total amount of interest expenses due to loans taken on during the h-th accounting period and represented by the $M^{(V)}$ symbol.

$_eT_h$: total tax amount (taxes, duties, etc.) incurred during the h-th accounting period.

q_{t_h}: amount of amortization and depreciation recognized during the h-th accounting period, which contributes to the amount of depreciation funds $\underline{q_{t_h}}$ as a liability component.

g_{t_h}: total amount of reserves for generic risks set aside during the *h*-th accounting period, contributing to the formation of the $P_{t_h}^{(G)}$ reserve fund as an equity component.

$_eP_h^{(S)}$: remuneration to shareholders (dividends) during the *h*-th accounting period.

$N'_{t_{h-1}}$: net value of the working capital at the start of the *h*-th accounting period (net value of the working capital at the end of the *h-1* accounting period).

$+N_h$: positive change in the working capital at the start of the *h*-th accounting period (increase in cash, cash equivalents and operating receivables, decrease in operating debts).

$-\underline{N_h}$: negative change in the working capital at the start of the *h*-th accounting period (decrease in cash, cash equivalents and operating receivables, increase in operating debts).

N'_{t_h}: amount of working capital at the end of the *h*-th accounting period.

$M_{t_{h-1}}^{(V)'}$: total loans at the start of the *h*-th accounting period (amount of loans at the end of the *h-1* accounting period).

$+\underline{M_h^{(V)}}$: loans paid back during the *h*-th accounting period.

$-M_h^{(V)}$: loans obtained during the *h*-th accounting period.

$M_{t_h}^{(V)'}$: total loans at the end of the *h*-th accounting period.

Q_{t_h}: amount of tangible and intangible assets at the end of the *h*-th accounting period (gross of depreciation and amortization accumulated); for the sake of simplicity, the entire movement for the *h*-th period is not represented.

$\underline{q_{t_h}}$: total amount of amortization funds at the end of the *h*-th accounting period (for the sake of simplicity, the change in depreciation funds for the *h*-th period is not separately represented).

$P_{t_h}^{(G)}$: amount of reserves for generic risks coverage recognized in the equity section at the end of the *h*-th period (for the sake of simplicity, the change in reserves for the *h*-th period is not separately represented).

As Masini stated, the parenthesis of the first member of the identity

$$(-\Pi_{t_{h-1}} - {_e}C_h - {_e}P_h^{(L)} - {_e}I_h - {_e}T_h + {_e}R_h - q_{t_h} + \Pi_{t_h} - g_{t_h} - {_e}P_h^{(L')} - {_e}P_h^{(S)})$$

equalling 0 represents the net income of the *h*-th accounting period on the assumption that no income was retained and that the remuneration for interested stakeholders (employees and shareholders) has been settled; the values in parentheses of the first member have a mutual relationship and represent the elements of a dynamic system.

The second member contains the set of working capital components

$$(N'_{t_{h-1}} + N_h - \underline{N_h} - N'_{t_h})$$

and the set of loans

$$(-M_{t_{h-1}}^{(V)'} + \underline{M_h^{(V)}} - M_h^{(V)} + M_{t_h}^{(V)'}).$$

The algebraic sum of the values contained inside the parentheses of the second member produces, for both, a value of 0; highlighting them means highlighting the movements that have led to the calculation of the year-end balances (N'_{t_h} and $M_{t_h}^{(V)'}$) during the *h*-th accounting period.

Outside the parentheses, the second member stands for the equity and the values expressing the production conditions that can be linkable to ongoing operations and processes; the overall amount of the net capital is indicated by the first member outside the parentheses, in $_{t_h}P_{t_h}^{(S)}$, where the symbol t_h on the right indicates that the structure of the elementary components (referred to the second member of the identity) is the determination of the *h*-th accounting period (Masini 1979: pp. 145–146).

Masini suggests these symbolic and mathematical representations of the company's economic performance for several types of entities (in addition to companies, the specificities of credit institutions, family-run businesses and public administration entities are also examined); furthermore, as regards companies, the rationale underlying the "general revaluation" referred to in Section 2 is being examined, while reaffirming the need to achieve adequate homogeneity across the system of accounting values on a regular basis.

As previously mentioned, the dominating rationale behind Carlo Masini's works hinges upon the concept of financial statements as a "behavioural tool" made available to the subject(s) managing the company (see Section 1.2.2., *supra*). This vision also affects the construction of the mathematical identities briefly outlined earlier. That being said, regardless of any inherent peculiarities, the overall methodological scope of the processes suggested here concerning the symbolic and mathematical formalization of the system of corporate accounting values can be appreciated from different perspectives:

1 Understanding the existing mathematical relationships between the components of the system of accounting values allows us to interpret the company's economic performance.
2 Thanks to mathematical formalization, all the relationships linking all the elements of the system of corporate accounting values are clarified, thus giving us a global financial picture (both income and equity).
3 The key accounting values (net income and equity) are jointly interpreted in their relationships, in their composition and performance.
4 The symbolic representation has the added advantage of highlighting the nature of the values. For instance, those values which in the income figure (in the first member inside parentheses) are indicated with the symbol "*e*" (accounting period) on the left are negotiated values (the sum of prices multiplied by volumes), whereas the other ones are merely estimates. This is important as it helps understand the earnings quality. Furthermore, those

values indicated by "*e*" were formed during the reporting period: their relationships therefore reflect, albeit not fully, a whole host of corporate circumstances and environmental conditions, i.e. indicative of homogeneous values, unless in the specific reporting period such extraordinary events occurred as to render this homogeneity assumption baseless. However, it would be extremely difficult to estimate financial statements values in the latter scenario.

In addition to what we have outlined so far, it is worth noting how the symbolic and mathematical representations, adopted by Carlo Masini as early as the mid-1950s to analyse the dynamics of the system of corporate accounting values,[18] can also provide a useful formal tool for an extremely wide range of applications by means of modern software dedicated to the management and control of corporate operations based on business intelligence and Enterprise Resource Planning (ERP) systems.

Indeed, as some authors pointed out (Galassi and Cilloni 2006, 2010, 2012), mathematical logic applied to the system of corporate accounting values forms the conceptual basis of modern corporate information systems and this appears increasingly more important if we consider the subsequent developments these applications can facilitate.

5 Conclusions

This chapter has afforded us the opportunity to underline, on several occasions, how the contributions made by Carlo Masini have stood out for being ahead of their time, proof that his "scientific vision" was indeed farsighted. Even so, these concluding remarks are aimed at emphasizing a further aspect that has seemingly emerged as one "constant", as it were, helping develop the previous treatise: Carlo Masini's thinking is thus characterized by his wide-eyed attention to the *systemic vision*, which leads him – albeit in the footsteps of Zappa's paradigm – to do significant progress, spurred by his constant need to interpret the "part" as a component of the "whole", where only the "whole" can help us understand the part.

This finds its ultimate expression, as far as Carlo Masini's works are concerned, in the field of financial accounting: the corporate systems of accounting are merely an "*of which*" forming part of the wider corresponding corporate system, whose management and organizational dynamics are the necessary prerequisite for any calculations, while providing the area of primary use of any derived information. Which also reflects in scientific terms where the "Economia Aziendale" feeds off any organizational and managerial phenomena sooner than any calculations relating thereto, and never labelled with the term "accounting", which is reminiscent of the arid technicality implied in data collecting. Still, even when directing our attention only to the data-collecting system, regardless of the management being scrutinized, the main focus remains on the "system" of accounting values and never on the single calculations seen from an atomistic perspective; the focus is therefore never on the income or equity, but on the co-determination of the income and equity, in keeping with the systemic logic that permeates every concept expressed and every argument advanced by the author.

Likely, this highly original and rigorous scenario painted thus far has helped create a school of thought originating in Masini, a school which today, though it has its epicenter at Bocconi University, has many exponents of his thinking in countless other Italian colleges and universities.

Notes

* Although this chapter is the result of shared thoughts on the subject, S. Corbella wrote paragraphs 1 and 3, while P. Andrei wrote Sections 2 and 4. The concluding remarks in paragraph 5 are a joint effort of the authors.
1 Because the focus is on Italy, where Carlo Masini worked and published his works, the biographical references mentioned in this chapter mainly concern Italian authors and Italian-language publications.
2 In Italy, the view of the financial statements as a "behavioural tool" may primarily be ascribed to "classical theory" of financial statements, typical of the narrative leading up to the 1960s and 1970s (D'Oriano 1993; Canziani 1997).
3 According to the countless authors that have dealt with this subject matter, financial statements are defined as "information (or knowledge) tools" in Dezzani (1974: pp. 18–19). It is also worth noting that, to this day "there is no such thing as a 'neutral' financial statement, i.e., merely aimed at divulging information without also being a behavioural tool for the company" (Cattaneo and Manzonetto 1992: p. 38); "financial statements continue to be also a 'behavioural tool' that can be used by the compilers to steer the judgments and behaviours of certain categories of readers of the document"; this is primarily because "qualifying financial statements as a behavioural tool in relation to certain players interacting with the company, appears to have an 'intrinsic character'" (Marasca 1999: p. XVI; p. 19).
4 The idea of a single financial statement is eloquently expressed, among others, by M. Cattaneo: "The financial statement is one and only one because it refers to the search for a basic knowledge offered to all the stakeholders concerning a company's ability to operate under conditions of dynamic equilibrium" (Cattaneo and Manzonetto 1992: p. 92).
5 As regards the constraints inherent in the expression "realized income" and all the due caution characterizing its interpretation, see Galassi 1967; indeed, the author (Galassi 1967: pp. 250–251) points out that:

> the income of an accounting period can never be defined as "realized" in absolute terms, "genuinely achieved", "true and real", i.e., measured against costs and revenues "earned" monetarily, insofar as assets and liabilities are recognized among its components, whether estimated or projected and expressing ongoing production processes, to varying degrees of completion, even when taking into account all revenues. ... Strictly speaking, the income is thus "realized" once the company has been liquidated.

6 Masini, too, cogently expressed his views on the existing relationships between the accounting period evaluations and the general revaluation process of the system of accounting values (see Masini 1957, 1961, 1970, 1978, 1979).
7 Concerning the subject matters dealt with in this Section and, more specifically, on the possible use of current values and economic values in the compilation of financial statements, see, among others, Andrei 2004, some of whose observations have been taken up and elaborated on later in this chapter.

8   If kept constant or subject to variability according to the performance targets for each accounting period, the value of the assets acquired in a certain period are doomed to become an expression of obsolete conditions and, after some while, can no longer be accepted as part of the balance sheet to be used as a meaningful basis for future accounting periods.

(Coda 1986: p. 79)

9   The general revaluation of the capital is not only necessary if radical changes occur in the productive combination, but also each and every time that, despite slow changes in the company's economy and environment marking subsequent accounting periods, the traditional evaluation criterion cannot express economically homogenous values in its main accounting figures.

(Viganò 1979: p. 41)

10   The methodology used to determine the net income and the equity comprises two different evaluation techniques that are jointly applied to the values within the same category: one technique which leads to the recognition of the "income" for each accounting period in a consistent way within a company, and one technique which, through general non-recurring revaluations, makes a number of accounting periods more consistent. The shared aim and objective link the two evaluation systems. A specific purpose sets them apart: the year-end evaluation process is aimed at calculating accounting period figures ..., while the non-recurring general valuation makes available the system of accounting values for future period evaluations.

(Masini 1955: p. 433)

11   For accounting periods characterized by an intense variability both in the environment and within the company, it might be necessary to perform a general revaluation at the end of each operating period. By contrast, it is worth noting that this process would pose several difficulties, especially in terms of the extreme volatility of corporate results in case the variations deriving from such process were to be included in the income statement. In fact we agree with the following assertion:

The suggestion to carry out, at the end of each reporting period, a general capital revaluation to enable, among other things, a recognition of a "variation in the revaluation capital", which, being realized in the year under examination, would integrate the concept of the net income ... cannot be accepted.

(Coda 1986: p. 80)

See in the same sense also Viganò 1979: p. 42.

12   As for the concept of "extraordinary" appreciations or depreciations of plant fixed assets when compiling financial statements, see Onida 1951: pp. 381–396.

13   As to the rationale behind Masini's "general revaluations" and its possible interpretation within the framework of financial statements prepared according to the IAS/IFRSs, see De Cicco 2006.

14   As for the main problems arising from the adoption of the *fair value* when compiling financial statements, see also Andrei (2008), Andrei and Quagli (2010).

15   For the purposes of the general revaluation,

there shall be an assessment of distinct elements which, however, should be considered as components of a single dynamic complex: the company's economy as represented by the accounting values, with particular reference to the implementation of all management processes. The meaning of general revaluations assigned here should be understood elliptically as "general valuation of corporate capital".

(Masini 1955: p. 415)

16 In mathematics the identities are equalities between two expressions where more variables occur and where these variables are true for all the values that can be attributed to the variables themselves. In this case, as Lino Azzini states, financial statements "equations" "are identities because they are composed of the same values, directly or indirectly in different aggregates" (Azzini 1978: p. 225).
17 The representation of the system of corporate accounting values by means of symbolic and mathematical formalizations is also present in Masini 1955: pp. 357–463, 1961: pp. 39–60, 1970: pp. 85–169, 1978, later completed and expanded in Masini 1979: pp. 104–239.
18 The representation of the system of corporate accounting values by means of mathematical formalization has been carried out also by Lino Azzini through methods that partially differ from those adopted by Carlo Masini, while still being based on similar assumptions (see in particular, as regards the summary of operations, Azzini 1978: pp. 201–241).

References

Andrei P. (2004), *Valori storici e valori correnti nel bilancio di esercizio*, Milan: Giuffrè.
Andrei P. (2008), "Fair value, significatività e attendibilità dell'informativa di bilancio", *Rivista Italiana di Ragioneria e di Economia Aziendale* 9–10.
Andrei P. and Quagli A. (2010), "Il fair value nel bilancio di esercizio: potenzialità e limiti nella prospettiva della dottrina economico-aziendale italiana", in Airoldi G, Brunetti G, Corbetta G. and Invernizzi G. (eds), *Economia Aziendale & Management. Scritti in onore di Vittorio Coda*, Milan: Egea.
Azzini L. (1978), *Istituzioni di economia d'azienda*, Milan: Giuffrè.
Campanini C. (1991), "Due concezioni del reddito nel bilancio d'esercizio: opposte ma (quasi) convergenti secondo una recente impostazione" , in AA.VV., *Scritti in onore di U. De Dominicis*, Trieste: Lint.
Canziani A. (1997), "Per il ritorno a una concezione classica in tema di bilancio di esercizio", in AA.VV., *Scritti di Economia Aziendale in memoria di Raffaele d'Oriano*, Padua: Cedam.
Cattaneo M. and P. Manzonetto (1992), *Il bilancio di esercizio*, Milan: Etaslibri.
Coda V. (1986), "I bilanci 'interni' di esercizio e di rivalutazione", in Coda V. and Frattini G., *Valutazioni di bilancio. Principi economici, norme civili, norme fiscali e direttive comunitarie*, 3rd edn, Venice: Libreria Universitaria Editrice.
Coda V. (2015), "Carlo Masini", Intervento al convegno "Il pensiero di Carlo Masini nella realtà odierna", Milan, Bocconi University, 20 November, 2015.
Dezzani F. (1974), *La certificazione del bilancio*, Milan: Giuffrè.
D'Oriano R. (1993), "Sulla visione 'classica' del bilancio d'esercizio", in AA.VV., *Scritti in onore di Carlo Masini*, Milan: Giuffrè.
De Cicco R. (2006), *Mercati dei capitali e informativa dei bilanci d'impresa e consolidati. Impostazione tradizionale e IAS/IFRS a confronto*, Turin: Giappichelli.
Galassi G. (1967), "Il postulato della 'realizzazione' nella dottrina aziendale nord–Americana", *Rivista dei dottori commercialisti* 2.
Galassi G. and Cilloni A. (2006), "Momento del reddito e logica ricorsiva in contabilità e in economia d'azienda. Le equazioni di Lino Azzini e di Carlo Masini: sviluppi metodologici", *Rivista Italiana di Ragioneria e di Economia Aziendale* 7–8.
Galassi G. and Cilloni A. (2010), "Sintesi, determinazioni quantitative ex-post, ex-ante, e variabili stocastiche in Economia Aziendale. Le equazioni di Lino Azzini e di Carlo Masini. Ulteriori sviluppi metodologici", *Rivista Italiana di Ragioneria e di Economia Aziendale* 5–6.

Galassi G. and Cilloni A. (2012), "Determinazioni analitiche e di sintesi, quantità fisiche e monetarie, nella logica di ottimizzazione economico-aziendale. I software applicativi. Le equazioni di Lino Azzini e di Carlo Masini: nuovi sviluppi metodologici", *Rivista Italiana di Ragioneria e di Economia Aziendale* 3–4.

Lionzo A. (2005), *Il sistema dei valori di bilancio nella prospettiva dei principi contabili internazionali*, Milan: Franco Angeli.

Marasca S. (1999), *Le valutazioni nel bilancio di esercizio*, Turin: Giappichelli.

Masini C. (1946), *Economia delle imprese industriali e rilevazioni di azienda*, Milan: Giuffrè.

Masini C. (1955), *La dinamica economica nei sistemi dei valori d'azienda: valutazioni e rivalutazioni*, Milan: Giuffrè.

Masini C. (1957), *I bilanci d'impresa. Principi e concetti*, Milan: Giuffrè.

Masini C. (1961), *L'ipotesi nella dottrina e nelle determinazioni dell'economia d'azienda*, Milan: Giuffrè.

Masini C. (1970), *Lavoro e risparmio. Economia d'azienda*, 1st edn., Turin: UTET.

Masini C. (1978), *Il sistema dei valori d'azienda. Un problema di calcolo economico nelle imprese. Razionalità e metodo*, Milan: Giuffrè.

Masini C. (1979), *Lavoro e risparmio. Economia d'azienda*, 2nd edn., Turin: UTET.

Onida P. (1951), *Il bilancio d'esercizio nelle imprese. Significato economico del bilancio. Problemi di valutazione*, Milan: Giuffrè.

Provasoli A. (1974), *Il bilancio d'esercizio destinato a pubblicazione*, Milan: Giuffrè.

Verona R. (2006), *Le politiche di bilancio. Motivazioni e riflessi economico-aziendali*, Milan: Giuffrè.

Viganò A. (1979), *Le immobilizzazioni tecniche investigate nella dinamica economica d'impresa (principi e concetti)*, Milan: Giuffrè.

9 Financial valuations in Domenico Amodeo's thought

*Sara Saggese, Adele Caldarelli and
Riccardo Viganò**

1 Introduction

Over the twentieth century, Italian accounting theory underwent a strong development fuelled by the so-called "zapparian revolution" (Bianchi 1984; Canziani 1994; Galassi and Mattessich 2004; Zan 1994) and the foundation of "Economia Aziendale" (business economics) as a unified and autonomous science (Viganò and Mattessich 2007; Viganò 1998).

At that time, the Neapolitan school of accounting provided an important contribution to the debate around business economics (Siboni 2005). The pivotal role played by this prominent research tradition had its climax in the studies of Domenico Amodeo as leading figure of the school and most eminent disciple of Lorenzo de Minico (Potito 2003).

Since his earlier studies, this profound scholar investigated the issues of capital evaluation in financial statements (Amodeo 1938), extending Zappa's and de Minico's thoughts (Fiume 2007). In this sense, he supported the dominant "income-oriented" approach for bookkeeping of "zapparian" heritage but criticized the notion of "Azienda" in Zappa's theorization (Amodeo 1964; Siboni 2005). The result was a more comprehensive definition of Azienda and a breakthrough interpretation of its economics in terms of business cycle, role of financial statements, and relationship between income and capital beyond the "zapparian" primacy of income (Amodeo 1956). The proposed evaluation model improved the framework illustrated by de Minico (1945) and strongly affected later developments of Italian accounting theories (Fiume 2007), opening up new avenues in the research field.

On the basis of these premises, this chapter aims to shed light into the theorization of the eminent scholar of the Neapolitan school of accounting by discussing his main contributions in terms of theoretical arguments and conclusions about financial valuation issues.

2 Notion of Azienda and role of financial statements

To fully appreciate the breakthrough contribution of Amodeo's theorization to the accounting theory, it is important to focus on some key issues in the Italian accounting debate in the first decades of the twentieth century, as already presented in earlier chapters of this book.

At that time, in Italy the income-oriented approach grew out of opposition to the "patrimonialistic" school of Fabio Besta (1922). The cornerstone of the argument was the notion of "Azienda" and the meaning of its operations. Indeed, under the atomistic approach of "patrimonialists", the Azienda was conceived as a mass of independent and detached components characterized by their own value. Differently, the "zapparian revolution" (Bianchi 1984; Canziani 1994; Galassi and Mattessich 2004; Zan 1994) opened the door to a more holistic notion of Azienda (Viganò and Mattessich 2007) as a dynamic and natural entity whose economic events were addressed towards predetermined aims, and linked to one another in a unitary and coordinated whole so as to reflect the main features of Italian firms (Viganò 1998).

These conflicting interpretations were also reflected in different accounting systems. The "patrimonialistic" approach emphasized the capital as the main and ultimate accounting reality. It conceived income as the accounting measurement of the change in capital over time, and identified the "balance sheet" as the main account of financial statements, relegating the "profit and loss" to a mere addition. Opposite conclusions were drawn by the income-oriented scholars. Indeed, by relying on the theoretical principles of unitary and non-atomistic view of Azienda, the income-based accounting system highlighted the supremacy of income over capital and conceived net worth as a static and derived concept (Viganò and Mattessich 2007). On the basis of these premises, a new notion of financial statements was introduced by the "zapparian" scholars (Bianchi 1984; Canziani 1994; Galassi and Mattessich 2004; Zan 1994). Under their theorization, financial statements were conceived as systems of values aiming to measure the income available for consumption in a perspective of maintenance of the entity (Alexander and Servalli 2011). Nevertheless, these tools were still internal-oriented and tried to report the economic reality performed by operations with no regard to external information, as the published financial statement was a mere legal obligation (Viganò 1998).

The Neapolitan school of accounting provided an important contribution to this debate through the studies of Domenico Amodeo (Potito 2003). The great significance of his thought for the accounting discussion can be learned looking at the scope of his theorization ranging from the notion of entity to the meaning of financial statements. In this respect, the most eminent disciple of Lorenzo de Minico completed the definition of Azienda provided by Besta and Zappa, and emphasized its durability, unity and finalism in respect to the aim of the entity (Amodeo 1956, 1964). In this sense, extending Zappa's notion, the author supported the dominant "income-oriented" approach (Siboni 2005) but interpreted its economics going beyond the "zapparian" primacy of income over capital (Amodeo 1956) and the traditional concept of financial statements.

In this respect, the contribution of his theorization to the evolution of the debate in the Italian accounting doctrine can be learned examining the evolutionary pattern of aims and scope of financial statements. Under the classic accounting theory, financial statements were reporting tools that synthesized bookkeeping recordings trying to reproduce the economic reality performed by operations (Amodeo 1955). Accounting was devoted almost exclusively to the internal financial statement as the most important information source for owners on the economic evolution of the entity. Indeed, at that time, Italian firms were typically medium or small in size, and often based on a sole or one-family proprietorship. In addition, the Italian capital markets and stock exchanges were rare and poorly functioning. Thereby, owners were overlapped to managers and the issues of selecting and evaluating their activity did not arise, limiting the role of financial statements to internal reporting (Viganò 1998).

Starting from these premises, Amodeo reinterpreted the concept of financial statement as an instrument of knowledge by emphasizing the entity's income as the main purpose of this tool, and the main object of accounting information. In this respect, the financial statements became a starting point for prospective premises aimed to conjecture about the future profitability of the entity. In the same vein, the net worth determination was directed to the need of measuring the entity's wealth in terms of income (Amodeo 1938, 1964). This role hailed from both the notion of Azienda provided by the author and his support to the "zapparian" income-oriented approach. Indeed, under Amodeo's theorization, the central dogmatic concepts of unity and inseparability of Azienda had a twofold effect. On the one hand, they produced a change in the accounting theory in terms of rejection of the central and static dimension of net worth illustrated by "patrimonialists" (Besta 1922). On the other hand, they provided a stronger support to the dynamic notion of income as more able to reveal the prevalence of coordination over the individuality of wealth elements (Alexander and Servalli 2011).

3 Relationship between income and capital in financial statements

In Amodeo's theorization, the role of financial statements and the issues of financial valuation hailed from the meaning and the relationship between income and capital as the cornerstones of his thought.

According to the eminent Neapolitan scholar, income was a pivotal knowledge instrument rooted into the aim of financial statements. For Amodeo, the primacy of income stemmed from the concept of business enterprise as an autonomous and real organism living over time (Viganò 1998). In fact, according to the author, over time only income existed in the form of "global income" (Amodeo 1955). All negative and positive changes raised by the events occurring in an Azienda were elements of income (Amodeo 1964). In particular, in line with the "zapparian" system, income was nurtured by the economic combination of costs and revenues through external dynamic operations. The former were conceived as negative elements of income connected to the obligations rising from the availability of goods and services, both in cases of direct production and exchange. The latter were identified as positive elements of income linked to the benefits of transferring goods and services to third parties (Amodeo

1952, 1956, 1964; Cinquini and Marelli 2002). Given the unitary nature of the Azienda through space and time suggested by his concept of entity (Amodeo 1964), in a systemic perspective Amodeo conceived the above-mentioned events as inseparable over the entire life of Azienda (Amodeo 1938). In the same vein, the author envisaged income as a holistic notion of wealth produced by the whole entity for its entire life. Under this concept, costs and revenues coordinated over time. As a consequence, only the totality of all costs could have been compared to the overall revenues, and no single or specific cost could have been matched to single or specific revenue. This is because each cost contributed to the overall revenues and did not generate any particular item in this category. Similarly, a single revenue did not hail from the contribution of a single cost item but from all the incurred costs (Viganò 1998).

It is worth noting that, under Amodeo's theorization, the "global income" was only one of the possible configurations of wealth produced by the entity. Indeed, according to the author, practical reasons led to temporarily limit the holistic nature of income, even if never for periods shorter than a year, and not to measure partial or interim/segmental results. In this sense, Amodeo acknowledged a periodic and discrete configuration of wealth represented by the "yearly income" that he defined as the increase or decrease of firm capital due to operations occurred over the full operating cycle of the Azienda. However, given the central dogmatic notion of unity of this entity and its related operations, in the author's thoughts also income had to be considered unitary. As a result, its yearly measure could have been only interpreted as a portion of the "global income" (Amodeo 1964). Thereby, compared to the classic accounting doctrine, the acknowledgement of a periodic configuration of entity wealth made Amodeo's thoughts more opened towards the financial statements as a medium of external information. In this perspective, by envisaging the "yearly income" notion, the financial statements were included in a multi-year observation window and their typical measure of income reflected more than ever the future-oriented accounting policies (Viganò 1998).

In Amodeo's thought, the measurement of the annual wealth was a strategic choice driven by the aim to quantify a "reasonable" configuration of income. As discussed in his first study *Contributo alla teoria delle valutazioni nei bilanci di esercizio* – "Essay on the theory of valuations in financial statements" (1938), and in the following research *Intorno alla teoria generale del bilancio di esercizio delle imprese* – "Essay on the general theory of financial statements" (1955), the assignment of income to the period had to be shaped in accordance with a conservative approach so as to secure the future entity profitability. In this sense, according to the eminent scholar of the Neapolitan school of accounting, the suitability of the entity means of production had to be evaluated only on the basis of their ability to produce wealth. Thereby, the reasonable income was the real objective of financial statements and its yearly measure could have been tested through the economic value of capital.

On the basis of these premises, Amodeo considered capital as an abstraction (Amodeo 1943). In particular, in line with the income-system of Zappa (1950), he saw net worth as a derived, static and artificial concept whose value could have been only referred to a given moment and measured in relation to income. While income was associated to ended operations, capital was conceived as dependent on the continuous and ongoing flow of the activities that unload onto the following periods. In this respect, capital was far removed from the dynamic nature of the Azienda. It was the instant picture of the entity ongoing operations, and represented the scale of its own whole future potentiality to produce income in terms of future profits and losses (Amodeo 1938). In this vein, the assets and liabilities, that qualitatively compose capital, did not have a unique independent value since their worth depended upon their contribution to the generation of income. Indeed, similarly to Schmalenbach's theorization of dynamic accounting (1926), except for monetary items, net worth was interpreted as a set of deferred costs and revenues rather than assets and liabilities (Amodeo 1964). As a result, in line with the "zapparian" income-system approach (Zappa 1950), the financial statements were centred on the profit and loss account, and the balance sheet was conceived as a static account derived from it (Viganò and Mattessich 2007).

In Amodeo's thought, the unique cause of the accounted capital had to be sought out in the lack of synchrony between monetary and non-monetary events occurring in an Azienda (Potito 1999, 2003). As discussed in his work *Intorno ai concetti di rateo e di risconto e alla loro generalizzazione* – "Essay on the notions of accrual and deferral and their generalization" (Amodeo 1946), the origin of every capital item different from its early monetary elements stemmed from the lag between monetary and gainful events. In this sense, the author broadened the notion of accruals and deferrals to every occurrence caused by the above-mentioned lag (Amodeo 1946). Before his eminent contribution, under the classic accounting doctrine, accruals and deferrals were conceived only in connection with non-recurring income items accruing over time (e.g. rents, interests). Thus, compared to his peers, the Neapolitan scholar provided a breakthrough interpretation of net worth. The innovativeness of his thought is even more emphasized by his conclusions on the meaning of capital as a set of accruals and deferrals in a broader sense (Amodeo 1946, 1964).

In Amodeo's theorization, also the economic meaning of net worth stemmed from its connection to income. In line with Zappa's thought (Zappa 1937), the author emphasized that capital resulted from the capitalization of future income. However, he enlarged this notion clarifying that its measure depended on the present value of the (discounted) average future income properly modified by the expected trend (Amodeo 1943; Fiume 2007). In this sense, the reference to the present value reflected the author's notion of an Azienda that was assumed to be everlasting and able to produce wealth over an indefinite future time frame, in line with mainstream accounting theory. As a result, the capitalization of average future income was infinite and based on a normal rate covering both the pure capital investment and the enterprise risk (Viganò 1998). Moving from these premises, the economic value of capital theorized by Amodeo was characterized by a bivalent meaning. On the one hand, it represented the global value of the enterprise. On the other hand, it was conceived as a pivotal benchmark to test the accounted net worth (Amodeo 1955). In this sense, Amodeo's thought was in line to Zappa's position on the relationship between economic capital and net worth resulting from the balance sheet, as this author also suggested periodical comparisons of both values and subsequent compensating revaluations of assets to foster their overlapping (Zappa 1937).

4 Accruals and financial valuation issues

The notion of income and capital and their relationships cannot be separated out from the pivotal and complementary issue of financial valuation.

For the classic doctrine, the entity's profitability was a pivotal capital characteristic. In this sense, net worth was meaningless if it lacked any income prospect (de Minico 1946). Thereby, the determination of income was a prospective issue as the dogmatic notion of the entity durability stemmed from its aptitude to produce future income.

For the scholars of the Neapolitan school of accounting, this approach was reflected both in the thoughts of de Minico and his disciple Amodeo. The former highlighted that the maximum value to assign to the capital depends on the variables rooted in future elements to evaluate (i.e. future revenues, future costs, and normal future income) (de Minico 1945). The latter emphasized the need to develop a configuration of income able to secure the future entity profitability, as previously discussed. It is the so-called "normal income" (Amodeo 1943), determined following prudence considerations in financial valuations (Amodeo 1964). In this respect, under Amodeo's theorization what is going to happen in the future is critical as these events give value to the firm. To this aim, the income figure assigned to each single year had to be of such an amount as will not impair the future firm's ability to produce a satisfactory (i.e. normal) repayment of the invested capital as measured by its accounting value. On the basis of these premises, the scholar emphasized that the capital at the end of period had to be evaluated in order to guarantee such a physiological configuration of future wealth, considered as the only one able to assure the survival of the entity. In this respect, according to Amodeo, capital had an economic meaning only in connection to the "normal income" (Amodeo 1943).

This approach underlines the pivotal role played in Amodeo's thought by the dogmatic notion of the going concern as also reflected in the financial valuations. According to the theory of the "normal income" determination, to not compromise the future entity's profitability, every single item had to be evaluated in connection to all other capital's items, since all their values contribute to the determination of a complex wealth that had to be consistent with the future length of the entity's life (Amodeo 1956). In this vein, financial accounting was not an automatism but a rational procedure of income assignment to the period (Amodeo 1964), since end of period evaluations had to depend on their effects on the "normal income" (Amodeo 1943).

The conventional historical cost-based valuations were clearly inadequate for this purpose. In this sense, Amodeo was very critical in respect to the use of historical costs as an incontrovertible approach (Alexander and Servalli 2011). In fact, as for the valuation of inventory, the eminent scholar of the Neapolitan school highlighted that the cost was not always suitable for measuring and representing the periodic income. The same conclusions were applied to the current value at the end of the period, opening up to the future realization as a value able to avoid the limits of both backward looking valuation and contemporary values (Amodeo 1956).

The issue of depreciation, meant as "Ammortamento", was similarly tackled in Amodeo's thought. Indeed, the eminent scholar proposed to leave the classic historical cost approach and coordinate depreciation and income assignment policies. In this respect, according to the author, the Ammortamento raised an economic appraisal issue in terms of amount of costs that could have been assigned to future periods without jeopardizing both the current and the future entity profitability (Amodeo 1956, 1964). Following this approach the Ammortamento was seen as a tool able to assure the gradual restoration of the asset cost through revenues. In other words, the depreciation charge had to assure that the resulting residual value of asset was properly covered in the future periods through the correlated revenues. Therefore, to be appropriate, the depreciation charge had to guarantee the future profitability perspectives at the end of each year. As a result, under Amodeo's theorization, assets had to be evaluated not on the basis of their productive efficiency and life expectancy but according to the amount that could have been postponed to the future Ammortamento, taking also into consideration all costs of the entity. In this sense, according to Amodeo the assets' depreciation was closely related to the so-called "power of Ammortamento" as the capability of future revenues to recover the costs in line with the "normal income" (Amodeo 1964).

In this vein, any financial accounting policy was seen as a tool to safeguard the future income of the entity by the accurate recognition of evaluation criteria and the proper accounting choices in terms of anticipations and deferrals of costs and revenues. On the basis of these premises, according to the eminent Neapolitan scholar, aside the Ammortamento, the provision was also extremely effective for this purpose. In this respect, accounting policies aimed to increase the retained earnings in periods with greater profitability, and to limit their increase in years with low profitability, were acceptable when driven by good faith and accuracy (Amodeo 1964).

The problem to assigning the income to the period, and the strong connection between capital and income in Amodeo's thought, raised the accrual issue. In fact, under his theorization, at the end of the period the accountant came across two opposite masses of income items: all the costs incurred from the beginning of the entity life, and all the revenues earned over the same observation window. However, not all costs and revenues contributed to determine the annual income as some of them would have measured future income.

On the basis of these premises, according to Amodeo, yearly costs and revenues could only have been indirectly measured, and the accountant had to look at the future instead of focusing on the past. In particular, the author proposed to determine the income of the period focusing on the costs and revenues of deferred allocation and to subtract them from the overall costs and revenues known by the accountant. Following this approach, the resulting mass of residual costs and revenues constituted the periodic economic items to be compared in order to measure the yearly income. Differently, the costs and revenues of deferred allocation represented assets and liabilities at the end of the period (Amodeo 1956, 1964). As a result, this theorization strengthened the notion that capital was instrumental in separating costs and revenues of the period from costs and revenues of deferred allocation.

The eminent scholar of the Neapolitan school of accounting did not follow the functional interpretation elaborated by de Minico (1935), adapting Fisher's economic concepts to the firms' dynamics (Fisher 1912), and highlighted that his Master overstated the practical applicability of his model based on the concept of income as a "flow of services" (Amodeo 1956). Despite its strong explanatory power and relevant practical application (Cinquini and Marelli 2002), the same Zappa strongly criticized the functional approach of de Minico especially in respect to the interpretation of costs and revenues in terms of dynamics of services, defined as the contribution of resources to the production process (de Minico 1935). However, even Zappa's "business cycles theory" was not free from criticism. In this respect, the author conceived the business operations as a set of cycles made of costs and revenues that could have been accrued only at the end of the cycle. Under this theorization, the difference between yearly and deferred allocation items of income respectively stemmed from the presence and the lack of income correlation phenomena between costs and revenues (Zappa 1927). From a theoretical standpoint, this correlation was in contrast with the dogmatic notion of unity and inseparability of the entity operations.

Therefore, the merit of the breakthrough contribution provided by the residual theory of Amodeo was twofold. On the one hand, it extended his theorization to income items that had been neglected by the alternative accrual approaches that did not consider costs and revenues respectively concerning services still used or released, but not yet incurred or earned as not yet correlated with cash outflows and inflows. On the other hand, it strengthened the notion that all the past and the future operations of the entity are linked in a continuous flow. Indeed, under Amodeo's theorization, the items involved in measuring the yearly income stemmed from the past (as costs and revenues deferred at the end of the previous period) and from the present (as incurred costs and earned revenues in the period), but extended their influence towards the future through costs and revenues of the period that would have been financially recognized (as cash inflows and outflows) in the future (Amodeo 1955, 1962).

5 Goodwill and hidden financial statement reserve

The prudence considerations in financial valuations to safeguard the "normality" of future wealth not only reflected on the periodic income determination but also on the value of net worth.

For the classic Italian accounting doctrine, the value of the capital at the end of the year was conceived as a tool to assign costs and revenues to the period under an accrual basis, according to evaluation conjectures on the future entity's profitability. In this respect, the measure of net worth was the outcome of two opposite effects related to the relationship between future and present profitability. Indeed, the overstatement of present income was reflected in the overstatement of entity capital to the detriment of future income. On the contrary, the containment of yearly income was reflected in a symmetric limitation of the entity capital to the benefit of future profitability. Thereby, the value of the capital at the end of the period was a sort of compromise between the opposite needs stemming from the conjectures on the future operations and the yearly income (de Minico 1946). Under this theorization, the difference between the value of the capital measured on the basis of the future prospects of "normal" income and the accounted net worth was conceived as the measure of the entity Goodwill.

Under Besta's theorization, Goodwill was already conceived as a differential value. It was interpreted as the greater value of the prosperous firm assets due to their profitable combined use producing an over the "normal" income (Besta 1922). As a result, it was measured as the present value of "excess" earnings (i.e. the difference between yearly income of the firm and yearly income of comparable underprivileged firms), discounted by the interest rate of medium or long term sound investments (Borrè 2008).

This notion implicitly acknowledged that Goodwill was an autonomous asset to be added to the value of all single firm resources. Differently, in Amodeo's thought, there was no room for a notion of Goodwill as complementary asset (Viganò 2001). Besides the issues of choosing the comparable underprivileged firms and the number of periods to calculate the present value amount, according to the Neapolitan scholar the above-mentioned concept clashed with the application of the systemic notion of Azienda (Amodeo 1964). Indeed, following the theorization of Besta, the capital was split into two groups of values. The former was characterized by all assets without Goodwill and all liabilities representing the net worth leading to the "normal" income. The latter was constituted by the Goodwill producing the "excess" earnings. According to the eminent scholar of the Neapolitan school of accounting, the capital could not have been separated into different parts distinguishing between the elements that produce "normal" income and "excess" earnings. As a consequence, Goodwill could not have been added to the goods of the entity on the basis of its ability to produce "excess" earnings. It resulted from the indistinct surplus of the economic value of capital (V_e) compared with the book value of capital (V_b) (Amodeo 1964). In this sense, the economic value of capital was obtained as a whole and its difference with book value was only a matter of recording or disclosure (Ferrero 1966; Guatri 1994; Viganò 1998; Viganò 2001).

On the basis of these premises, harking back to the theorizations of Vianello (1928) and Cerutti (1926), Amodeo supported the identity between Goodwill and hidden financial statement reserve since both relied on the gap between V_e

and V_b. Under his theorization, the hidden financial statement reserve existed over the business activity and appeared only when the capital was intentionally evaluated. Unlike the classic accounting doctrine, according to the Neapolitan scholar, the hidden financial statement reserve did not stem from the underestimation of assets and the overestimation of liabilities, but from the gap between book and economic value of capital. In particular, it was conceived as a voluntary phenomenon that emerged whenever the book value of capital was lower than the whole value it was assigned with a view to the future income (i.e. $V_b < V_e$). Differently, Goodwill was accounted only on the occasion of firm acquisition since, in this circumstance, the value of the going concern was higher than its book value. Indeed, in the case of favourable events, the present value of the expected future income stemming from the above-mentioned capital was higher than its book value, as the financial statements conveyed only historical accounting information. Therefore, in Amodeo's theorization there was no room for a notion of "endogenous" Goodwill. This item was conceived as a denial of historical appraisals since it provided evidence on the changes to the early accounted values due to the economic coordination of the entity and the presence of peculiar circumstances that characterized its operations. Thereby, Goodwill was considered as the odd disclosure of pre-existing hidden financial statement reserves (Amodeo 1964).

Under Amodeo's theorization, symmetrical conclusions were drawn in respect to the opposite case of book value of capital higher than its economic value (i.e. $V_b > V_e$). In this respect, the Neapolitan scholar interpreted the phenomenon as the effect of a hidden loss or "capital watering" that existed over the business activity and appeared only when the capital was intentionally evaluated. Thereby, unlike the classic accounting doctrine (e.g. Onida 1971), Amodeo broadened his conclusions to the negative Goodwill (i.e. the so-called "Badwill") as a consequence of his opposition to the classic notion of Goodwill connected to the "excess" earnings. In this sense, denying the existence of a Badwill was unreal for Amodeo since unfavourable events (e.g. at the beginning of the entity's lifecycle) could have hampered and jeopardized the economic coordination of the entity, leading to an economic value of the capital lower than its book value (Amodeo 1964).

The acknowledgement of Badwill by Amodeo's theorization completed the assimilation of hidden financial statement reserves (or hidden loss) and Goodwill (Badwill), thus delivering to the accounting theories one of the most innovative contributions in the field of study.

6 Concluding remarks

Scholars and practitioners have long debated the pivotal role played by the accounting valuations for investment decisions of financial statement users (Barth 2000; Watts and Zimmerman 1986).

The theoretical arguments and the conclusions on financial valuation issues in Domenico Amodeo's thought provided a strong contribution to this debate leading to major changes in the research field at the time his studies were pub-lished. Indeed, his breakthrough theorization suggested new theoretical approaches and opened up additional avenues for later research providing new ground to bridge the gap of Italian accounting theory in respect to the inter-national arena. The innovative scope of his contributions can be learned looking at the prevailing conformism at the time of his studies, when the Italian account-ing scholars were split into two opposite schools of thought: on the one side the supporters of the "patrimonialistic" school of Fabio Besta (1922), on the other side the disciples of the "income-oriented" school following the outbreak of the revolutionary theorization of Gino Zappa (1927), the Master of modern account-ing theory (Bianchi 1984; Canziani 1994; Fiume 2007; Galassi and Mattessich 2004; Zan 1994).

Despite the eminent Neapolitan scholar supporting the dominant "income-oriented" approach of "zapparian" heritage, he provided innovative insights into the Azienda and the issues raised by the evaluation of its operations. This was especially true not only in reference to his more comprehensive notion of entity (Amodeo 1956), but also with regard to his theorization that went beyond the "zapparian" primacy of income over capital. In this respect, his residual theory to determine the income of the period (Amodeo 1956, 1964), his notion of capital (Amodeo 1946, 1964), as well as his interpretation of accruals and defer-rals (Amodeo 1946), were harshly criticized (Potito 1999). Although with less momentum, the same conclusions applied to his interpretation on the meaning of Goodwill and its identity with the hidden financial statement reserve (Amodeo 1964).

The strong contribution provided to the accounting doctrine by Amodeo's thought was also connected to his continuous research efforts to examine in depth the financial accounting issues, and to make proper deductive generaliza-tions aimed to enrich the framework of the income-oriented approach (Potito 1999, 2003). In this respect, his research produced a twofold effect on the fol-lowing studies. On the one side, his sensibility to the Azienda and the financial valuations impressed his disciples and remained one of the characteristics of the Neapolitan school of accounting (Catuogno 2003; De Sarno 1997; Macchioni 1996; Potito 2000; Viganò 1967, 2005, 2001; Viganò *et al.* 2000). On the other side, his openness to the international dimension of accounting studies acquired from his Master de Minico resulted in later valuable research on international accounting (Caldarelli 1997; Viganò 1990). In this sense, one of the most rel-evant merits of Amodeo's theorization was that it fuelled the adoption of an international qualification by both Italian accounting scholars and practitioners. Indeed, the most eminent disciple of de Minico was very much engaged in the world of enterprises as business consultant. In addition, he supported the cre-ation of an Italian standard-setting body and the introduction of both nationally accepted accounting principles and auditing standards as President of the Italian national board of chartered accountants (Fiume 2007; Potito 2003).

This contribution was especially important when the international financial community started to require a public financial statement more externally oriented also for legal and fiscal purposes in response to the harmonization process (Arena *et al.* 2014; Viganò 1998). In this respect, accounting scholars were not fully aware of the international developments in accounting research and practice due to the nature of "Economia Aziendale", the success of Italian accounting scholarship and the peculiar features of the Italian setting in terms of ownership structures and company access to capital (Viganò 1998; Viganò and Mattessich 2007). As a result, the international debate on the role of accounting information and financial reporting to acquire resources and limit information asymmetries (Watts and Zimmerman 1986) was almost completely neglected, leading to a gap between accounting theory and practice (Arena *et al.* 2014). Amodeo's openness towards the international accounting practice and the relevant concepts debated in the global arena opened up new avenues for the more recent development phase of Italian accounting theory, breathing fresh life into the research field.

Note

* This Chapter was jointly written by the authors. However, it is possible to mainly allocate Sections 1 and 6, to all three authors; Sections 2, 3, 4 and 5, to Sara Saggese.

References

Alexander, D. and Servalli, S. (2011), "Economia Aziendale and financial valuations in Italy: Some contradictions and insights", *Accounting History* 16, 291–312.

Amodeo, D. (1938), *Contributo alla Teoria delle Valutazioni nei Bilanci di Esercizio*, Naples: Arti Grafiche ' Italia Imperiale'.

Amodeo, D. (1943), "Di alcune posizioni limite nel campo di una teorica generale dei sistemi", *Rivista Italiana di Ragioneria* 8–9–10, 125–149.

Amodeo, D. (1946), "Intorno ai concetti di rateo e di risconto e alla loro generalizzazione", *Economia Aziendale* 3–4–5, 1–14.

Amodeo, D. (1952), *Elementi di Ragioneria. Appunti ad Uso Esclusivo degli Studenti*, Naples: Giannini.

Amodeo, D. (1955), *Intorno alla Teoria Generale del Bilancio di Esercizio delle Imprese*, Naples: Giannini.

Amodeo, D. (1956), *Le Gestioni Industriali Produttrici di Beni*, Turin: Utet.

Amodeo, D. (1962), *Scritti di Ragioneria*, Naples: Giannini.

Amodeo, D. (1964), *Ragioneria Generale delle Imprese*, Naples: Giannini.

Arena, C., Saggese, S., Sarto, F. and Viganò, R. (2014), "Accounting in Italy", *European Accounting Association Newsletter* 2, 15–17.

Barth, M.E. (2000), "Valuation-based accounting research: Implications for financial reporting and opportunities for future research", *Accounting and Finance* 40, 7–31.

Besta, F. (1922), *La Ragioneria*, 2nd edn, Milan: Vallardi.

Bianchi, T. (1984), "The founding of Concern Economics: The thought of Gino Zappa", *Economia Aziendale*, 3, 255–272.

Borrè, L. (2008), *L'Avviamento in Aziende con Carenza di Reddito*, Milan: Giuffrè.

Caldarelli, A. (1997), *L'informazione Societaria e di Bilancio in Danimarca*, Padua: Cedam.

Canziani, A. (1994), "Gino Zappa (1879–1960) Accounting Revolutionary", in Edwards, J.R. (ed.), *Twentieth-Century Accounting Thinkers*, London: Routledge.

Catuogno, S. (2003), *Configurazioni di Reddito a Valori Correnti e Modelli di Capital Maintenance*, Padua: Cedam.

Cerutti, A. (1926), *Ammortamenti e Riserve nelle Aziende Industriali*, Milan: Società Anonima Libraria Italiana.

Cinquini, L. and Marelli, A. (2002), "An Italian forerunner of modern cost allocation concepts: Lorenzo de Minico and the logic of the 'flows of services'", *Accounting, Business & Financial History* 12, 95–111.

De Minico, L. (1935), *Elasticità e Relazioni Dinamiche dei Costi nelle Imprese Industriali*, Naples: Rondinella.

De Minico, L. (1945), *Lezioni di Ragioneria. I Fondamenti Economici della Rilevazione del Reddito*, Naples: Pironti.

De Minico, L. (1946), "Una picconata all'Avviamento", *Economia Aziendale* 3–4–5, 1–15.

De Sarno, M. (1997), *Economia dell'Impresa in Liquidazione*, Padua: Cedam.

Ferrero, G. (1966), *La Valutazione Economica del Capitate di Impresa*, Milan: Giuffre.

Fisher, I. (1912), *The Nature of Capital and Income*, New York: Macmillan.

Fiume, R. (2007), "Lorenzo de Minico's thought in the development of accounting theory in Italy: An understated contribution", *Accounting, Business & Financial History* 17, 33–52.

Galassi, G. and Mattessich, R. (2004), "Italian accounting research in the first half of the 20th century", *Review of Accounting and Finance* 3, 62–83.

Guatri, L. (1994), *La Valutazione delle Aziende*, Milan: Egea.

Macchioni, R. (1996), *L'operazione di Scissione. Un'analisi Economico-Aziendale*, Padua: Cedam.

Onida, P. (1971), *Economia d'Azienda*, Torino: Utet.

Potito, L. (1999), "In ricordo dell'opera di Domenico Amodeo", *Rivista Italiana di Ragioneria e di Economia Aziendale* 99, 144–48.

Potito, L. (2000), *Economia delle Operazioni Straordinarie d'Impresa. Profili Strategici, Valutativi, Contabili, Fiscali*, Padua: Cedam.

Potito, L. (2003), "Ritratto di un maestro: Domenico Amodeo", *Contabilità e Cultura Aziendale* 3, 148–53.

Schmalenbach, E. (1926), *Dynamische Bilanz*, Leipzig: G.A. Gloeckner.

Siboni, B. (2005), *Introduzione allo Studio di Storia della Ragioneria attraverso il Pensiero e le Opere dei suoi Maestri*, Milan: Franco Angeli.

Vianello, V. (1928), *Istituzioni di Ragioneria Generale*, Roma: Albrighi Segati.

Viganò, E. (1967), *La Natura del Valore Economico del Capitale d'Impresa e le sue Applicazioni*, Naples: Giannini.

Viganò, E. (1990), *L'impresa e il Bilancio Europeo*, Padua: Cedam.

Viganò, E. (1998), "Accounting and business economics traditions in Italy", *European Accounting Review* 7, 381–403.

Viganò, E. (2005), *Il Valore dell'Impresa nella Successione Familiare*, Padua: Cedam.

Viganò, E. and Mattessich, R. (2007), "Accounting research in Italy: Second half of the 20th century", *Review of Accounting and Finance* 6, 24–41.

Viganò, E., Viganò, R., Caldarelli, A., Cinque, E., Sannino, G., Macchioni, R., Manes Rossi, F., Aversa, B., Palumbo, R., D'Amore, M., Maglio, R., Fiume, R., Andreottola, F., Tizzano, R., Vagnoni, E., Capalbo, F., Forte, W., De Sarno, S., Sensini, L., Tommasetti, A., Martina, R., Di Taranto, G., Kunz, A., Catuogno, S., Tartaglia Polcini, P., Farneti,

G., Mariniello, L.F., Bisogno, M., and De Sarno, M. (2000), *Azienda. Contributi per un Rinnovato Concetto Generale*, Viganò, E. (ed.), Padua: Cedam.

Viganò, R. (2001), *Il Valore dell'Azienda. Analisi Storica e Obiettivi di Determinazione*, Padua: Cedam.

Watts, R.L. and Zimmerman, J.L. (1986), *Positive Accounting Theory*, Englewood Cliffs, N.J.: Prentice Hall.

Zan, L. (1994), "Towards a history of accounting histories: Perspectives from the Italian tradition", *European Accounting Review* 3, 255–310.

Zappa, G. (1927), *Tendenze Nuove negli Studi di Ragioneria*, Milano: Istituto Editoriale Scientifico.

Zappa, G. (1937), *Il Reddito d'Impresa: Scritture Doppie, Conti e Bilanci di Aziende Commerciali*, Milan: Giuffrè.

Zappa, G. (1950), *Il Reddito d'Impresa*, Milan: Giuffrè.

10 Paolo Emilio Cassandro and the rational valuations

*Stefano Adamo, Pierluca Di Cagno and Francesca Imperiale**

1 Short biography

Paolo Emilio Cassandro was born in Barletta on 9 January 1910. After having earned the technical school-leaving certificate, he graduated at 20 years old from the Royal Superior Institute of Economic and Commercial Sciences (*Regio Istituto Superiore di Scienze economiche e commerciali*) in Bari, presenting a dissertation on Accounting with the title "Economia aziendale in the foreign Countries and the recent Italian trends" (*L'economia aziendale nei Paesi stranieri e le recenti tendenze italiane*), Professor Benedetto Lorusso was the supervisor of his thesis.

In 1933 Cassandro won the competition for a teaching tenure in Accounting in the School Institutes, and thanks to a scholarship from the Ministry for Public Education, he spent two years in Germany for a study trip (1933–1934), attending courses in *Betriebswirtschaftslehre* at the *Handelshochschule* (business high school) in Berlin.

When he came back to Italy, after a short period teaching in Technical and Trading Institutes, in 1940 he started his academic career at the University in Bari, where, before as Graduate Assistant and after as appointed Teacher for the course of *Ragioneria Generale e Applicata*, he conducted teaching and research activity.

In 1950–1951, at the University of Catania, he won the competition for Full Professor and he gained a Full Professor tenure in *Ragioneria generale e applicata* in the Faculty of Economy and Trading (*Facoltà di Economia e Commercio*) at the University of Bari. He conducted an intense teaching activity, in several universities (in 1965 he was one of the founders of the Faculty of Economy and Trading of the University of Pescara) and in important national institutions (among these the ENI – Ente Nazionale Idrocarburi's Superior school).

At the University of Bari he attained important academic positions (as Director of the Department, Dean, Vice-Chancellor) until 1971–1972 when he was appointed as Full Tenured Professor in the course of *Ragioneria generale e applicate* at the University La Sapienza of Rome where he taught until 1985, even after his retirement in 1980, also holding the position of Director of the

Institute of Accounting and Economic and Business Researches (*Istituto di Ragioneria e di Ricerche Economico-Aziendali*).

Paolo Emilio Cassandro died in Rome on 2 October 2004.

2 Scientific position

Cassandro's scientific works consist of 32 books and about 140 articles and essays, published not only in his native language, but also in English, German and Portuguese.[1] The first work (a short essay about Leone Gomberg) was published when he was still a student (Cassandro 1929).

Cassandro was an academic whose scientific role revealed many original details and a significant autonomy with respect to the dominant school of thought existing in Italy in the first half of the twentieth century: that is the patrimonialist school of Fabio Besta (1909) and later the Income School of Gino Zappa (1927).

For this reason, thanks to the direct and unfiltered study of foreign accounting doctrines, favoured by a long stay in Germany, Cassandro's education is unavoidably characterized by his own opinions on the contents of the business administration science, overcoming Besta's approach (even if its root always remains in Cassandro's thought) and embracing, in an evolutionary crux, the greater part of Zappa's innovations.

Indeed, since his first works Paolo Emilio Cassandro felt the need to join Zappa's theory with the widespread Fabio Besta's doctrine, in which Cassandro always recognized the merit to be a precursor of Zappa's *Tendenze Nuove*.

Cassandro especially esteemed the evolutionary perspective of Zappa's approach as expressed by Aldo Amaduzzi, who was a direct disciple of Gino Zappa. Cassandro met Amaduzzi in 1940 and this interaction was certainly crucial for his academic and scientific growth (they both taught at the University of Bari until 1947 and after at the University of Rome since 1971). Indeed, Aldo Amaduzzi (as presented in Chapter 6) elaborated a theory considering the management in its economic and financial issues and including the manifestation of the Azienda's life in a time and space system, moving from a vision of the entity as an "accounting system" to a vision of the entity as an "economic system" in which capital and income derive from the real facts (which produce the system of the business operations) with the consequent development of a theory founded on the conditions for the equilibrium of the entity (Amaduzzi 1949a; Cassandro 1949). The acceptance by Cassandro of Amaduzzi's theory is clear.

Cassandro's research activity was characterized by an interdisciplinary approach with frequent use of mathematical and statistical tools, and above all with incessant references to foreign doctrines: starting in the 1930s for the German works (in particular of Schmalenbach and Nicklisch), to which French works and in particular Anglo-Saxon works (among which Littleton, Moonitz and Paton) were added since the second half of the 1940s. This constant updating of the accounting and economic trends and of international business phenomena led Cassandro to deal with some avant-garde subjects well in advance with respect to the national context, where these issues would be considered only years after. In this sense, the systematic work on group accounting dated 1954 stands out, and it is the first treatise on this topic published in Italy (Cassandro 1954).

Finally, Cassandro's scientific thought comes clearly to light, showing how it is decisively characterized by Besta's influence, even if the former is developed in an advanced dimension. This allowed Cassandro to arrive at a personal framework in which the static and structural conception (Besta 1909) is combined with the dynamic and managerial one (Schmalenbach 1919; Zappa 1937) in a perfect equilibrium.

A prominent role in Cassandro's thought was played by the ethical and social issues that permeate the entity, conceived as a "community" (Cassandro 1958a: pp. 182–184; reference in Nicklisch 1920), and by the specific economic and financial effects produced by the management of business activity, because the safeguarding of the entity as "driving force of the economy" (*centro motore dell'economia*) is not related only to the entrepreneur figure, but to the entire community, directly or indirectly involved. From this comes the clear reference to the need to combine the equilibrium of the entity with the income (*reddito*) policy (Cassandro 1967a: pp. 3–4).

This interpretation constantly recurs in Cassandro's works, with the issues concerning the assessment of the fundamental economic quantities (income and capital). The need to combine the income production with its distribution among those who contributed to its creation in a variety of ways, led Cassandro to recognize the absolute centrality of the safeguarding of the entity's capacity to produce income, through a process of renewal and regeneration favoured by the integrity of the capital or of the substance (*substanzerhaltung*) of the entity.

The fairness in the stakeholders' remuneration (not only the shareholders) is a need subordinated to the respect of the equilibrium conditions of the entity (Cassandro 1967a: p. 19).

In this regard, it is important to consider two issues:

1   Paolo Emilio Cassandro was a committed liberalist (Benedetto Croce and Luigi Einaudi are his anchorage).
2   His theoretical work on business' community and on profit was formed in the historical period (about the 1960s), immediately preceding the turbulent autumn of 1968 and the energy crisis of the 1970s.

In the end, Amaduzzi's lesson concerning the combination of different interests meeting in the entity (Amaduzzi 1949b) is considered by Cassandro's thought as the interpretation of the entity as a system that creates income for the benefit not only of the owner, but of the entire business community and in general for all the national community.

From this comes the possibility to identify the social income, to be referred not only to the entrepreneur, but also to the entire business community and country. In this regard, the significance attributed to economic quantities different from the income, among which the valued added has an absolute pre-eminence (Cassandro 1967b), should be considered. Strictly connected to this is the recurring reference to the "administrative rationality" constantly and in a variety of ways having repercussions on the activities into which the business administration is divided (management, organization, accounting).

With reference to what we will consider below concerning Cassandro's doctrinal approach, it is important to highlight how Cassandro's thought was formed in a period (1946–1978) in which the framework of financial statements was subjected to changes passing from the conception considering the financial statements an information tool with a prevailing internal significance and a public legalistic significance (1942–1970), to a conception considering the financial statements an information tool with an external significance in the wide range of corporate disclosures (1970–1995). This is a period where at an academic level a conflict arises between those who support different financial statements for different needs and those who are in favour of a neutral and single set of financial statements.[2]

3 Works on financial reporting: the annual financial statement

The research branch to which Cassandro paid specific attention consisted of accounting recordings,[3] which, identified in a systemic approach, are characterized by the following issues (Adamo 2009: p. 455):

- the unitary consideration of the entity as a system of elements;
- the prevailing, even if not exclusive, quantitative and monetary dimension of the related values;
- the inclusion of the preparatory accounting recording and the completion of the real accounting bookkeeping (elementary recording and cost assessment).

Considering the subject of financial statements in the wide scientific production of Cassandro there isn't an essay or a treatise uniquely dedicated to financial statements. However, this could give a deceptive impression, because this subject is one analysed in most depth by Cassandro. Indeed, with particular reference to valuations, we can identify several works concerning the annual and consolidated financial statements (among which the most important are Cassandro 1946, 1950, 1954, 1971), and the subject is also developed in his monographs dedicated to specific types of entities such as agricultural (Cassandro 1953a), and insurance ones (1957a), in addition to an innumerable series of minor works written in the period between 1950 until 1975 and to which we also refer in this Chapter.

In Cassandro's conception, the annual financial statements are an accounting recording represented by a periodical summary of the accounting entries of the period. Finally, financial accounting, through its common and widespread tools (accounts and double-entry method), and with other kinds of recording (inventory recording and budgeting), favours the assessment of the fundamental quantities able to express the system formed by the business operations (capital and income).

With reference to this topic, it appears useful to verify Cassandro's contribution considering the following issues:

- the relationship existing between accounting methodology and financial statements;
- the purpose and the object of financial statements;
- the concept of income and the valuation logic.

3.1 Relationship between accounting methodology and financial statements

In Cassandro's interpretation, the annual financial statements (that is the regular financial statements) must be considered part of the accounting recording, as a synthetic expression of the recording of the accounting period. The strict connection existing between the complex accounting recording and the financial statements (the latter comes from the former) clearly arises from the definitions, already existing in the early works, that find definitive form in the work concerning accounting bookkeeping (Cassandro 1971):

- Annual recording: accounting recording entered in the normal business life in order to know the economic quantities concerning the single business operations, and in order to methodologically classify, organize and summarize these original quantities with the aim to periodically assess (usually referring to annual intervals of time) the economic result of the entity or of some business operations.
- Financial statements: documents having the aim to demonstrate, in a synthetic way, the results of the business entity in the period to which these financial statements refer.

According to Cassandro, the main financial statements (balance sheet and profit and loss account) are two recapitulatory accounts, obtained by double-entry recording, in which positive and negative quantities are compared and from which two final values of income and of capital arise (Cassandro 1962). Following Aldo Amaduzzi, Cassandro asserts the strict relationship existing between the two parts of the financial statements because, as is well known, the income of an accounting period cannot be stated without assessing the capital. These are two interdependent quantities representing the complex of the complementary assets and of the related economic movements that have occurred in the accounting period.

3.2 Purpose and object of the financial statements

Preliminary to the process of formation of the financial statements is the identification of the object and of the purpose attributed to the financial statements, then the object to which the accounting recordings themselves is addressed and the related purpose is assigned.[4]

Furthermore, in Cassandro's model an illusory likeness between object and purpose of the financial statements appears. Financial statements are defined as a:

> system of monetary values having the aim to determine the partial results of a production process underway ... whose main aim is to assess the income of the accounting period and the connected capital, because the former cannot be assessed without the latter.
>
> (*sistema di valori monetari che mirano a dar contezza dei risultati parziali di un processo produttivo in corso di svolgimento ... il cui scopo preminente è quello della determinazione del reddito di esercizio, determinazione che implica pure quella del capitale, non potendosi determinare il primo senza il secondo.*)

(Cassandro 1957b)

Considering this definition, it is possible to identify the complete agreement with Amaduzzi's approach, according to which the phase for the determination of the income is interlaced with the capital one. In relation to this, Cassandro takes care of assessing the informative function of the financial statements, highlighting, however, further specifications on the unavoidable limits.

Indeed, even if the prevailing purpose of the financial statements is the determination of periodical income, it is necessary to understand the final aim in practice of this determination, and this leads Cassandro to highlight the distinction existing between (Cassandro 1957b):

- The internal financial statements, representing the economic and financial trend of the business, with the objective to realize the management policy designated to stabilize the capacity of the entity to produce income. This leads to the interpretation of the financial statements as a tool of the administration board.
- The public financial statements, that is the document knowable by third parties and presented to different users who must examine it, and which is used, depending on the case, as the basis for the dividend distribution to shareholders or to assess profit taxes.

In this regard, Cassandro seems not interested in the juxtaposition of internal and public financial statements; instead he is interested in the quality (in the form and in the substance) of the related assessed quantities (capital and income) which assessment should not be made in relation to specific stakeholders' needs. In this manner Cassandro highlights the need for neutral financial statements assigned to the calculation of an "economic income", then to an income determined in relation to the need to know, with the better possible approximation, "what is the effective increase (or possibly decrease) of the capital in the accounting period considered" (*ciò che è effettivo accrescimento (o eventualmente decremento) del capitale nell'esercizio considerato)* (Cassandro 1957b).

It is clear that this point of view doesn't ignore the increasing information needs of stakeholders who, following the evolution of the socio and economic context, not only embrace the traditional users (shareholders, tax authority), but also further classes of persons that for different reasons have interest in the business (workers, banks, financiers, customs, suppliers, etc.) (Cassandro 1973).

Finally, we can assess that Cassandro's approach doesn't disregard the theory assessing the existence of different financial statements in relation to the knowledge need (Besta 1909; Pantaleoni 1925; Zappa 1937; Onida 1940), but he limits its range.

In particular, given that the differences in financial statements come from the different purpose/object (normal operating condition, liquidation, transfer, etc.) there are no doubts that financial statements are different, but when the reference is made to a specific information purpose (the normal operating condition of the entity) the unavoidable range of discretion in the value attribution to the several assets cannot be bent to the achievement of purposes different form the "rational" calculation of economic income and of the related operating capital.

Valuations appear "rational" when they are coherent with the systemic nature of the entity and with the object to which the information need is directed: economic, financial and patrimonial effects of the management operation system, set according to an operating perspective.

Therefore, according to this point of view, the financial statements are a knowledge tool addressed to verify the management trends of the business; their formation is independent of the specific information needs of the various stakeholders (shareholders, treasury, financiers, …) being a document representing the entity objectively considered.

For this reason Cassandro is inclined towards the development of types of financial statements elaborated following the issues characterizing the several types of business (industries, banks, insurances, etc.). In this regard, Cassandro constantly and early identifies the usefulness of proceeding through the study of business sectors *(tipizzazione)* in order to favour the spread of clear and uniform financial statements on the formal and on the substantive perspective (for example Cassandro 1949, 1953b, 1957b, 1958b, 1968, 1973).

This stance highlights a need already supported by the German doctrine during the 1920s and perceived in the economic contexts of North America in the 1930s and the 1940s, and decisively ignored in the Italian doctrine existing at that time, and in this sense Cassandro can be for sure considered a precursor of the harmonization process characterizing the European Directives of the 1970s.

3.3 The concept of the "rational income": general standards and the valuation logic of the financial statements

As mentioned above, Cassandro's thought is characterized by a recurring reference to the administrative rationality needed for the development of all the administrative business activities. Evidently, the financial statements are not an exception and rationality dominates the entire construction of the financial statements and above all their valuation logic in order to mitigate the unavoidable discretion existing in the valuation processes (Di Cagno 2008).

Even if we have already highlighted the preeminent significance of the "value added" (*valore aggiunto*) quantity in relation to the valuation processes of the financial statements, Cassandro unavoidably paid more attention to the annual income that, jointly with the operating capital, is the traditional reference quantity in financial reporting researches.

According to Cassandro "the income is the result of the operational activities to which personnel resources, assets and the business organization all contribute" (*il reddito è il risultato della gestione, ossia delle operazioni aziendali, nello svolgimento delle quali confluiscono le forze personali, i mezzi aziendali e la componente organizzativa del sistema*) (Cassandro 1958a: p. 179).

Starting from this definition, Cassandro develops a conceptual framework where a series of principles are identified and the latter clearly anticipate the *image fidèle* (true and fair view), and other principles[5] that will be introduced by the European Commission. These principles (already presented at an early stage in Cassandro 1957c) are stated as follows in a work published in the 1970s (Cassandro 1973):

- The principle of *clearness*, put into effect through the adoption of standardized financial statement sheet structures able to favour a sufficient level of analysis in the classification (homogeneous) in the balance sheet and in the profit and loss account, as well as through the adoption of a clear and unequivocal terminology, and through the introduction of further disclosure reports.

- The principle of *faithful representation* (*chiarezza sostanziale*), which, being related to the appropriateness of valuation criteria in respect to the represented items (capital and income), should favour the assessment of "truthful" values able to be "a faithful representation of the entity's reality, in order to allow the financial statements to be a mirror that does not distort that reality" (*una fedele rappresentazione della realtà aziendale, in guisa che il bilancio sia uno specchio non deformante di quella realtà*) (Cassandro 1973: p. 844).

When one moves to consider issues typically involving valuation, it appears coherent with the systemic framework of the different order of accounting data to pay attention to inventory accounting. Indeed, inventory accounting appears "needed" in order to assess the income of the accounting period, through the valuation of different assets favouring the "adjustment" (reverse, transfer, adjusting and addition entries) of exchange values accounted during the accounting period.

According to Cassandro, the need to obtain a "rational income" is established in order to allow a fair interpretation of the business trends, and above all in order to avoid dangerous dilution of capital able to jeopardize the capacity of the business to operate in normal and balanced conditions (Cassandro 1971: pp. 124–125). Therefore, the rational income must represent a real increase of the initial net worth, certainly avoiding misleading measures that, combined with income distribution, rather produce the dangerous distribution of capital. Ultimately, the "rational income" defined by Cassandro is a form of "distributable income" assessed for the continuity of the going concern, and for the safeguard of the capital integrity (Cassandro 1971: p. 125).

The safeguard of the capital integrity is the focus of this approach or, as Cassandro wrote, borrowing the term from the German, the substance (*substanzerhaltung*) to which valuations should be "rationally" oriented, implying to consider acceptable the creation of "hidden reserves", at least until it leads to illegality, or it distorts the clearness of the financial statements presentation (Cassandro 1946: p. 9).

As a consequence we deduce that Cassandro's intent is not so much to identify a specific valuation criterion, but to identify a limiting criterion for valuations.

Finally, we can assert that Cassandro takes care to identify a control system (we would say today an impairment test) that cannot be rationally overcome. As a consequence "maximum" valuation limits (for assets) and "minimum" valuation limits (for liabilities) are identified, and when they are overcome, valuations enter in the irrational range with the related risk to damage the capital integrity.

In the logic of rational valuations, the limits are identified considering, first, the point of view of the going concern. These limits, in a dynamic dimension, are respectively identified in future estimated cash receipts and payments (Cassandro 1962): this allows to identify a financial-perspective valuation logic already existing in Zappa's theory, and that is elaborated by Aldo Amaduzzi (Amaduzzi 1939) and by Cassandro who asserts "it is not so much the physical size of the different resources which is important, but their capacity to produce income in the future, which means, and gives rise to, their value" (*non è tanto la consistenza fisica dei vari fattori, quanto la loro prospettica capacità di rendimento economico che conta e attribuisce loro valore*) (Cassandro 1950: p. 22).

At first sight, the valuation limits of assets consist of the following parameters (Cassandro 1971: pp. 128–129; and in compliance with Amaduzzi 1939, pp. 25–26):[6]

• For assets, the future estimated realizable values direct (for assets intended to be sold) or indirect (for assets intended to be used), when entirely used in the productive process. These values are limits that should not be reached and, therefore, it is prudent to stay below them due to the uncertainty in the estimation, and in order to consider the period of time existing until the moment in which they will be realized (discounting back), as well as the potential sale expenses and expenses needed to complete the production.

• For liabilities, the limit is identified in the estimated amount to be paid for their settlement, also in this case amended in order to consider uncertainty involved in the estimate, as well as the duration and the potential settlement expenses.

This framework leads to the general valuation principles recognized by Cassandro, that is going concern and prudence principles, the latter applied in an administrative sense, as needed, and as a preventative measure to take under control the uncertainty involved in the estimates. In addition, the matching principle, recalled to take account of the ongoing operations at the end of the accounting period, is considered more a technical accounting matter than a general accounting principle.

From this approach a valuation logic arises in line with the systemic vision of the entity, where the complementary use of the productive resources is joined with the time dimension of management activity giving rise to a perfect combinatory effect.

According to Cassandro the ideal approach should avoid the inconvenience to assess specific valuation rules that, even if they could be acceptable in some cases, in other cases they could not be so (Cassandro 1971: p. 477). The estimate of general limits, instead, is compatible with specific valuation criteria that, each time, entities could apply on the basis of the concrete circumstances and particular sectors in which they operate.

As mentioned above, in Cassandro's interpretation, for an adequate approximation, the business type (*tipizzazione*) is fundamental, that is the creation of models of financial statements in relation to the particular characteristics of specific entities operating in given activity sectors, with the effect to consider as many financial statement models as there are types of businesses to be standardized, in this manner favouring the drawing up of consolidated financial statements (Cassandro 1954: p. 337 ss.).

In relation to this standardization process of the financial statements (Cassandro 1973):[7]

- The subject, the aim, the postulates and the general principles are the ones typical of the operating financial statements.
- Structure and form of the financial statements, as well as the valuation criteria, could change depending on the type of business considered, this in order to allow a better formal clearness and faithful representation.

4 Financial valuation in Cassandro's approach

As highlighted by Cassandro, if theoretically the recalled "rational limits" do not have particular problems in their assessment, on the practical level difficulties appear extremely clear (Cassandro 1971: p. 126).

In this regard, however, it is useful to point out how the natural pragmatism and the immediacy characterizing Cassandro's approach take him to not consider only theoretical implications of the analysed concepts (in Zappa's theory there were meagre practical applications, just for uncertainties existing in calculation).

Indeed, Cassandro, far from falling back on accommodation solutions or on unquestioning agreements on legal dispositions existing at that time (oriented to the adoption of historical cost as valuation criterion), decisively rejects references to historical cost, and to current values, actually attempting, instead, to calculate the estimated future realization value.

Interlacing the managerial accounting and cost controlling tools with inventory entries and financial accounting, he tried to take advantage of Amaduzzi's studies on the entity as a "bridge between past costs and current and future prices, between 'old' and 'new' exchange values" (*ponte tra prezzi passati e prezzi attuali e futuri, tra "vecchie" e "nuove" ragioni di scambio*) (Amaduzzi 1949a: p. 62) and this required exactly the combination between historical data (elaborated as standard cost) and prospective data, in order to identify correct reference parameters (Cassandro 1950: p. 39).[8]

4.1 The valuation of production factors with a long useful life

Starting from the examination of valuation criteria for production factors having a long life, it is possible to discern two phases in Cassandro's studies:

*   A first one where the position of our scholar decisively followed Zappa's theory, even if filtering the latter with the fully-evolved thought of Aldo Amaduzzi (Cassandro 1946 and 1950).
*   A second phase starting from the middle of the 1950s, when he improves and strengthens his own interpretation, intended to firmly maintain the logic of future values.

First phase (1946–1950)

During this phase, Cassandro pays attention to the determination of the contribution of assets having a long useful life to the economic result of the accounting period, combining the latter with the related accounting types that favour their representation in the profit and loss account.

Specifying that this economic contribution consists in the expression of the price/value in use of these production factors and that accounting methods and types used do not only consist in depreciation procedures, the point of view of the Author is clear: identify the value that can be attributed to the economic use of the resources (value in use), in order to allow to maintain this value through the regeneration (economic and financial) favoured by the enterprise production (Cassandro 1950: pp. 21, 33–34).

In this approach, the regenerating process is necessarily based on the following issues (Cassandro 1950: pp. 92–93):

*   measurement of the gains obtained by production in a quantity sufficient to (re)acquire equivalent production factors (economic restoration);
*   availability, at the moment of this replacement, of financial resources needed to allow it (financial restoration).

In order to realize this, it is necessary that revenues attributed to each accounting period are able to cover "not only costs attributable to the period, but also the contribution rates correctly calculated" (*oltre a tutti i costi imputabili al periodo anche le quote d'incidenza correttamente calcolate*) (Cassandro 1950: p. 35).

From this view unavoidably arises Cassandro's interest in the perspective to be considered that is the one of future costs, as "to base this calculation on a retrospective and historical vision (past costs) ... means to subtract from the contribution calculation any economic meaning" (*fondare tale calcolo su una visione retrospettiva e storica (costi passati) ... significa togliere al calcolo dell'incidenza ogni significato economico*) (Cassandro 1950: p. 39).

The rational basis of this calculation for the assets having a long useful life is, therefore, the reference to a prospective view considering going concern, even if this does not imply totally to neglect the retrospective base of past costs. Consequently, in this approach past and future costs are both considered in order to identify the appropriate parameter to be used for the determination of "value in use" of the analysed production factors.

From a strictly accounting point of view, the representation of this contribution is expressed through the combination of the following "accounting types" (*istituti contabili*, Cassandro 1950: p. 44 ss.):

1   The allocation of historical costs made through the depreciation procedure.
2   The advanced allocation of future renewal costs, modernization, etc. connected to future estimations based on future replacement costs (setting up renewal provisions adequately calculated on the basis of experience, or other appropriate methods).
3   The determination of costs for the maintenance and for repair (setting up maintenance and repair provisions).

As proof of the influence exercised by Zappa's theory, it is clear how Cassandro's stance is intended to assess the contribution on the economic result, exclusively operating on accounting procedures directly involved in the income calculation and leaving behind the asset valuation problem.

The economic reference to the future is, in any case, absolutely noticed because the recall of future replacement costs or reproduction costs is explicit, even if it is made in order to assess the "appropriate" accounting calculation of income. In this sense, the analysis of issues determining this future perspective (technological changes, the regularity of production processes, the business size, etc.) becomes clear (Cassandro 1950: p. 105).

He does not neglect the possibility to account with a direct entry, in the balance sheet, for the future replacement cost (and its related allocation) which,

> even if it has a rational economic basis, it presents ... the inconvenience not to have a general relevance (in the case of the expected reduced amount of reproduction cost it would appear appropriate to base the calculation on this lesser cost?), and it joins or confuses in a singular accounting presentation, the distribution of historical costs, that is the distribution of costs already incurred, with the distribution of prospective costs one estimates to bear.

(*se ha indubbiamente un razionale fondamento economico presenta ... l'inconveniente di non avere una portata generale (nel caso di previsto minore costo di riproduzione sarebbe opportuno fondare il calcolo su tale minore costo?) e di congiungere o confondere in un unico istituto contabile, il riparto dei costi storici, che è riparto di costi già sostenuti, col riparto dei costi prospettivi, che sono costi che si presume di sostenere.*)

(Cassandro 1950: p. 101)

Summarizing:

- If the future replacement cost is higher than the historical cost, the historical cost reference must be adjusted through appropriate integration considering higher renewal costs and maintenance and repair costs.
- If the future replacement cost is lower than historical cost, no integration will be made.

Second phase (1958–1973)

In the following development of his research, Cassandro reaches the personal belief consisting in the rejection of any reference concerning past cost or market values, or combination of these values with the future realization values. Starting from the end of the 1950s, Cassandro's position is exclusively based on these latter values, highlighting their utility to represent a rational superior valuation limit for assets.

In Cassandro's model the reference to rational limits, identified in the future realization/extinction values, is strengthened and fixed in the approach of our scholar (in this regard see e.g. Cassandro 1958a, 1962, 1967b, 1971).

In these studies, Cassandro considers the problem of financial valuations inside the inventory entries, where, as just highlighted, the identification of future realization/extinction values is the only explicit reference. It substantially means "to be able to distinguish, in the estimated realization value of goods, to whose production those activities, as production factors, related, how much represents recovered or returned value of the same activities" (*di riuscire a discernere, nel valore presunto di realizzo dei beni, alla cui produzione quelle attività, come fattori produttivi, hanno concorso, quanta parte rappresenta recupero o ritorno del valore delle attività stesse*) (Cassandro 1971: p. 140).

To this end, managerial and control tools become fundamental and in particular cost accounting. Through the use of production cost configurations as a function of the determination of selling price, specific technical coefficients are identified that, given a sellable quantity of goods and a related average price, allow to the identification of (as anticipatory quantity) the total amount of realizable revenues within a given period of time. This amount, appropriately compared with the useful economic life of the production factor, with the estimated annual average price and with the annual average quantity of production, will represent the superior limit for the valuation of the related asset (Cassandro 1971: pp. 140–144).

Identification of this superior limit, to be necessarily revised annually, is needed for prudence reasons to stay below this limit due to uncertainties connected to the estimates (administrative prudence), and due to taking account of the time to be spent until the complete use of the asset: thus the reference to an estimated discounted future realization value becomes clear.

Furthermore, Cassandro pays attention to the reasons leading him to reject the alternative parameters of historical cost and of the current estimated realizable value (Cassandro 1971: pp. 145–148):

- With reference to historical cost, he thinks that to consider the historical cost as maximum inventory value has not an economic sense when, due to the estimated trends of the entity, it is not possible to assess the revenues, with all the other costs, able to restore, among the other costs, the ones incurred for the assets having a long useful life.
- About the current estimated realizable value (substantially the market value), the judgement is more problematic because in this case a prejudicial logic exists, indeed these goods, like other goods intended to be used, are not intended to be sold and therefore the hypothesis of a direct realization doesn't match with reality and cannot be considered as a basis for valuation.

Moreover, the consideration of market values is totally excluded (even if the value is lower than the realization values), instead the historical cost is considered acceptable only if the book value, after all depreciations, is not higher than the superior limit consisting in the indirect estimated realization value.

However, the need for an economic and financial restoration persists and, then, the opportunity to assess annual rates for the contribution of the production factors, able to safeguard both the recovering of past cost, and the rates for greater renewal and maintenance costs, implicitly allow Cassandro's propensity for future replacement costs to be identified.

Finally, and summarizing very briefly what is mentioned above, in the end Cassandro's approach for assets having a long useful life is as follows:

1   It is considered rational to assess a superior valuation limit (for assets).
2   This superior limit consists in the indirect future discounted realizable value, to be used both as reference criterion and as impairment for other potential valuation criteria.
3   The combination of depreciation rates, greater renewal, maintenance and repair costs, indicates a propensity towards the criterion of future replacement cost that appears compatible with the indirect future realization values.

4.2 The valuation of production factors with a short useful life

The production factors classified in this group are all factors whose economic utility is consumed in only one production process, and, then, they naturally have a short duration. Among these, in the industrial and trading businesses, stock goods intended to be sold (goods and finished products) and those intended to be used in order to produce finished products (such as raw materials and work in process products) have particular relevance.

In relation to this, if for goods intended to be used Cassandro repeats, with due differences, the considerations made for the assets having a long useful life (this because these are factors that only indirectly will generate revenues for the entity), for assets intended to be sold (goods and finished products) the reasoning is different.

According to our scholar, for this group of assets, the superior valuation limit, consisting in the estimated direct realizable value, is not difficult to assess. In fact, he thinks that for a "rational" identification of this value:

> it will be sufficient to refer to average market prices of an appropriate period of time predicting the inventory entry, and on this basis, considering the trends of the market, it is possible to estimate the net realizable market value that will be the superior valuation limit.
>
> (*basterà riferirsi ai prezzi medi di mercato di un congruo periodo di tempo precedente l'epoca dell'inventario, e sulla loro base, tenendo presenti le tendenze di mercato, prevedere il presumibile valore netto di realizzazione, che costituirà appunto il limite superiore di valutazione.*)
>
> (Cassandro 1971: p. 136)

Having assessed the superior limit it is considered appropriate, for prudence, to consider a value below this superior limit for an amount that takes account of uncertainties connected in the estimation, of costs and expenses to be incurred for the future realization. The time in which the realization is estimated has less impact in this case, because the period of time is generally short.[9]

After this clarification, Cassandro explains the motives for the rejection of historical cost and of the current market price, placed inside the "lower value rule". According to Cassandro, even if this rule is certainly explained by prudence reasons, this prudence can be also obtained assessing only the logical limit of the estimated realization (Cassandro 1971: p. 137).

Indeed, Cassandro highlights the irrationality of the logic of lower value because,

> it is not clear why even when the cost is lower than the current price, one should consider the former as superior valuation limit. The cost is always a historical past, and in this sense, it is superseded; the danger of dilution arises only when an asset is valued at a value superior to the amount that could represent the estimated realization.
>
> (*non si vede, perché, anche quando il costo è inferiore al prezzo corrente, ci si debba attenere al primo come a un limite superiore di valutazione. Il costo è pur sempre un fatto storico e, come tale, superato; un pericolo di annacquamento si ha solo quando un bene viene valutato in misura superiore a quello che può essere il presumibile realizzo.*)
>
> (Cassandro 1971: pp. 137–138)

Furthermore, even considering the supposed higher objectivity of cost or of market value in relation to the direct realization values, Cassandro highlights the "uncertainty" of these two criteria, because (Cassandro1971: pp. 138–139):

- For historical cost, different measures of costs to which reference can be made exist (prime cost, technical cost, full cost, etc.), each of these measures is characterized by unavoidable elements of uncertainty and subjectivity (existence of indirect costs).
- About the current market price, as in the case of future realization values, it is always the result of forecasts and of estimates, even if founded on a starting objective amount, as in the case of current prices at the moment of inventory entry.

More illogical appears the reference to these criteria for not sellable stock goods intended to be used inside the entity (raw materials, work in process products, etc.) This is the reason explaining the greater rationality of the rule based on the indirect estimated realizable value (Cassandro 1962).

5 Conclusions

In order to identify the impact generated, at different levels, by Paolo Emilio Cassandro's studies, it is useful to point out the different profiles existing in his works: the theoretical doctrinal profile and the practical technical one.

Under the academic point of view, it is known how the scholar has a personal and independent scientific placement that is the result of the combination of different influences: Fabio Besta's influence based on accounting issues and the influence exercised by Eugen Schmalenbach and Gino Zappa's theories based on "Economia Aziendale" (with reference to Zappa's theory the influence is mainly exercised by Aldo Amaduzzi's development of the theory).

The constant updating of the doctrine and of economic and accounting practices at international level, critically considered by Cassandro, leads this scholar to become an acute propagator of the innovative trends arising in the more advanced contexts, favouring an early introduction in Italy of phenomena that have had only a later influence. Under this point of view, Cassandro's work that can be considered the most relevant is certainly that one concerning holding groups dated 1954 (this is the first treatise published in Italy on this subject).

With reference to the financial statements, Cassandro's thought can be summarized as follows:

- The financial statements are a system of values intended to represent the effects of the system of managerial operations.
- They are a tool for the knowledge of the management: trends of the entity reflected in the interrelated quantities of income and capital.
- Starting from the conception of the entity as a "community" and as a "centre and driving force of the economy" the assessment of these quantities must

be done following "rational" and neutral procedures, in order to allow the achievement of business equilibria, without being influenced by specific interests and needs.

• In relation to this, the complex of several financial statements/several purposes finds a limit inside the singular information need. Then, the operating financial statements in an economic sense, even if consisting of values unavoidably subject to subjectivity, are conceptually unique, namely having the aim to represent the rational calculation of the income and of the related operating capital in the view of business equilibrium verification.

• Reliability and clearness of financial statements are efficaciously obtained through the introduction of models elaborated according to the issues characterizing each type of business (industrial, banking, insurance, etc.). Then, a specific type of financial statements for each specific sector of activity, and not several financial statements for each business.

• Rationality in valuation is obtained without the adoption of rigid and detailed criteria, but using general valuation criteria as a reference basis and at the same time as limits not to be overcome (rational limits).

• In this approach, the estimated direct and indirect future realizable values consist in the coherent and rational reference with respect to the analysed subject: the management trend of the entity.

• At a practical level, the related calculation is based on the concrete use of different levels, (a system) of accounting data (financial accounting, inventory entries, budgeting and costs). In this manner historical data (elaborated as standard costs) and prospective data obtained estimating the profitability of the production (factors having a long useful life and factors with a short useful life to be used inside the entity) or the estimated direct realizable values (factors with a short life).

On a technical and practical level, the well-chosen scientific insights and the profound knowledge of the innovative trends on accounting at an international level allowed Cassandro to earn several recognitions, but also prestigious positions in institutional bodies. Among the others, it appears useful to point out the role assigned to Cassandro during the years 1972–1973 in the Ministry of State Investments of the Italian Republic, concerning the formulation of specific studies in the field of accounting. In particular, these studies used in Italy as a basis for the drawing up of the European Union (EU) Directives concerned the following issues:

1   The financial statements of the entity owned by the State with reference to the reform of joint stock companies and to the EU Directives.
2   The guidelines for the drawing up of the financial statements of companies being part of the EGAT (Ente autonomo di Gestione delle Aziende Termali), EFIM (Ente partecipazioni e Finanziamento Industrie Manifatturiere) and EGAM (Ente Gestione Attività Minerarie) groups and of the consolidated financial statements.

Notes

* This Chapter was jointly written by the authors. However, it is possible to mainly allocate Sections 1, 2 and 3.2 to Stefano Adamo; Sections 3.1 and 3.3 to Francesca Imperiale; Section 4 to Pierluca Di Cagno and Section 5, to all three authors.
1 For an illustration of the scientific profile of Paolo Emilio Cassandro, see several essays contained in Aa.Vv. 2008. Furthermore, see Faccia (2007).
2 For a literature review on the different approaches see Adamo (2006).
3 Accounting recording is defined by Cassandro (1958a: p. 62) as "a vital and intellectual process of management" (*processo vitale e d'intelligenza dell'amministrazione aziendale*).
4 Object and purpose of the financial statements are connected through a kind of bi-univocal relationship, because the representation of a given object can satisfy different purposes; at the same time any information purpose unavoidably needs a preliminary identification of the same object.
5 Furthermore, as we will discuss below, Cassandro contributed to the drawing up of European dispositions through specific institutional tasks assigned by the Italian State.
6 On closer inspection, Cassandro already made reference to rational limits for asset valuations in a minor work dated 1958 (Cassandro 1958b).
7 In compliance with this approach, as already remembered above, Cassandro developed during his research activity different works attaining the sectorial analysis of agricultural business (1953a), and insurance businesses (1957a). In addition to these works there is also an essay related to hydrocarbons published after his death *Le aziende produttrici di idrocarburi* (manuscript dated 1968–1969) and edited by Nicola Di Cagno in 2008.
8 This procedure shows similarities with some North-American approaches (Mobley 1967).
9 The first approach of Cassandro (1946: p. 24) appears close to Zappa's one, when the former suggests the current price as an acceptable approximation of the estimated future realizable value.

References

Aa.Vv. (2008) *Atti del Convegno della Giornata di studi in memoria di Paolo Emilio Cassandro*, Bari: Cacucci.
Adamo, S. (2006) Dalla conoscenza alla comunicazione: il ruolo dell'informazione periodica di bilancio, in riferimenti Storici e Processi Evolutivi dell'Informativa di Bilancio tra Dottrina e Prassi, *Atti dell'VIII Convegno Nazionale SISR – 2005*, Roma: Rirea.
Adamo, S. (2009) Il sistema delle rilevazioni secondo Paolo Emilio Cassandro, *Rivista Italiana di Ragioneria e di Economia Aziendale*, n. 7/8.
Amaduzzi, A. (1939) *Aspetti di problemi di valutazione nelle imprese commerciali*, Padova: Cedam.
Amaduzzi, A. (1949a) *Il sistema dell'impresa nelle condizioni prospettiche del suo equilibrio*, Roma: Signorelli.
Amaduzzi, A. (1949b) *Conflitto ed equilibrio di interessi nel bilancio dell'impresa*, Bari: Cacucci.
Besta, F. (1909) *La Ragioneria*, Milano: Vallardi.
Cassandro, P.E. (1929) Un precursore Leone Gomberg, *Rivista Italiana di Ragioneria*, nn. 3–4.
Cassandro, P.E. (1946) *Le riserve occulte*, Giovinazzo: Andriola.
Cassandro, P.E. (1949) Il sistema dell'impresa, *Rivista Italiana di Ragioneria*, nn. 5–6.

Cassandro, P.E. (1950) *L'incidenza dei fattori produttivi a lungo termine sul risultato economico di esercizio nelle imprese*, Bari: Cacucci.

Cassandro, P.E. (1953a) *Le gestioni agrarie*, Torino: Utet.

Cassandro, P.E. (1953b) Metodologia contabile ed economia d'azienda, *Prolusione al Corso di Ragioneria dell'Università di Bari – 1951*, Bari: Cacucci.

Cassandro, P.E. (1954) *I gruppi aziendali*, Bari: Cacucci.

Cassandro, P.E. (1957a) *Le gestioni assicuratrici*, Torino: Utet.

Cassandro, P.E. (1957b) Bilancio, *Enciclopedia ENI*.

Cassandro, P.E. (1957c) Tecnica contabile e analisi economica, *Annali della Facoltà di Economia e Commercio dell'Università di Bari, Vol. XIV*.

Cassandro, P.E. (1958a) *Le aziende. Principi di ragioneria*, Bari: Cacucci.

Cassandro, P.E. (1958b) Su di un nuovo sistema di bilancio per le grandi imprese, *Rivista di Politica Economica*, n. 10.

Cassandro, P.E. (1962) Fondamenti di Economia aziendale e Ragioneria, *La Scuola in Azione a cura della Scuola di Studi Superiori sugli Idrocarburi dell'ENI*, n. 7.

Cassandro, P.E. (1967a) L'equilibrio dell'impresa e la politica dei redditi, *Rivista di Politica Economica*, n. 1.

Cassandro, P.E. (1967b) Il profitto dell'impresa e la sua determinazione, *Rassegna Economica*, n. 5.

Cassandro, P.E. (1968) Modelli e tipi nello studio economico-aziendale, *Rivista dei Dottori Commercialisti*, n. 2.

Cassandro, P.E. (1971) *Le rilevazioni aziendali*, Bari: Cacucci.

Cassandro, P.E. (1973) La tipizzazione dei bilanci annuali delle società per azioni, *Rivista dei Dottori Commercialisti*, n. 5.

Cassandro, P.E. (2008) *Le aziende produttrici di idrocarburi*, Appunti delle lezioni a.a. 1968/9, Bari: Cacucci.

Di Cagno, N. (2008) Il bilancio di esercizio nella visione di Paolo Emilio Cassandro, *Aa.vv., Atti del Convegno della Giornata di studi in memoria di Paolo Emilio Cassandro*, Bari: Cacucci.

Faccia, F. (2007) *Paolo Emilio Cassandro. Contributo all'evoluzione delle teoriche aziendali*, Roma: Aracne.

Mobley, S.C. (1967) Revenue experience as a guide to asset valuation, *The Accounting Review*, n. 1.

Nicklisch, H. (1920) *Der Weg aufwärts!: Organisation*, Stuttgart.

Onida, P. (1940) *Il bilancio d'esercizio nelle imprese. Significato economico del bilancio. Problemi di valutazione*, Milano: Giuffrè.

Pantaleoni, M. (1925) Alcune osservazioni sule attribuzioni di valori in assenza di formazione di prezzi di mercato, *Erotemi di Economia*, vol. II, Bari: Laterza.

Schmalenbach, E. (1919), *Dynamische Bilanz*, Leizpig: Duncker & Amblot.

Zappa, G. (1927) *Tendenze nuove negli studi di ragioneria*, Prolusione all'inaugurazione dell'anno Accademico 1926–1927 del Regio Istituto Superiore di Scienze Economiche e Commerciali di Venezia, 13 novembre 1926, Milano: Istituto Editoriale Scientifico.

Zappa, G. (1937) *Il reddito d'impresa, Scritture doppie, conti e bilanci di aziende commerciali*, Milano: Giuffrè.

11 Insights into the notion of goodwill from the Italian theoretical contribution

Roberto Di Pietra

1 A short premise

In this chapter we will start from the definition and determination of goodwill in Guido Ponzanelli's theoretical contribution, before considering it in relation to the broader and more demanding question of the passage from Accounting to *Economia Aziendale*.[1] This topic will be dealt with from the point of view of historical research and, more specifically, the history of doctrines. We will look in particular at the broad question of the shift from Accounting to *Economia Aziendale*, taking advantage of the fact that debate on this matter has recently lost much of the divisive force it possessed but a few years ago (Coronella 2010: p. 62).

In the manifesto of the Italian Society of Accounting History the history of doctrines is deemed to be an area of research typical to the History of Accounting, and is defined as the "analysis and comprehension of the evolutionary line followed in time by doctrinal theorization" (SISR 1995: p. 26). This thematic area is undoubtedly difficult to delineate, as it does not necessarily possess the characteristics of historical research and is often directly connected to the present, being close in time to events, the people involved and the ideas examined (Antonelli 2012: p. 5).

In identifying the research topics that come under the Accounting History umbrella, some scholars have deemed the presence of the history of doctrines interesting (Previts *et al.* 1990: pp. 140–141), while others (Carnegie and Napier 1996) do not consider it to be explicitly included. The marked doctrinal and theoretical characterization that took place in Italy in the twentieth century favoured the identification of a specific line of research among history studies, although this was not mirrored on the international scene. In this sense the existence of a specific area of research dedicated to the history of doctrines constitutes, in the facts and literature we will be citing, a specific cultural expression of the situation in Italy. We will make further reference to this cultural quality as this study unfolds.

2 Debating in a complex theoretical context: from one paradigm to another

The Accounting and *Economia Aziendale* theories that evolved in Italy from the end of the nineteenth and throughout the twentieth century were intended to offer scholars a structured and complete set of definitions of a general nature, on the basis of which more specific and operative concepts could gradually be developed. The theoretical positions that have characterized *Economia Aziendale* studies include a series of concepts regarding the definition of an *azienda* (a business entity, e.g. a firm or a company), of its main objectives and of the elements that allow it to assess its performance; these prompt a whole series of necessarily coherent approaches, criteria and methods of accounting disclosure, logics of valuation and forms of representation in financial statements (Catturi 1989).

The definition of such theories is the result of the historical context in which they were formulated, or in other words of the prevailing characteristics of the economic and business scene (Catturi 1989).

In this sense some scholars have interpreted the development of *Economia Aziendale* upon the foundations of Accounting as the process of "scientific revolution" illustrated by Kuhn and based on the idea of paradigms. In his celebrated work *The Structure of Scientific Revolutions*, Kuhn (1996) identifies two phases in the development of knowledge. The first is a phase of cumulative growth, in which a high degree of specialization is achieved in a given sector of research; the second is a phase of evolutionary growth, in which periods of revolution and reconstruction of the theoretical corpus in a given sector of research take place. Aside from Popper's criticism of this approach, his reference to Kuhn's epistemological paradigms is particularly interesting in the case of *Economia Aziendale* (Popper 2002; Fuller 2004). The shift from one theoretical paradigm to another is fully grasped within Kuhn's vision, especially with reference to the progressive shift from the paradigm to a model of the disciplinary matrix, which is seen as a precondition of knowledge (D'Amico 1999: pp. 26ff.; Consorti and Palumbo 2005: pp. 509–512; Palumbo 2005).

Along the same interpretative line, from the point of view of its development, accounting theory can be interpreted as a theory of the different accounting paradigms that have dominated the history of Accounting, following a path coherent with Kuhn's thesis of "revolutionary" theoretical evolution, i.e. a succession of paradigm revolutions (Perrone 1997: p. 85). Within this context, Palumbo (2005: p. 4) states that Accounting evolves through non-cumulative processes.[2]

According to this approach, the shift from Besta's scientific Accounting to Zappa's *Economia Aziendale* constitutes a revolutionary change of paradigm. Obviously not all scholars agree with this interpretative approach. Giannessi (1980) and, more generally, the Tuscan School, see the development of Accounting as cumulative. According to Giannessi, certain elements of Besta's theory herald Zappa's theory, and there is therefore a phase of transition between Besta's contribution and the definition of Zappa's theory.

In short, there was no break or revolution, but a "continuity of studies". The interpretations of Catturi (1989, 2008), Bertini (1990) and Ferraris Franceschi (1991, 1994) are along the same lines. The first maintains that the entity (or income-based) system constitutes an evolution of the proprietorship system; the second identifies elements of Besta's work that anticipate the systemic concept brought to light by Zappa; the third underlines that the tendency towards specialization, which is typical of cumulative development, has allowed for both more in-depth knowledge and the formation of research areas that have gradually distanced themselves from each other.

In reality, the field of hypotheses regarding the relationship between *Economia Aziendale* and Accounting, or rather the position of Accounting in relation to *Economia Aziendale*, is much broader and can be separated into six distinct, and perhaps extreme, positions:

a   Accounting is a part of a whole, represented by *Economia Aziendale*;
b   Accounting has an interdependent and equal relationship with *Economia Aziendale*;
c   *Economia Aziendale* is part of Accounting;
d   the subject of Accounting is entirely absorbed by *Economia Aziendale*;
e   Accounting is an independent discipline formed of three parts;
f   Accounting should be considered as a body of knowledge that lacks autonomy and scientific rank (Antonelli 2012).

If looked at from the point of view of the shift that took place, we believe that the abovementioned terms regarding the position of Accounting in relation to *Economia Aziendale* can be helpfully simplified (with all the limitations that this entails) into two different main approaches. On the one hand are those in favour of the paradigm approach, and on the other are those that support a line of continuity in the development of *Economia Aziendale*.

Here we shall refer to the particular case of goodwill, being a topic of study that apparently falls perfectly into a paradigm shift logic, as a proprietorship and an entity approach are both clearly identifiable. The two approaches and the relative methods of goodwill valuation fit conveniently within the theoretical positions of both Besta and Zappa.

Reading and analysis of Guido Ponzanelli's contribution on the notion of goodwill introduces a series of elements that place this paradigm shift in crisis. As we shall clarify in greater detail below, in his definition of goodwill Ponzanelli uses a vision that necessarily brings the proprietorship perspective closer to the entity perspective, even adopting a mode of determining goodwill that involves using a method typical of the entity approach within a proprietorship-type conceptual system.

This chapter will develop as follows: in the second section we shall illustrate how the definition of goodwill fits into the accounting theories developed in Italy; in the third section we shall present the concept of goodwill proposed by Guido Ponzanelli; in the fourth we shall refer to his particular method of determination. In the fifth section we will seek to make some brief concluding remarks, which we hope will help clarify the debate that sets the supporters of the paradigm shift approach against those who prefer a vision of continuous development.

3 Accounting theories and the definition of goodwill

The debate on the concept of goodwill (regarding its definition, the methods to be used for its determination, and its identification, valuation and disclosure in financial statements) is ongoing and seems to be closely connected to the different theoretical positions adopted over time. Thus, we can observe how this subject emerged in the literature, constituted the subject of heated debate and was then temporarily set aside. In this sense, we can refer, for example, to the numerous articles published in the most long-running Italian Accounting journal on the subject of goodwill. In almost 100 years of publishing (from 1901 to 2000) the *Rivista Italiana di Ragioneria e di Economia Aziendale* (RIREA – the Italian Journal of Accounting and *Economia Aziendale*) published 11 articles on the subject, mainly in three particular decades (the 1910s, 1960s and 1990s). The subject of goodwill recurred in relation to its conceptual definition, its determination, and its accounting treatment based on the laws issued for the preparation of financial statements (Baldi and Di Pietra 2014). It is of particular interest that, from the nineties onwards, the regulatory impact of the European Union (EU) and the International Financial Reporting Standards (IFRS) played a dominant role regarding the definition of goodwill and its mode of representation in the financial statements.

The remarks proposed in the previous paragraph allow us to place Guido Ponzanelli's contribution on the concept of goodwill in context, in relation to both debate on the concept itself and, more generally, to the debate regarding the shift from Accounting to *Economia Aziendale*.

To this end, we can refer first and foremost to the viewpoint of Fabio Besta, who maintained that goodwill is independent of a company's tangible assets and regards only intangible assets. At the same time, goodwill is triggered by the fact that a company's tangible assets have a greater value because they are inter-coordinated. The sum of the phenomena, negotiations and relationships used by Besta to define the concept of *azienda* (a business entity) nonetheless presupposes reference to a set of assets that constitutes a distinct whole, from which their greater value arises (Besta 1909, Vol. I: p. 422).

For Besta goodwill can be determined independently, due to the conjunction of the company's tangible assets, the use of which results in higher than usual profits, or "extra-profits".

To state that goodwill is definable as the capacity to obtain a result that is better than normal implies that one knows what the normal profit should be. This means that we can say a "super" profit has arisen because we estimated or predicted (in some way) what amount of profit was deemed "normal" (Ceccherelli 1960: p. 176).

As mentioned above, in Besta's theoretical vision, goodwill is considered as an intangible good from which a certain result is obtained, together with other elements of capital: in the specific case of goodwill this result is qualified as super profit (or, as Besta terms it, an "excess of fruits").

Besta's approach, which considers the entity of goodwill to be determinable independently, contrasts with that of Gino Zappa. In other words, for Zappa the existence of super profit does not coincide with the determination of goodwill, but simply signals the presence of the latter. This idea is in line with Zappa's theoretical position, which attributes to the definition of *azienda* and the related concept of capital a character that does not permit the independent determination of goodwill (Zappa 1939: p. 678). The company's capital is an economic entity for the purpose of production, which therefore presupposes that the firm is functioning. Valuation of this established economic entity determines goodwill as its future capacity to generate income (Zappa 1939: p. 96).

Coherently with his theoretical vision, Zappa's definition of goodwill follows a logic that identifies the company's economic value as lying exclusively in its capacity to generate income, and part of this value includes goodwill (Amodeo 1964; Ferrero 1966; Onida 1975; Amaduzzi 1992: pp. 275–284).[3]

The theoretical divergence between Besta and Zappa's visions leads in the first case to a vision based on proprietorship and concerned with the quantitative determination of goodwill, and in the second to an income-based vision, concerned with the qualitative evaluation of the same entity. These two visions have lead (not so much in the two Masters as in their disciples) to two distinct and opposing methods of determining goodwill: the proprietorship and entity methods (as they are traditionally known in the doctrine and in current accounting practice).

As amply debated in the History of Accounting, the passage from Besta's theoretical position and his Scientific Accounting to Zappa's theory and his *Economia Aziendale* can be related to an effective and important change of paradigm. And as in all cases of paradigm-related revolutions, this passage manifests all the signs that precede and follow the change of paradigm. Hence, in the numerous contributions dedicated to the birth and development of *Economia Aziendale* in Italy it is possible to observe both arguments that heralded the conceptual elements, which would find their logical place in Zappa's theory and, on the other hand, arguments that denounced the problems with Besta's theory (even in Besta's own work).

In other studies the debate has been developed by scholars who adhere to Zappa's doctrine in a more zealous manner and with greater conviction than even Zappa himself: scholars who have taken his thought in directions that he himself may never even have imagined, and who have become bearers of a theoretical paradigm that would necessarily eliminate its predecessor. Similarly, but as a form of resistance, other studies have sought to highlight the limitations of Zappa's theoretical vision, while highlighting the strong points of Besta's vision.

This situation of clear contrast was part of a dynamic in which one of Besta's disciples laid the foundations for his Master's theoretical paradigm to be superseded, triggering a contrast between the pre-existing school of disciples and a not-yet-defined "new" school. In this sometimes bitter contrast we can distinguish between: the assiduous guardians of the previous faith; the zealous and staunch assertors of the supervening paradigm; and the inhabitants of a middle ground, partly oriented towards a quest for "improbable" forms of conciliation between the two theoretical paradigms and partly towards accepting the new while keeping hold (as far as possible) of elements of the original paradigm.

We believe that the case of goodwill fits into this last situation. As mentioned previously, due to its elusive nature this entity can belong to either a proprietorship or an entity vision. This very nature has meant that goodwill is one of the few cases in which (aside from the affirmation of Zappa's theoretical paradigm in Italy) a proprietorship vision has survived and ended up coexisting alongside an entity vision, at least in accounting practice.

4 The concept of goodwill according to Ponzanelli

Guido Ponzanelli's contribution to the question of goodwill should be considered above all in the context of his opinion on the position of Accounting in relation to *Economia Aziendale*. For Ponzanelli only Accounting really focuses on company life and *Economia Aziendale* is encompassed within its theoretical system (Catturi 1989: p. 197; Antonelli 2012: pp. 66–71). Ponzanelli (1961: pp. 9–13) explicitly states that "Accounting constitutes the synthesis of systems of company review", and even that "no change of name was necessary to indicate what has for centuries been known as Accounting" (Ponzanelli 1988: p. 960).

Considering this general approach and the conflict between the proprietorship and entity methods, Guido Ponzanelli can be said to belong to the first (Ianniello 1995). In particular, he is influenced by Alberto Ceccherelli's (1960) idea that a strictly proprietorship vision of goodwill, and therefore the capacity to produce super profit, should in any case result in an added value.

For Ponzanelli the existence of goodwill is clearly independent in relation not only to the existence of a company's own tangible assets, but especially to a particular real situation that gives a company hope in its future profitability (Ponzanelli 1960: p. 436).

In other words, goodwill is connected to super profit, but there is a part of goodwill that only arises because the company, which has been running for some time, has already demonstrated its capacity to function and therefore incorporates a value greater than any other similar but newly created company. This is because a company that has existed for longer has already developed its own capacity to organize itself and adapt to the economic context.[4] In short, Ponzanelli goes beyond the mere proprietorship concept, to see goodwill as deriving from super profit, but also from the company's capacity to function as a result of the organization it has developed and its adaptation to the economic environment.

On the basis of this already heterodox approach, Guido Ponzanelli makes his own considerations on the concept of goodwill, involving elements of a psychological nature i.e. factors related to human relations.

In line with the affirmations of Alberto Ceccherelli (1946, 1962: p. 4), Guido Ponzanelli attributes a central role in company life to people and to their behaviours both inside and outside the company (Ponzanelli 1975). In this context, Ponzanelli brings in elements of work and consumer psychology and highlights the importance of the motivations behind employees' behaviour, such as their personal, family, union-related, political and religious aspirations etc. Coherently with the introduction of these elements, he deems it important to specify that the maximization of company productivity does not necessarily coincide with the maximization of profit.

In relations between production companies, or between a company and its suppliers, it is important to identify the best way of rationalizing the processes that bind their respective activities; similarly, in relations between companies and clients increasing attention needs to be paid to market research, in order to grasp changes in preferences and favour each company's capacity to satisfy consumer demand quickly and effectively (Ponzanelli 1959: p. 748).

For Ponzanelli these psychological aspects introduce elements of uncertainty to the determination of the value of a company's activities. This uncertainty constitutes a risk factor for investors, which consequently requires adequate compensation. This risk (known as company risk) must be compensated in relation to the coordination of production factors, the capital invested and the possible loss of capital originally invested. The compensation for risk is known as normal profit or minimum business income and is justified by the need to indemnify the investor for the company risk sustained (or to attribute interest on the capital invested, considering the capital risk run).

In addition to this is the need to guarantee compensation for the management activities carried out. Normal profit may be greater or less than the profit effectively realized and disclosed in accounts. Estimating normal company profit is a non-accounting exercise conducted through statistics-based review, in which the value of effective income needs to be considered (which, in turn, can be current or prospective), as well as the value of average profit (which, for example, could be sectorial) (Ponzanelli 1959: pp. 755–756; Cassandro 1962: p. 177).

For normal profit to be estimated the company has to already be established. This means that it exists from a legal viewpoint, has already defined its organization and is capable of functioning as a production unit. Moreover, an already established company is characterized by its own specific organization of the production factors available to it, which allows it to function and establish a network of relations with subjects that today we usually call financers, public administration, employees, suppliers and clients – in a single word, stakeholders.

The development of these relations brings about the economic and financial situation that characterizes a company in any given moment. By valuing these relations, we can define the concept of goodwill, which, according to Ponzanelli (1959: p. 758), coincides with the reputation that the company builds within its environment, thanks to its organization. Reputation-building is mainly entrusted to the capacity of those in management positions, and is therefore connected to the subjective factors of fairness, prudence, sense of opportuneness, aptitude for perceiving and predicting aspects and circumstances, and the ability to understand others' interests.[5]

While Ponzanelli's proposed definition of goodwill belongs to the proprietorship method and therefore has a quantitative accounting character, it stands out due to its introduction of a series of qualitative elements regarding, above all, the "people factor". Reference to fairness and prudence are related to a subjective and dynamic company attitude, aimed at comprehending different and coexisting internal and external interests (Coda 1963).

In the same definition, Ponzanelli refers to another company approach, aimed at learning and organizing in relation to changes in the environment that the company is an active part of. Intuition, the ability to predict aspects and circumstances, and the ease of comprehension of others' interests are characteristics that define a company's sense of opportuneness.

Ultimately a company, in the sense of an organization that measures itself against its environment, develops its own reputation, and this is what Ponzanelli means by goodwill. This implies its reputation from the point of view not only of clients, but also of all subjects that the company has relations with. In this approach goodwill confirms its nature as an intangible resource whose existence depends on qualitative subjective factors. The latter manifest themselves through the organizational and management function and, as a single aspect, in relation to the economic environment in which the company operates.

As mentioned above, the concept of goodwill proposed by Ponzanelli certainly fits within the proprietorship vision and the consequent method of determination. However, it moves away from this vision in the fact that this scholar introduces a series of qualitative elements, which differ from the quest for super profit as they focus on the idea of reputation and presuppose the logic of an established company. Ponzanelli himself openly cites Zappa when he affirms that "the firm has become an active part of the environment" and thus the expression "ongoing economic coordination" appears entirely confirmed. This, as we shall see, poses significant problems for the determination of goodwill.

5 Ponzanelli on the determination and disclosure of goodwill

While Ponzanelli's proposed definition of goodwill may seem interesting and in some ways innovative from a conceptual viewpoint, it appears difficult to apply for the purposes of determining this entity. Indeed, it is not simple to achieve a reliable quantification of the qualitative and subjective factors he refers to. They are not transferable, and if they were it seems unconvincing to assume that they could be maintained in time. Moreover, their maintenance would be conditioned by the presence of the same people in organizational and management positions (Ponzanelli 1959: p. 759).

In short, the subjective factors and the network of relations that the company establishes are theoretically the very determinants of its reputation, i.e. of its goodwill, but they cannot be used to determine it.

The quantification of goodwill in monetary terms, for the many real reasons that demand the valuation of a company, must be achieved in a different way. In this context Ponzanelli specifies that in all such situations efforts must be made to give a value to the company's organization, rather than estimating possible future profits (as provided for in the entity method).[6] The value to be attributed to the company's organization derives from the expenses incurred during the setting up phase and throughout the company's lifetime. These expenses did not materialize in any specific object of the company's property (be it tangible or intangible), but contributed to creating the best conditions in terms of efficiency of the company's organization, and to maintaining them in time (i.e. the above-mentioned established company and its reputation).

The creation of this condition of efficient organization is a gradual process, which depends upon the company's management and constant adaptation to its environment (Ponzanelli 1960: p. 444). The subjective factors that characterize the company's organization also orient how it is managed. Through its management the company enters into contact with its environment and adapts to it. Via this contact the company gains a series of experiences that influence the subjective factors and hence its organization, in what Ponzanelli refers to as a "virtuous circle". This process allows a company to generate its own differential value in relation to other companies.

From the point of view of the determination of goodwill, Ponzanelli adopts the idea according to which the value of a capital good is equal to the sum of the current individual values of the services that it can provide in the future. In the same way, the flow of potential services of any given capital stock corresponds to its revenue. Thus goodwill can be determined by calculating revenue (simple or perpetual).

Valuing capital stock based on the services that it will provide in the future makes it possible to identify the cost to be incurred by the company for its acquisition on the market (we shall call this cost "C"). From the same capital stock we expect a revenue, distributed over the course of years ("R"). The ratio of revenue to cost determines the value of the annual unit revenue (the rate "i") (Ponzanelli 1960: pp. 446–450).

Following this logic, "R" corresponds to the super profit, or to what remains of the current (or prospective) effective revenue once the normal profit is deducted, while the rate "i" is selected bearing in mind the specific and generic risks of the given company (Ponzanelli 1959: pp. 767–768; Ferrero 1966: pp. 179ff.).

While the mode of calculation adopted is that typical of the entity method, the logic followed by Ponzanelli in determining goodwill is nonetheless grounded in the proprietorship method. The values of the capital elements are only added to the goodwill value for the purpose of the calculation, i.e. in order to obtain the economic capital value, although the contrary is conceptually and necessarily true, i.e. the values of the elements of the working capital are subtracted from the value of the economic capital to obtain goodwill.

From the point of view of disclosure in financial statements, Ponzanelli suggests that goodwill should be recorded among the balance sheet assets, as traditionally provided for by the Italian Civil Code's laws on financial statements and on the basis of the EU's Accounting Directive. However, Ponzanelli makes an unusual provision regarding this inclusion among the balance sheet assets: he suggests offsetting the value of goodwill by including a special entry among the balance sheet in the liability and equity side that serves to neutralize the effect of goodwill on the net capital value. The intention pursued with this special entry or reserve (no better defined) is to prevent a company's wealth in accounting terms from being increased by a value that derives from an uncertain, and in some senses unjustified, process of valuation.[7]

The form of disclosure proposed by Ponzanelli is foreseen in the case of purchased goodwill, and therefore in relation to extraordinary operations that trigger the determination of goodwill. However, it appears evident that this solution could also be adopted in the case of disclosure of the original goodwill in balance sheets, i.e. the goodwill produced by the company preparing its own balance sheet. In this case we would be confronted with an even more novel and peculiar situation, given that no regulatory system governing the preparation of financial statements provides for the possibility to include original goodwill.

The laws of the Italian Civil Code, the Italian accounting standards (OIC 24) and International Accounting Standards (IAS 38) all establish that goodwill generated internally cannot be recorded among a company's assets, as it does not constitute an identifiable resource (it is not separable from the company that generated it).

From the point of view of depreciation, national laws are known to differ from international ones. Based on article 2426 of the Italian Civil Code (point 6) goodwill paid for must be amortized according to its economic life or, when it is not possible to determine it, within a period of ten years. If adequately justified by the administrators in a supplementary Note, the amortization period may be extended, but cannot exceed the set duration specified for the use of this intangible activity.

Based on IFRS 3 purchased goodwill cannot be amortized. The company that purchased it must verify on an annual basis whether or not it has decreased in value (in relation to specific events or changes in circumstances, as provided for by IAS 36), and consequently devalue it. In some ways the substance of this approach does not seem far removed from Ponzanelli's proposal to offset the value of goodwill with a special reserve among the equities, in order to prevent it from determining an unjustified greater net capital value.

6 Concluding remarks

In Italy, almost 90 years after Gino Zappa's celebrated inaugural address (Zappa 1927), the debate on the real significance of the shift to *Economia Aziendale* still appears to be unresolved. Indeed, the gradual opening up of Accounting, Management, Finance and Organization studies etc. to the international scene has brought to light many doubts about the nature and effective content of this ground-breaking change in the current scenario and its uniqueness (Antonelli 2012).

Over the last 20 years debate on the nature of the shift from Accounting to *Economia Aziendale* – on its meaning, on the boundaries and contents of *Economia Aziendale*, and on the effective existence of these contents – has been abundant and even increased, especially in relation to the international scene (Viganò 1967; 1996: pp. 209–243). In some ways comparison with the international scene (think, for example, of the impact of the recent research assessment processes) has attenuated the very significance of *Economia Aziendale*, as it has been impossible to find fully (or even partially) corresponding forms, and terms of comparison with specific disciplines such as Accounting or Management, or even specific areas of research (Financial Accounting, Management Accounting or Public Sector Accounting) have had to be abandoned (Antonelli 2012: p. 1).

As mentioned in the paragraphs above, the positions adopted are very diverse. Nonetheless we believe that they can be synthesized in the visions of those who consider Zappa's theoretical paradigm to prevail over that of Besta, or those who see a gradual development from Besta's Scientific Accounting to Zappa's *Economia Aziendale* following a path of continuity.

The case of the definition and determination of goodwill fits perfectly into this scenario. The great debate that has taken place on this issue has left us with two clear theoretical approaches: a proprietorship vision and an entity vision of goodwill. In this context, whatever one's position in the debate on the relationship between Besta and Zappa, it is certainly true that the way goodwill is conceived mirrors these different theoretical standpoints. However, the fact that the two conceptions have survived within accounting practice over time as effectively alternate methods attenuates the point of view of those who support the affirmation of one theoretical paradigm over the other.

The specific nature of goodwill becomes even more important if we consider the original and innovative character of this notion and its determination taking into account Guido Ponzanelli's proposal. On foundations characterized by proprietorship, Ponzanelli introduces elements regarding people, subjectivity and the qualities that determine the value of goodwill based on the super profit approach, but he does so using the formula of simple or perpetual revenue typical of the entity logic. Ponzanelli's approach to goodwill therefore seems coherent with the idea not of one paradigm prevailing over the other, but rather of development through accumulation. A series of qualitative elements are grafted onto the notion of goodwill of a proprietorship origin, including reputation and the importance of an established company's organization, which in Ponzanelli's words recall the concept of "ongoing economic coordination". Goodwill is therefore an emblematic case that seems to confirm the form of development through accumulation.

Notes

1 Throughout this chapter we will use the Italian term *Economia Aziendale*, avoiding translating it. There have been several attempts to translate this term but no one is able to comprehend its exact meaning. Some authors have translated *Economia Aziendale* as Business Administration, Accounting and Business Administration, Business Economics or Concern Economics. Recently the Accademia Italiana di Economia

Aziendale (AIDEA) (which is the official association representing this research and teaching area) has adopted the translation of "Italian Academy of Business Administration and Management".

2 In an international context, Kuhn's approach has been used to illustrate the evolution of Accounting, as he identifies how changes in accounting paradigms have taken place when the disciplinary crises that have preceded scientific revolutions were overcome. In this sense see the Accounting History contributions of Glautier (1983: pp. 51–68) and Cushing (1989: pp. 1–41).

3 As explained in Chapter 9, Section 5, Amodeo considers goodwill as a hidden financial statement reserve. The same author has also stressed the idea that there are some conditions in the economic life of a business entity determining a negative goodwill (the so-called "Badwill").

4 On this point Guido Ponzanelli (1960: p. 437) affirms that as soon as the company has passed the preparatory phase, i.e. as soon as it is technically capable of carrying out its activity, relations initially entered into are consolidated and others are created, which serve to lend recognition to the functioning company and prove its capacity to achieve its ends.

5 Ponzanelli (1960: p. 438) offers the following definition of goodwill:

> Goodwill coincides with the reputation, made possible by organization, that the company forms within its environment, which is primarily dependent upon the capacity of those in charge of management and is thus connected to the subjective factors of fairness, prudence, opportuneness, faculty of intuition and prediction, perception of aspects and circumstances, ease of comprehension of others.

6 On this point Ponzanelli (1960: p. 411) specifies that neither does this mean:

> attributing value to possible future wealth, but to the company's organization, to achieve which expenses were incurred, in the establishment phase and beyond, that do not materialize in the form of any specific object that contributes to creating the best conditions of efficiency and maintaining them over time.

7 On this subject Ponzanelli (1960: p. 453) points out:

> That entry, or special reserve, could be gradually reabsorbed into the net capital if, and in as far as, while the super profit becomes fully effective from one financial year to another, the "goodwill" entry among the assets could also be considered effectively amortizable.

References

Amaduzzi A. (1992), *L'azienda nel suo sistema e nei suoi principi*, Torino: Utet.

Amodeo D. (1964), *Ragioneria Generale delle Imprese*, Napoli: Giannini.

Antonelli V. (2012), *Ragioneria ed economia aziendale, Osservazioni in prospettiva storico-dottrinale sulle controversie in tema di posizionamento*, Rirea Historica, Roma: Rirea.

Baldi R. and Di Pietra R. (2014), Importing and "refracting" accounting: traces in over a century of a long-lived Italian accounting journal, *Contabilità and Cultura Aziendale*, Vol. 14, n. 2, pp. 79–106.

Bertini U. (1990), *Il sistema d'azienda, Schema di analisi*, Torino: Giappichelli.

Besta F. (1909), *La Ragioneria*, Vol. I, 2nd edn, Milano: Vallardi.

Carnegie G. D. and Napier C. J. (1996), Critical and interpretive histories: understanding accounting's present and future through its past, *Accounting, Auditing and Accountability Journal*, Vol. 9, n. 3, pp. 7–39.

Cassandro P. E. (1962), *Le aziende, Principi di ragioneria*, Bari: Cacucci.

Catturi G. (1989), *Teorie contabili e scenari economico-aziendali*, Padova: Cedam.

Catturi G. (2008), *Il pensiero di Paolo Emilio Cassandro sul posizionamento scientifico e sulla ripartizione disciplinare degli studi aziendali: attualità e prospettive*, in Atti del Convegno, Giornata di studi in memoria di Paolo Emilio Cassandro, Bari: Cacucci.

Ceccherelli A. (1946), *Economia e Amministrazione economica delle imprese*, Firenze: Universitaria Editrice.

Ceccherelli A. (1960), *Le funzioni professionali del commercialista*, Milano: Vallardi.

Ceccherelli A. (1962), *Istituzioni di Ragioneria*, Firenze: Le Monnier.

Coda V. (1963), *Introduzione alle valutazioni dei capitali economici d'impresa*, Milano: Giuffré.

Consorti A. and Palumbo R. (2005), I paradigmi contabili lineamenti per un'analisi storico-sistematica, in *Atti dell'VIII Convegno Nazionale della Società Italiana di Storia della Ragioneria*, Roma: Rirea, pp. 509–536.

Coronella S. (2010), *Compendio di storia della ragioneria*, Rirea Historica, Roma: Rirea.

Cushing B. E. (1989), A Kuhnian interpretation of the historical evolution of accounting, *The Accounting Historians Journal*, Vol. 16, n. 2, pp. 1–41.

D'Amico L. (1999), *Profili del processo evolutivo negli studi di economia aziendale, Schema di analisi per 'paradigmi' e 'Programmi di Ricerca Scientifici'*, Torino: Giappichelli.

Ferraris Franceschi R. (1991), La teoria economico aziendale di fronte alla crescente specializzazione degli studi, in Aa.Vv., *Continuità e rinnovamento negli studi economico-aziendali*, Atti del Convegno AIDEA, Bologna: Clueb.

Ferraris Franceschi R. (1994), *Il percorso scientifico dell'economia aziendale, Saggi di analisi storica e dottrinale*, Torino: Giappichelli.

Ferrero G. (1966), *La valutazione economica del capitale d'impresa*, Milano: Giuffré.

Fuller S. (2004), *Kuhn vs Popper, The Struggle for the Soul of Science*, New York: Columbia University Press.

Giannessi E. (1980), *I precursori in economia aziendale*, (quarta edizione), Milano: Giuffré.

Glautier M. W. E. (1983), Searching for accounting paradigms, *The Accounting Historians Journal*, Vol. 10, n. 1, pp. 51–68.

Kuhn T. S. (1996), *The Structure of Scientific Revolutions*, Third Edition (first edition: 1962), Chicago and London: The University of Chicago Press.

Ianniello G. (1995), Il contributo di Guido Ponzanelli in tema di avviamento d'impresa, in Aa.Vv., *Guido Ponzanelli, La Sua dimensione umana e scientifica*, Padova: Cedam, pp. 125–145.

Onida P. (1975), Osservazioni sulla valutazione delle aziende di produzione in esercizio, stimate come complessi oggetti di trasferimento giuridico, in *Studi di Ragioneria, organizzazione e tecnica economica in memoria di A. Riparbelli*, Vol. II, Pisa: Pacini.

Palumbo R. (2005), *Approcci prospettivo, retrospettivo e prudenziale nella elaborazione dei paradigmi contabili, Sviluppo scientifico e conflitti di paradigma*, Torino: Giappichelli.

Perrone E. (1997), *La ragioneria ed i paradigmi contabili*, Padova: Cedam.

Ponzanelli G. (1959), Sul problema dell'esistenza, della determinazione e della contabilizzazione del valore dell'avviamento nelle imprese, *Rivista dei Dottori Commercialisti*, Vol. 11, n. 2, pp. 53–77.

Ponzanelli G. (1960), Sul problema dell'esistenza, della determinazione e della contabilizzazione del valore dell'avviamento nelle imprese, in *Studi di Ragioneria e Tecnica Economica*, Firenze: Le Monnier, pp. 427–453.

Ponzanelli G. (1961), *Lineamenti di economia generale delle aziende*, Firenze: Tipografia S. Davite.

Ponzanelli G. (1975), *La determinazione e la rilevazione dei costi di produzione nelle imprese industriali*, Siena: Ticci.

Ponzanelli G. (1988), Sintesi del pensiero scientifico sul contenuto della ragioneria e sulla sua evoluzione, in *Scritti di economia aziendale per Egidio Giannessi*, Pisa: Pacini.

Popper K. R. (2002), *The Logic of Scientific Discovery*, (Routledge classics), London: Routledge.

Previts G. J., Parker L. D. and Coffman E. N. (1990), An accounting historiography: subject matter and methodology, *Abacus*, Vol. 26, n. 5, pp. 126–158.

SISR (1995), Manifesto della Società Italiana di Storia della Ragioneria, in *Società Italiana di Storia della Ragioneria, 1984–1994*, Pisa: Pacini.

Viganò E. (1967), *La natura del valore economico del capitale d'impresa e le sue applicazioni*, Napoli: Giannini.

Viganò E. (1996), *L'economia aziendale e la ragioneria, Evoluzione – Prospettive internazionali*, Padova: Cedam.

Zappa G. (1927), *Tendenze nuove negli studi di Ragioneria*, Milano: S.A. Istituto Editoriale Scientifico.

Zappa G. (1939), *Il reddito di impresa*, Seconda Edizione, Milano: Giuffré.

12 "Consumable income" according to Edoardo Ardemani's thought

Alessandro Lai

1 Edoardo Ardemani's career

Born on 9 April 1914, Edoardo Ardemani graduated with honours in 1937 in Economic and Commercial Sciences at the Catholic University of Milan. His supervisor was Pietro Onida, with whom he started the first milestones of his university career (Vv.A.a, 1997, p. V). He was assistant professor and lecturer at this university for a period of over 25 years. In 1964 he won a university chair competition at the University of Venice "Ca' Foscari".

After a few years, in 1967, he moved to the University of Padua, where the Economic Faculty was located in the Verona branch. Here he held the Chair of Accounting until 1989 and introduced the teaching of "Economia Aziendale" in 1978, as an innovation if compared to the traditional accounting courses taught for many years.

His main accounting disciples were Professor Giorgio Brunetti (who has been professor of Economia Aziendale and professor of Accounting at the University of Venice and at Bocconi University) and Professor Antonio Tessitore (who has been professor of Economia Aziendale and professor of Accounting at the University of Venice, at the University of Padua in the Verona venue, at the Catholic University of the Sacred Heart in Milan, at the University of Verona).

His long career (he retired in 1989) led him to teach many generations of students: in addition to technical contexts, values of integrity and fairness were instilled into them. Instead of having paternalistic attitudes, he showed a deep interest and willingness in developing his student's research potential (Vv.A.a, 1997, p. V). He received the Gold Medal as a meritus of School, Culture and Art, awarded by the President of the Italian Republic; in 1989 he was appointed Professor Emeritus of Economia Aziendale at the University of Verona.

I had the privilege of a personal knowledge of Edoardo Ardemani for many years. In the early stages of my course of study at the University of Padua (in the Verona venue), having the intention to continue to do research, I turned to him for some advice. Thus, he guided me to Professor Antonio Tessitore, who had moved from the University of Venice to the University of Verona in the meanwhile. Professor Ardemani was my thesis second supervisor, and in the very early years of my research and teaching activities, he gave me important advice and suggestions. I can testify to his thought owing to many fruitful meetings with him, during which he spoke about his ideas. This direct knowledge makes it more effective for me to interpret his works, his papers or those of other scholars written in his honour.

He died in Milan on 31 May 2006.

2 The holistic culture of Edoardo Ardemani

The production of Edoardo Ardemani is entirely in tune with Zappa's vision (Zappa, 1927, 1950, 1957): his Master Professor Pietro Onida, one of the greatest Zappa's scholars, opened his mind to that paradigmatic view (Onida, 1971, p. 3 ss.). He was a respectful disciple. This led him to try not to deviate from the new ways of learning, and to follow a culture that at the time of his graduation was not yet completely taken for granted, as many Italian academic venues – at that time – continued to follow Besta's paradigm (Lai *et al.*, 2015, p. 273). Really, the inaugural lecture of Zappa (Zappa, 1927) and the start of the new stream that characterized Italy without interruption until the present day, had begun in 1927 (10 years before Ardemani's degree). Nevertheless, the Italian Academy was still imbued with Besta's patrimony culture (Besta, 1880, 1894); thus, joining the new trend – as Ardemani did – represented in itself a great innovation, especially if compared to the past.

The understanding of Edoardo Ardemani's thought cannot ignore the following consideration: the effort that the new Academia intended to propose, in a time of innovation, needed to go towards the deepening of the new paradigmatic movement, namely the development of the "multi-storey building" of which Zappa had laid down only the foundations (Coda, 2002). His closeness to the scientific proponents of the great innovation could lead him to stay inside the new paradigm and to prevent him taking further steps in different directions.

The "direct lineage" of Edoardo Ardemani's thought from Zappa's one has to be seen in this cultural background. At that time, it was common among academics to emphasize the relationships with their Masters as if they were parenthood. In this view, Ardemani can be seen as Onida's "son" and Zappa's "grandson". In the Italian Accounting academia at the that time it was common to qualify a disciple as a "son" and a Master as a "father". This direct descendence strengthened cultural orthodoxy, according to the habits and usages of that time: in other words, every effort aimed at bringing innovations just within the same paradigmatic stream (Lai *et al.*, 2015).

According to Zappa's own culture, the central vision is represented by the idea of the firm as a whole (Zappa, 1950, p. 13; 1957, t. I, p. 64): Ardemani, as a Zappa "grandson", had a full holistic view of the firm (Ardemani, 1971, 1978). This view was reinforced by his closeness to Pietro Onida's ("his father") contributions to the Economia Aziendale theory (Onida, 1971) and increased by a strong teaching attitude in widespread fields of accounting and management. So he got a systemic view of the Economia Aziendale and of its related discipline(s).

This is the culture in the light of which we can explain the scientific path that led him to consider the issue that is under discussion here.

Previous schools and those from foreign cultures saw the "azienda" either as a sum of facts or as a mere legal framework within which the processes producing new wealth were carried on (Canziani, 1994, p. 148 ss.; Lai, 2004, p. 24 ss.). Ardemani was far away from these cultures. He never missed the opportunity to emphasize, as an essential achievement of the new school, the unity "in space" and "across time" of the "azienda" and the related business decisions (Ardemani, 1982, pp. 69–82).

Unity "in space" means recognizing the connections among business choices in all functions, divisions, different areas of a firm or its subsidiaries. This is because the governance cannot avoid considering the economic interests of the company conceived in its identity as a socio-economic institution devoted to all its stakeholders: so we can consider itself as a unit overcoming even the identity of its stakeholders (Zappa, 1957, t. I, p. 80 ss.; 1962, p. 721; Coda, 2002, p. 26). Indeed it is ruled by an owner (economic subject) or by his agent that gives a coherent guidance, which in turn carries out all related measures, aimed at meeting the needs of its stakeholders, in the long term.

Zappa's revolution introduced a new idea pervading the whole new subsequent culture, which had huge implications both in research and in the business world (Canziani, 1994, p. 157 ss.).

According to the first point of view, there could not have been any properly grounded analysis in literature, no research nor scientific innovation effort, that could have ignored the relationships between different enterprise areas. As regard the second one, the search for levels of management efficiency and effectiveness was to be seen looking at the "azienda" as a whole and not considering its different parts as divisions, branches, subsidiaries and so on. All these circumstances are reflected on the result and consequently on the capital returns, as an effect of the contribution that management overall gives, and not of the single parts of the "azienda".

The management unity was also postulated "across time", as every choice and every decision taken had to be read and understood in the general system of corporate decisions. In every occasion the new culture reiterated the idea that these decisions are taken unitedly and that governance is addressed by a single economic subject (the owner or its agent), referring to just one economic institution and its continuity (Lai, 2004, p. 34 ss.). All this is consistent with the durability goal that an "azienda" naturally seeks, concerning the economic institution as a whole and not its parts (Zappa, 1957, t. II, p. 719).

This circumstance, for academics of the new stream, made difficult the recognition of the enterprise's partial results, even if referred to divisions, branches, corporate subsets or subsidiaries, as well as the research for efficiency regarding some business functions, divisions or even branches or subsidiaries (Zappa, 1957, t. I, p. 493 ss.). The same is true for the disclosure of financial results, which had to be referred to the firm as a whole. Every research that was not in tune with this idea of unity, could not find acceptance in the new doctrinal current. All the revenues and all the costs coming from management decisions and actions have to be juxtaposed to measure income. This position highlighted the differences of the new stream with Besta's patrimony school and with the previous administrative culture that conceived income as the result of the juxtaposition of value variations in individual elements of assets and liabilities. This is the cultural context in which Edoardo Ardemani gave a great development to the concept of consumable income that was – to some extent – "embedded" in previous scholars' works (Onida, 1971, p. 600 ss.) and evolved it in his own work (Ardemani 1978, §IV, pp. 125–208) as a further result of various positions expressed by other authors belonging to the Zappa tradition.

3 The background of the consumable income concept

Applying a kind of self-assessment process, Ardemani identified on his own the areas in which he believed he had provided significant contributions in the new lines of research, during the course of his academic experience, lasting for many years. So, before his retirement in 1986, Ardemani's students and colleagues received a book containing the main scientific discoveries and results that he thought to have achieved during his long research life (Ardemani, 1986).

In each chapter of this volume (*Studi e ricerche di ragioneria* – Accounting Studies and Researches), Ardemani wanted to raise the reasons of the steps undertaken "inside" Zappa's orthodox vision of the doctrine, as interpreted and deepened by his Master Pietro Onida. Looking at the text index, it is easy to understand the contributions provided, which characterize Ardemani's scientific works:

a accounting among other "Business Administration disciplines";
b the evolution of the "firm" and its accounting system;
c accounting measures connected to income and financial management;
d income in financial statements;
e self-financing management and its accounting;
f equity in financial statements;
g business control through financial statements;
h goodwill, equity and the value of the firm;
i added value accounting system;
j financial statements and their arrangement.

"Income in financial statements" is a significant chapter for the purposes of this chapter. This part is entirely focused on consumable income issues. This is a theme that characterized Ardemani's researches for many years, namely from the time of his first works, absolutely in tune with his ancestors. The position expressed by Ardemani can be better understood by considering two elements:

a the holistic view of the "azienda" arising from Zappa's culture, discussed above in Section 2, of which Ardemani is a direct expression;

b   the Italian system of companies, to which the research of accounting developed by Ardemani has been addressed. This system is characterized by:

  i   A widespread system of small and medium enterprises that have always composed the Italian industry, often governed by a person who is both the owner and the enterprise manager (Cattaneo, 1963, p. 61). This is therefore a situation in which the problems highlighted by the agency theory appear as secondary ones (Ardemani, 1971, p. 219), or at least they are confined to the management of the second level, or to situations in which various members of a family share the property of the same company. In these contexts, the property mainly gets its personal income directly from operations (as an entrepreneurial wage).

  ii   A limited number of large listed companies, where families play an essential role as they are mostly holding the majority of interests required for their government.

  iii   A small number of public companies, for which the remuneration issues of capital are similar to those observed in the Anglo-Saxon context.

  iv   Cooperative banks, very widespread in the national context. These are true public companies, in which the members are waiting for a suitable return on capital, but they can have just one vote during the shareholder's meeting, regardless of the capital held, pursuant to the principle "one person, one vote".

  v   A system of enterprises owned by the State or by public entities, born from the complex experience of holdings started in the 1930s of the twentieth century. As they were the expression of a public property, there were characterized also by priorities other than the achievement of income.

In a system like that summarized above, maximizing pay-out became a widespread temptation. In any kind of business (small, medium, large or listed), the family needs were much more important than the company ones. Therefore income was withdrawn, as much as possible, by family for its own various needs. This type of behaviour, that some Italian scholars have subsequently studied and summarized in the expression "poor company, rich family", has in fact represented and represents even today a threat to the business continuation, as a company like that cannot self-sustain its own development processes. Preferences to family needs and personal instances of owners represent a deep danger for companies.

4 The consumable income

This cultural and environmental context aids an understanding of Ardemani's accounting proposal, and the identification of "consumable income" as a benchmark (Ardemani, 1978, 1986), conceived as the "maximum value that has not to be exceeded to avoid damaging the future management". This approach would seem to have nothing new if the position was referring to the normal distribution process affecting each company. Certainly, the concern that the pay-out is not excessive determines expectations of behaviour that can be controlled at the time of the income distribution.

But Ardemani's proposal related to an earlier moment, not for expediency reasons, but in a way consistent with the corporate vision of his research: the qualification of "consumable income" concerns the income determination process, not the pay-out moment, and therefore relates to the evaluation of corporate assets and liabilities. This circumstance makes it interesting to understand the foundation of this position, which leads us to consider the overall needs of future management and the related asset and liabilities evaluation.

If we consider a wider position about income, according to Ardemani's thought and to the previous literature, the need to periodically account for it satisfies different purposes: its "abstract nature" depends on its purpose (Onida, 1971, §§99–100–101–102), in tune with the Italian "Economia Aziendale" tradition, and drives to account for it in many possible ways. Different determinations and measures of income do not contrast with one another but instead coexist as a result of the different purposes they have (Onida, 1971, p. 620 ss).

Different kinds of income differ mainly owing to the administrative problems to be solved through their determination and not just to the subjects interested in the financial statements, as previous researches conceived. It was accepted, and widespread in the literature of those times, that different stakeholders require different income accounting: Ardemani too shared the idea that each stakeholder would like to have his own disclosure, and possibly his own different result (Ardemani, 1971), even through different financial reports (internal ones, public one, for banks, for fiscal agency, etc.). But in this particular case, the underlying idea is a bit different.

Actually, according to his thought, income could be determined (Ardemani, 1986): (i) to have a periodical pay-out and to reward equity; (ii) to settle whether or not to invest in particular assets (able to give a sufficient income to reward the investment); (iii) to assess the return of investment and the entrepreneurial capabilities. In the first case, income has to be determined as a "consumable income of the period" that is considering "the highest amount one can withdraw without damaging the going concern and future management". According to this idea, consumable income is an amount that cannot be overcome, a maximum limit: while the financial reporting preparer has not to overpass it, at the same time he has not necessarily to reach it when determining the result of the period.

If the preparer overcomes this limit, he may damage future management, as the company shall reward equity, in subsequent periods, less than the shareholders expect, according to the plans and programmes that the company has developed and the shareholders know or figure out about the future. The underlying idea is that there is a sure continuity among incomes that the company is going to have in its subsequent accounting periods. Owing to this continuity, which is deeply related to the overall idea of "azienda", the board can move forward some profits or move back some losses (being more conservative, for example) just to assure to the future income the possibility to reward equity adequately. Really, the aim of any kind of "azienda" is to produce value (Tessitore, 1997).

Alternatively, the higher the amount that you choose for the current period's income, for instance through a lower use of conservative provisions, a reduced amount of depreciations and a generous and optimistic valuation of stocks, the higher the possibility that future results are not able to satisfy the rewarding needs for the future. This could cause some concern: most probably shareholders will sell their shares, which lose their value; according to Ardemani's thought, if you would like to keep the shareholders close to the company you don't need to adequately reward current equity, but just the future one. And the idea of consumable income suggests exactly managing earnings with this particular purpose.

This idea and position may recall the great amount of literature about earnings management that has been developed especially from the last 40/50 years all over the world (Healy and Whalen, 1999; Schipper, 1989). Actually, the international literature tries to explain the reason why financial report preparers manage earnings (and the tools used to do it) to perceive their own purposes, and suggest common behaviour about this issue, related to different situations to be solved: so, earnings management is commonly perceived as a way to manipulate company earnings towards a pre-determined target. This target can be motivated by a preference for more stable earnings (income smoothing) or by the need to cut off with a time in which different managers were responsible for the company (big bath), or by the opportunity to delay the recognition of possible losses, hoping for a recovery of a better situation able to bear these bad events without having a great impact on income. Many other possibilities could be considered as examples of earnings management (Healy and Whalen, 1999, p. 370 ss.). Whatever it could be, the earnings management literature deals with situations in which preparers neither respect the existing accounting standards nor manage at the edge of their correct interpretation to get their own expected results. So they have an effect on earnings quality (Leoni, 2013, p. 64 ss.).

On the contrary, in Ardemani's thought, accounting for "consumable income" is not a matter of behaving to avoid existing accounting standards. At the time in which he wrote, there was no accounting standard widespread in the Italian tradition, but just a civil law designing general principles which, in many cases, required further specifications that accounting literature (written mostly by academics and sometimes by professionals) could have provided. Only at the beginning of the 1970s, also in Italy, a greater awareness about generally accepted accounting standards arose, while the discussion about the implementation of the IV and VII EEC directives grew up: at that time, the idea of income gradually but generally moved to "income produced in the period", even if this idea was strongly contrasted by some of the professors more related to the "pure" theory coming out from the Zappa revolution.

In the Italian tradition, many academics have been dealing for a long time with principles to be followed in financial reporting: the prevalent idea of income was far from that of an "income produced in the period" and was more close to an "income assigned to a period": it means that the financial reporting preparer has to assign a certain amount of income to a period, considering both accounts and other issues. Ardemani's idea of "consumable income" followed exactly this stream and was able to give a solution to this issue (independently from its acceptance by professionals or other academics). Finally he affirms that we can conceive the "consumable income" as a forest: what is relevant is not the amount of wood produced in one year, but that (greater or lower than the former) you can cut without giving prejudice to a normal growth in the next years.

5 Determining the consumable income

The definition of "consumable income" had some implications (Ardemani, 1978, pp. 127–128):

a At first, it is useful to clear up what "future management" exactly means: just the subsequent period? All the periods after the current one? These solutions are both rejected by Ardemani as his idea is strictly related to future periods in which operations linked to the current one will develop, until the same operations will be over: it means that "future management" will be completed when current operations will expire. He means both operational and investment assets needed to pursue the purpose of the company, referring to operations that can be found in the financial reporting (particularly in the balance sheet).

b A second problem to be dealt with is to clarify how and when future management is not damaged. It depends on the possibility to assure "adequate rewards" to the capital invested by shareholders. About this theme, Ardemani admits that the adequateness depends on many issues related to: the amount of risk connected with future management, the reward assured to other companies in the same sectors, financial markets conditions but also other indirect advantages that the owner who control the company can get, and finally by the group rewarding policy.

c Finally, another issue is the amount of capital to be considered in order to appreciate the adequateness of rewarding. Ardemani doesn't say so much about that, but he proposes considering just the amount of equity put into the company by the shareholders, and not the full amount of equity at the time of the financial reporting. However, the reason for this suggestion is not so clear.

As the determination of the "consumable income" necessarily requires the examination of future periods to consider ongoing operations and their end, the "consumable income" is not just a final result of the period, nor a result definitively achieved. It depends on many forecasts and assumptions: that's why it is "hypothetical"; so it is more or less reliable, depending on many circumstances (Ardemani, 1978, pp. 128–130).

The first of these circumstances is the amount of the forecasts that the preparers of the financial reports have to organize and their related value, compared to the values coming from bookkeeping accounts regarding cash, receivables and debts: the lower the values related to these last accounts (that don't need forecasts), compared with the amount of stocks, inventories, fixed assets and financial investments, the lower is the reliability of income. The second is related to the difficulties to be dealt with, while forecasting future values, in connection with the length of the period to be considered and to the weight of tangible and intangible assets: the greater these assets and the longer their economic life, the more difficult forecasts are. The third is a result of what Ardemani calls "elasticity" of the firm, that is its capacity to follow the changing environmental conditions: the greater this elasticity, the lower the possibility that the company has to reduce its income owing to external conditions. Finally, the income reliability depends, according to Ardemani, on the weight of extraordinary revenues compared to revenues produced by ordinary management: the greater are the former, the lower the reliability.

Besides, the idea of "consumable income" is able, according to Ardemani, to find an actual use: so, he tried to give solutions to some questions, by setting his own "standards" useful for measuring this kind of income and giving a solution to the main issues related to revenues and costs recognition (Ardemani, 1978, pp. 130–133). According to his "consumable income" theory, the preparers have to distinguish operations completing within the same annual period from those embracing many periods. The first ones are to be attributed to the period without any discussion. The second ones have to be considered (a) at first individually and then (b) in their whole. When these operations are considered individually, several cases may happen:

- if in the period there is a cost which will match one or some revenues in future periods, this cost has to be postponed to the future at a value not greater than the related revenues;
- if in the period there is a revenue which will match one or some costs in future periods, this revenue has to be postponed to the future at a value not lower than the related costs;
- if in the period there are (just one or) some revenues which will match just one cost in future periods, this cost has to be anticipated to the current period at a value not lower than the cost itself;
- if in the period there are (just one or) some costs which will match just one revenue in future periods, this revenue has to be anticipated to the current period at a value not greater than the revenue itself.

However, in many times during a period there is a cost, while in the future periods there may be an indistinct amount of revenues which can be related to that cost just indistinctly; or, on the contrary, during a period there is a revenue, while in the future periods there may be an indistinct amount of costs which can be related to that revenue just indistinctly. In these situations, operations ongoing at the end of the period have to be considered not individually, but by recognizing costs and revenues just considering the economic possibilities of future periods. In other words, a cost must be recognized in a period when future periods will not be able to bear it, because it would prevent an adequate remuneration of future capital. Symmetrically, a revenue may be recognized in a period, if this recognition wouldn't prevent an adequate remuneration of future capital: otherwise, it has to be recognized in future periods. So costs and revenues have to be recognized in the reporting period with different criteria, as costs must be recognized, while revenues may be recognized, as "consumable income" needs to prevent future period from insufficient rewarding.

According to Ardemani's thought, after applying these main rules aiming at an adequate rewarding of invested capital in future reporting periods, the preparer has to deal with income smoothing (Ardemani, 1978, pp. 130–133) that he has to plan both for the current and for subsequent periods, to improve the company image among stakeholders; he has not to obtain the same incomes in future periods neither incomes strictly proportional to the invested capital: the need is to have some logical relationships with invested capitals, risks and rewards commonly obtained on financial markets for companies belonging to the same industry. So, according to Ardemani, besides appropriate investment and disinvestment choices during the period, managing earnings is fruitful for smoothing income: it can be obtained by enlarging depreciations, reducing inventories, increasing provisions and recognizing in the period some costs that could have a multiannual recognition. He thinks that this income smoothing is not damaging stakeholders – even those who would like to sell their stocks in the short run – because he says that they have no right to be rewarded for the income of the period, owing to the management unity along various periods (Ardemani, 1978, p. 134).

Forecast uncertainty determines the need to express future revenues and future costs, to be recognized in the current period, through ranges, rather than through punctual values. So, consumable income has to be determined in a range, expressing, from the top to the bottom, values less high but more reliable. The range is related to different levels of risk: the higher the selected income, the greater the need to have favourable management conditions in the future. On the contrary, the lower the selected amount of income, the higher the possibility of getting this result, even with poor future conditions. Earnings management permits choosing the value of income within that range, distinguishing risks to be considered during the income determination process and risks to be considered when the board agree about the pay-out.

So, Ardemani strongly affirms that between income determination and its pay-out there is not a clear conceptual difference (Ardemani, 1978, p. 135): both of them rely on the level of risk that is taken into consideration before or after income determination. Earnings management, aiming at smoothing results in subsequent periods, permits choosing among these different levels of risk. This choice is to be connected to secondary aims related to income recognition: a judgement about the boards' behaviour or managers' performance, the need to have a financial reporting to be presented to banks or investors to get more capital, the need to set product prices when the activity is controlled by regulators, the opportunity to satisfy shareholders' requests, etc.

Finally, Ardemani admits that the possibility of the earnings management practices depends on the amount of both overall and specific risks regarding management. The greater these risks, the larger the possibility to be left to the financial reporting preparers to use a greater range of values for income. Besides, the greater the dimensions of the firms, the greater their rigidity and so the harder the risk is on them: this is why earnings management, according to Ardemani's thought, has to be huge for larger firms. However he admits that the possibility of using earnings management to "correctly" measure the "consumable income" is strongly limited by the rules imposed by civil and fiscal law at the discretion of the preparer.

6 Conclusions

The idea carried on by Edoardo Ardemani has been fully developed in tune with Zappa's theory of the "azienda" and the new construction of the Economia Aziendale theory. To some extent, his view is a further development of his "father" (Pietro Onida) or "grandfather" (Gino Zappa) positions, with an appreciated capability to really deal with theoretical and practical problems embedded in the concept of this kind of income. In some handbooks of his, which he used in university courses with his students, he developed large parts about different processes to account for consumable income, with a lot of additional pages devoted to many kinds of assets and liabilities.

He spent many years spreading this idea to many generations of students in Milan, Venice and Verona, during his long and successful academic career. Many generations of students were fascinated by the coherence of this idea, which is the great construction that was built upon an understanding of the unity of management "in space" and "across time".

As far as I know, many students – even after many years – remember Ardemani's enthusiasm about consumable income, and his capability to convince them about its correctness and its adequacy to give a unitary view of the firm: that was his great purpose.

Even if this academic success is far from being formal, the possibility of using "consumable income" as a measure of income to be used in "real" financial reporting "formally" had a limited life. It is true that the Italian conditions (mainly small and medium firms, a few large public companies, a lot of family firms, financial reporting conceived mainly for fiscal purposes, etc., as discussed in Section 2) favoured the earnings management diffusion probably more than some other countries did, and – in any case – the earnings quality is a relevant issue (Leoni, 2013, p. 94 ss.). Most probably, it is true that in Italy, for a long period, earnings management was not considered to be criticized by many generations of academics and accounting professionals (Onida, 1971, p. 607 ss.), but the situation changed at the beginning of the 1970s when the principles discussed at the European level (and embedded in the fourth and seventh accounting directives) became well known also in Italy, thus decreasing the discretion in accounting for income.

So new figures of income arose, both in academic papers, books and handbooks, as developed by literature (Adamo, 2013, p. 552), and in practical mementos devoted to professionals. Most of these figures, while not denying the unity of the management "in space" and "across time", as the Italian Economia Aziendale posits, are related to the need to identify, with a lower subjectivity and without using formal earnings management, the measure of income to be referred to a period. Ardemani himself – in the last edition of his handbook, devoted to the students of the degree in Economics (Ardemani, 1982, pp. 123–129) – preferred to talk about an "economico-aziendale" income (i.e. an income measured in compliance with the Economia Aziendale principles), rather than to use again the concept of consumable income.

So consumable income progressively disappeared from books and papers used in academic or professional courses and, far from being used even by professionals, remained, at least in Italy, a fascinating idea to be investigated in accounting history researches.

References

Adamo, S. (2013) (ed.), *Le rilevazioni di esercizio delle imprese. Strutture complesse e sintesi periodiche*, Bari: Cacucci.

Ardemani, E. (1971), *La contabilità generale e il bilancio d'esercizio*, Milano: Marzorati.

Ardemani, E. (1978), *L'amministrazione delle imprese*, Milano: Giuffrè.

Ardemani, E. (1981), Il valore di presunto realizzo come parametro di riferimento, in Vv. Aa., *Bilancio di esercizio e amministrazione delle imprese. Studi in onore di Pietro Onida*, Milano: Giuffrè.

Ardemani, E. (1982), *L'impresa. Economia. Controllo. Bilancio. Vol. I. L'economia delle imprese*, Milano: Giuffré.

Ardemani, E. (1986), *Studi e ricerche di ragioneria*, Milano: Giuffré.

Besta, F. (1880), La ragioneria: Prolusione letta nella solenne apertura degli studii per l'anno scolastico 1880–81 alla R. Scuola superiore di commercio in Venezia, Tipografia dell'istituto Coletti, Venezia.

Besta, F. (1894), *La Ragioneria Scientifica e le sue relazioni con le discipline Amministrative e Sociali*, Roma: Loescher.

Canziani, A. (1994), Gino Zappa (1879–1960). Accounting Revolutionary, in Edwards, J.R. (ed.), *Twentieth-Century Accounting Thinkers*, London: Routledge.

Cattaneo, M. (1963), *Le imprese di piccole e medie dimensioni*, Milano: Istituto Editoriale Cisalpino.

Coda, V. (2002), "L'economia aziendale nella seconda metà degli anni '50: una rivisitazione delle "produzioni" e dell'opera postuma di Gino Zappa", *Contabilità e cultura aziendale*, 2(1): 6–33.

Healy, P.M. and Wahlen, J.M. (1999), "A review of the earnings management literature and its implications for standard setting", *Accounting Horizons*, 13(4): 365–383.

Lai, A. (2004), *Paradigmi interpretativi dell'impresa contemporanea. Teorie istituzionali e logiche contrattuali*, Milano: Franco Angeli.

Lai, A., Lionzo A. and Stacchezzini, R. (2015), "The interplay of knowledge innovation and academic power: Lessons from 'isolation' in twentieth-century Italian accounting studies", *Accounting History*, 20(3): 266–287.

Leoni, G. (2013), *L'informativa economico-finanziaria delle PMI italiane. Concetti e determinanti di earnings quality*, Roma: RIREA.

Onida, P. (1971), *Economia d'azienda*, Torino: UTET.

Schipper, K. (1989), "Commentary on earnings management", *Accounting Horizons*, 3(4): 91–102.

Tessitore, A. (1997), *Una riconsiderazione del concetto di azienda*, in Vv.Aa. (1997), *Economia e finanza aziendale. Scritti in onore di Edoardo Ardemani*, Milano: Giuffrè.

Vv.Aa. (1981), *Bilancio di esercizio e amministrazione delle imprese. Studi in onore di Pietro Onida*, Milano: Giuffrè.

Vv.Aa. (1997), *Economia e finanza aziendale. Scritti in onore di Edoardo Ardemani*, Milano: Giuffrè.

Zappa, G. (1927), *Tendenze nuove negli studi di ragioneria, Discorso inaugurale dell'a.a. 1926–1927 nel Regio Istituto Superiore di Scienze Economiche e Commerciali di Venezia*, Milano: Istituto Editoriale Scientifico.

Zappa, G. (1950), *Il reddito di impresa*, Milano: Giuffrè.

Zappa, G. (1957), *Le produzioni nell'economia delle imprese*, t. I–II–III, Milano: Giuffrè.

Zappa, G. (1962), *L'economia delle aziende di consumo*, Milano: Giuffrè.

Index

Page numbers in *italics* denote tables, those in **bold** denote figures.

.

For Product Safety Concerns and Information please contact our EU
representative GPSR@taylorandfrancis.com
Taylor & Francis Verlag GmbH, Kaufingerstraße 24, 80331 München, Germany

www.ingramcontent.com/pod-product-compliance
Ingram Content Group UK Ltd.
Pitfield, Milton Keynes, MK11 3LW, UK
UKHW021005180425
457613UK00019B/811